IMAGES
of America

LOUISIANA

On the Cover: The Citizen's Band performed at special events, parades, and civic functions in the late 1800s and early 1900s. A Grand Band concert was scheduled at the Burnett-Buell Theater one March evening to raise money for new uniforms, the flyer for which proclaimed, "A town without a band is sleeping."

IMAGES
of America

LOUISIANA

Betty Jane Allen and Martha Sue Smith

ARCADIA
PUBLISHING

ISBN 978-0-7385-9406-4

Published by Arcadia Publishing
Charleston, South Carolina

Printed in the United States of America

Library of Congress Control Number: 2012933464

For all general information, please contact Arcadia Publishing:
Telephone 843-853-2070
Fax 843-853-0044
E-mail sales@arcadiapublishing.com
For customer service and orders:
Toll-Free 1-888-313-2665

Visit us on the Internet at www.arcadiapublishing.com

To the Louisiana Area Historical Museum for its efforts to preserve Louisiana's history

To the Louisiana Public Library, one of the first 10 Carnegie libraries in Missouri

CONTENTS

ACKNOWLEDGMENTS

This book has been a community effort, and we thank everyone who has assisted us along the way. Specifically, we would like to thank the following people for sharing their knowledge and/or their photographs: John Wood, Carolyn E. Allen, Betty Asquith, Linda Ince Beer, Grace Jane Catlett, Sally Cropp, Dan DeCook, Sally Dinwiddie, Barbara Lee Fay, Rev. Pat Glenn, Bea Goodin, Charlotte Griffith, Irene Griffith, Jeff Guay, Eddie Holliday, Marilyn Johnson, Anne Keller, LaCrosse Lumber Co., Nathan Lilley, Louisiana Fire Department, Louisiana Area Historical Museum, *Louisiana Press Journal*, Louisiana Public Library, Trent Meyers, J. Note Mitchell, *People, Places, & Pikers*, Mary Perkins, Pike County Chapter National Society Daughters of the American Revolution, Preserve Louisiana's Images, Saint Joseph Catholic Church, Dorothy McCune Sansing, *Sesquicentennial, Louisiana, MO 1818–1968*, Gail (Gast) Sidwell, Lois Stark, Irene Steers, *The Stark Story*, Larry White, and John Wetzel.

INTRODUCTION

"Land of the Golden Hills" was the phrase used by early French explorers to describe the Louisiana area, and rightly so. Since the first settlers made their home here in 1808, many have found that Louisiana offers a quiet, peaceful atmosphere for raising a family and operating a business. Mississippi River charm, rolling landscapes, and gracious historic homes wrapped with down-home friendliness make the town an ideal tourist attraction. Louisiana is one of Missouri's oldest and most treasured towns.

Settlers were in the general vicinity of Louisiana as early as 1810, and some two miles southeast, a Daughters of the American Revolution Monument marks the site of Buffalo Fort, where 25 families took refuge during the War of 1812. It became a prominent supply stop for pioneers to the Salt River country and the city flourished as a river port until the coming of the railroads, when it became an early trade and industrial center.

The oldest town in Pike County, Missouri, Louisiana was founded by Joel Shaw and Samuel K. Caldwell and was originally settled by John Bryson, Esq., and John Walker. Louisiana was the county seat of justice until 1824, when the records were moved to Bowling Green. The Louisiana courthouse was the first brick house ever erected in the county.

Benjamin Templeton was noted as saying that the town was named in honor of Lucinda, a daughter of John Walker and a general favorite of the neighborhood at the time the town was laid out. Others believe that it was named for Walter Bayse, an attorney from St. Louis who is said to be the author of the Louisiana Purchase document. On the day the Louisiana Purchase document was signed in 1803, Walter Bayse's wife gave birth to a daughter in St. Louis and they named her Louisiana Bayse. The Bayse family moved to Pike County in 1816. When the town was looking for a name in 1818, they were so taken with young Louisiana Bayse that they named the town after her. The first mill of any kind in the county was a sawmill and gristmill a short distance west of Louisiana, built by John Bayse in 1818. The town was incorporated in January 1845 and obtained a city charter in March 1849. Louisiana was the principle shipping point for a large area of the county and its location offered superior advantages as a commercial and manufacturing center.

Louisiana blossomed as a prosperous business community, reaching a population of 7,000 by the late 1800s. In the mid-1920s, a ferryboat was operated 24 hours a day for river crossings, but service eventually ended following the completion of the Champ Clark Bridge in 1928. The bridge was operated as a toll bridge until 1952, when the toll was ended. The bridge continues to be the only span across the Mississippi River between St. Louis and Hannibal. In addition to commercial uses, the river has become a favorite spot for fishing and boating, sporting a new dock at Louisiana and the large Illinois Marina across the river. The third Missouri railroad bridge to cross the Mississippi River opened in 1873, and its large draw-span is still in use, enabling passage for barge traffic, excursion boats, and large pleasure crafts.

Tobacco was a major industry for Louisiana. At its peak in 1862, there were approximately seven tobacco factories doing business. In addition, there were a number of lumber mills; the Lyons Iowa LaCrosse Lumber Co. is the only one remaining.

Today, the population of Louisiana is approximately 3,800. Although no longer the city it once was, pride in Louisiana's rich heritage is reflected by the many old, stately churches and business buildings and homes. Several have been placed in the National Register of Historic Places, the most recent being the Bethel Chapel African Methodist Episcopal (AME) Church. Several blocks and more than 50 buildings make up the Georgia Street Historic District, the state's most intact Victorian streetscape.

Louisiana is home to the world-famous Stark Bro's Nurseries & Orchards Co., the largest nursery in the world and the oldest in America. James Hart Stark founded Stark Bro's Nurseries & Orchards Co. in 1819.

Champ Clark, the distinguished Speaker of the House of Representatives who narrowly missed the Democratic nod as a presidential candidate, opened a law office in Louisiana and was principal of the Louisiana schools.

A Carnegie public library was founded in Louisiana in 1904 and is in the National Register of Historic Places. A new addition houses a reading room for children made possible with a sizable donation from a private individual. It has been named "Libby's Room" after the benefactor's sister.

John B. and Mary F. Henderson signed a warranty deed on May 2, 1903, to the City of Louisiana giving land for a park. The city passed and approved Ordinance No. 1732 on June 5, 1903. Henderson, a Republican senator from Louisiana, was credited with authoring the 13th Amendment abolishing slavery, and voting for the acquittal of Pres. Andrew Johnson. Henderson Riverview Park is just one of several lovely parks in Louisiana, offering a pastoral view of the Mississippi River. The Louisiana Rotary Club dedicated the John B. Henderson historic marker on July 4, 1998.

One

Our Beloved Mississippi River

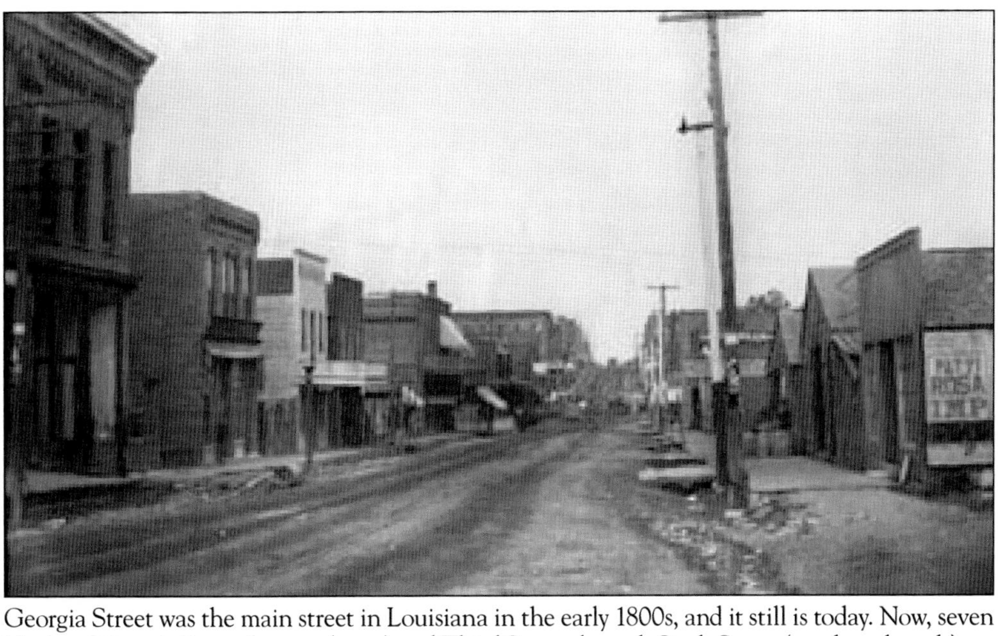

Georgia Street was the main street in Louisiana in the early 1800s, and it still is today. Now, seven blocks of Georgia Street (east and west) and Third Street through Sixth Street (north and south) are in the National Register of Historic Places. This photograph is taken from Seventh Street looking south to Third Street. Two more blocks south is the Mississippi River. (Courtesy John Wood.)

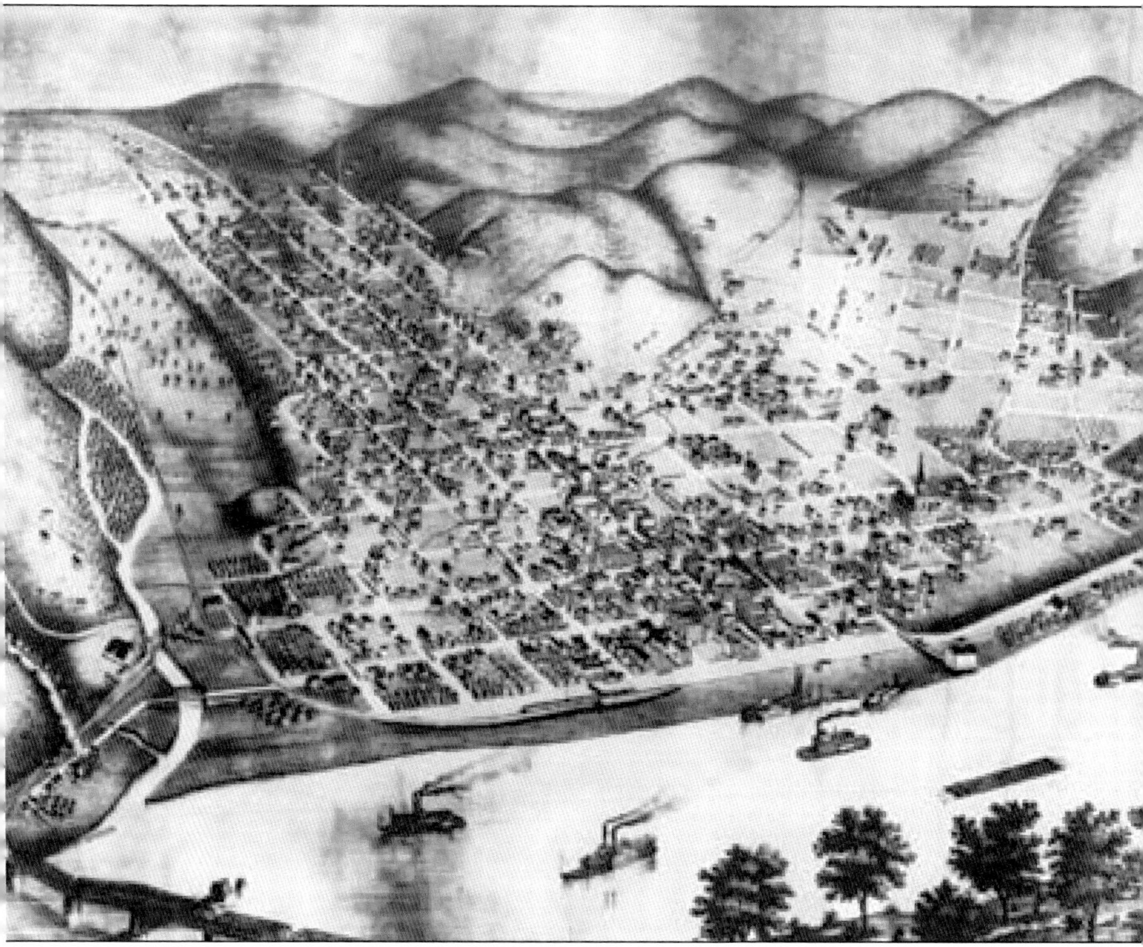

This lithograph of Louisiana was produced by the Chicago Lithograph Company in 1876. It has been copied and framed on notes, maps, and brochures. Jeff Guay, the manager of Press Journal Printing Company presented the Louisiana Public Library with a hand-colored copy, which is beautifully framed and hangs in the upstairs reading room. (Courtesy Betty Jane Allen.)

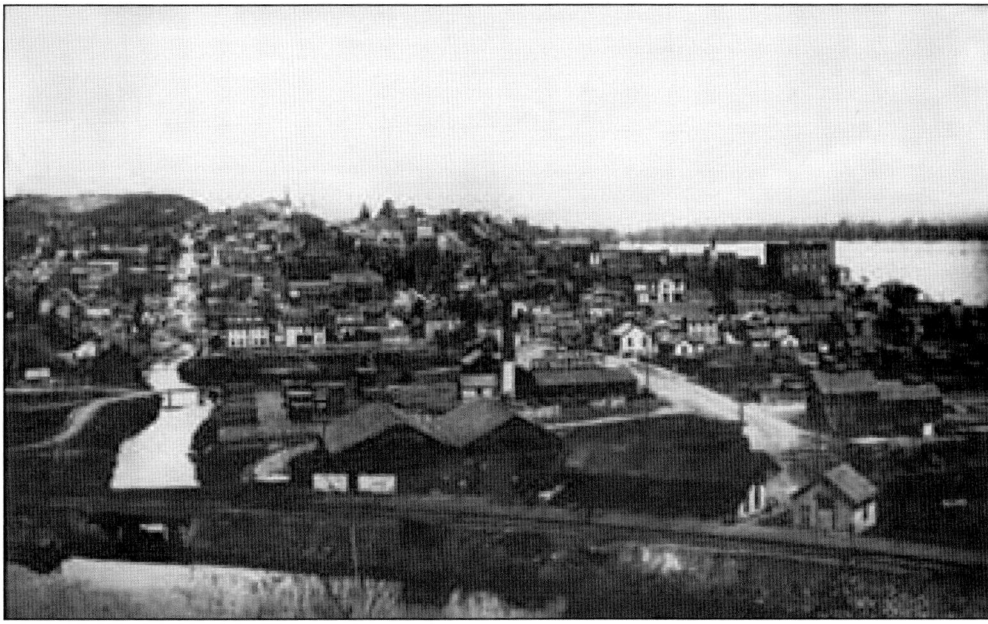

This closer look at Louisiana is a bird's-eye view from the mid-1800s. The Mississippi River on the right and the railroad in the foreground are two reasons why Louisiana thrived. (Courtesy Betty Jane Allen.)

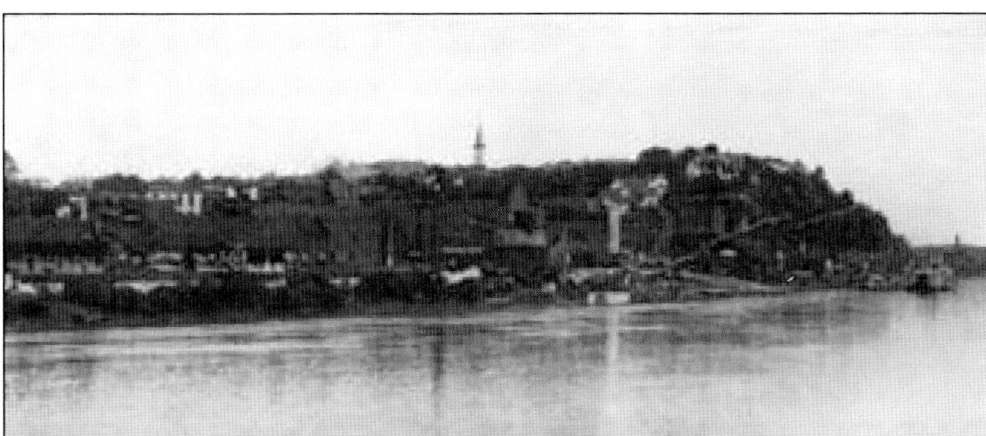

Shown is an early view of Louisiana from the Mississippi River. (Courtesy Betty Jane Allen.)

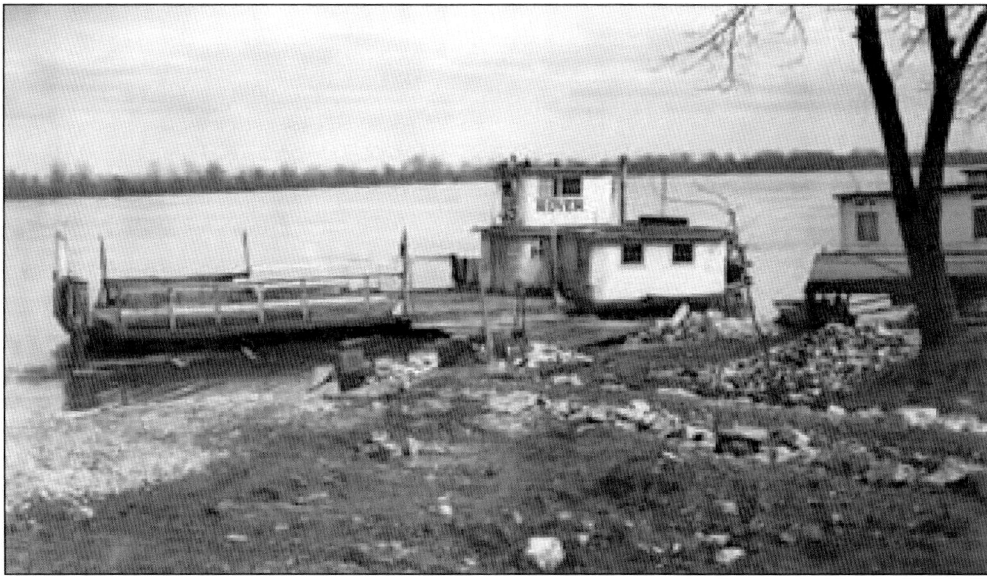

In 1821, prior to the construction of the Champ Clark Bridge connecting the twin Pike Counties of Illinois and Missouri, the steel-hull ferryboat *Rover* provided transportation across the Mississippi River. A single person's passage was 25¢, two-wheeled carriages were 75¢, and hogs, sheep, and goats were 6 1/4¢. Rover's Landing was at the foot of Tennessee Street in Louisiana. (Courtesy Betty Jane Allen.)

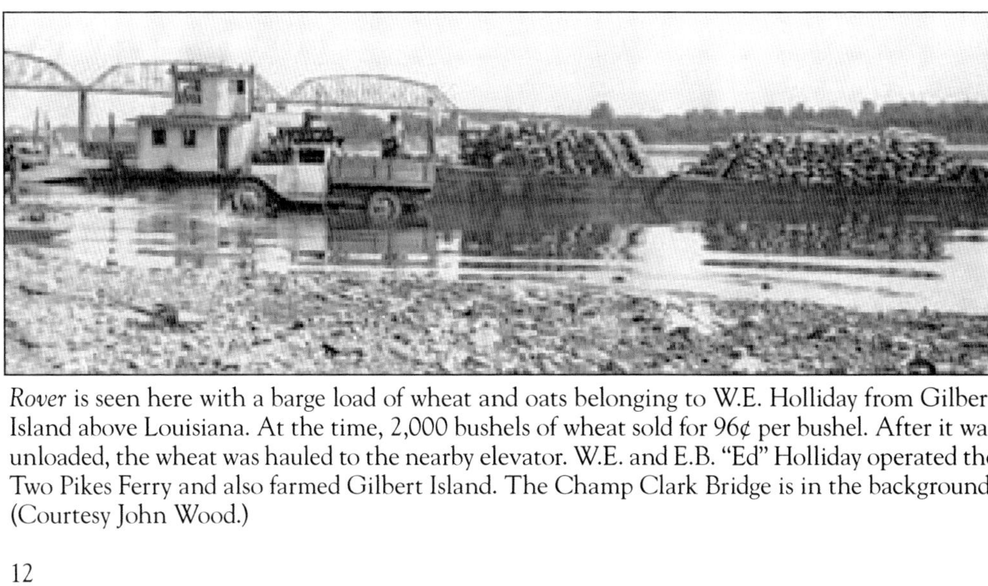

Rover is seen here with a barge load of wheat and oats belonging to W.E. Holliday from Gilbert Island above Louisiana. At the time, 2,000 bushels of wheat sold for 96¢ per bushel. After it was unloaded, the wheat was hauled to the nearby elevator. W.E. and E.B. "Ed" Holliday operated the Two Pikes Ferry and also farmed Gilbert Island. The Champ Clark Bridge is in the background. (Courtesy John Wood.)

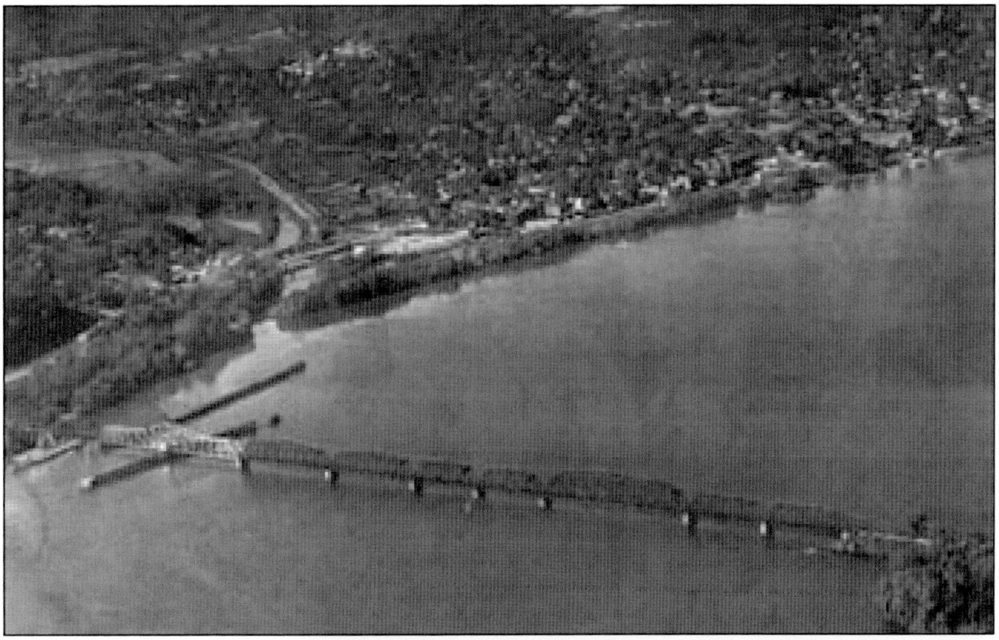

The above bridge was the third bridge built over the Mississippi River, in 1873. This early aerial photograph clearly shows the draw-span, the largest in the world at that time. The span opened to the right, allowing passage for barges, excursion boats, and private vessels. Louisiana was founded in 1818 on the bank of the river. Noix Creek, at the far left, empties into the Mississippi. (Courtesy John Wood.)

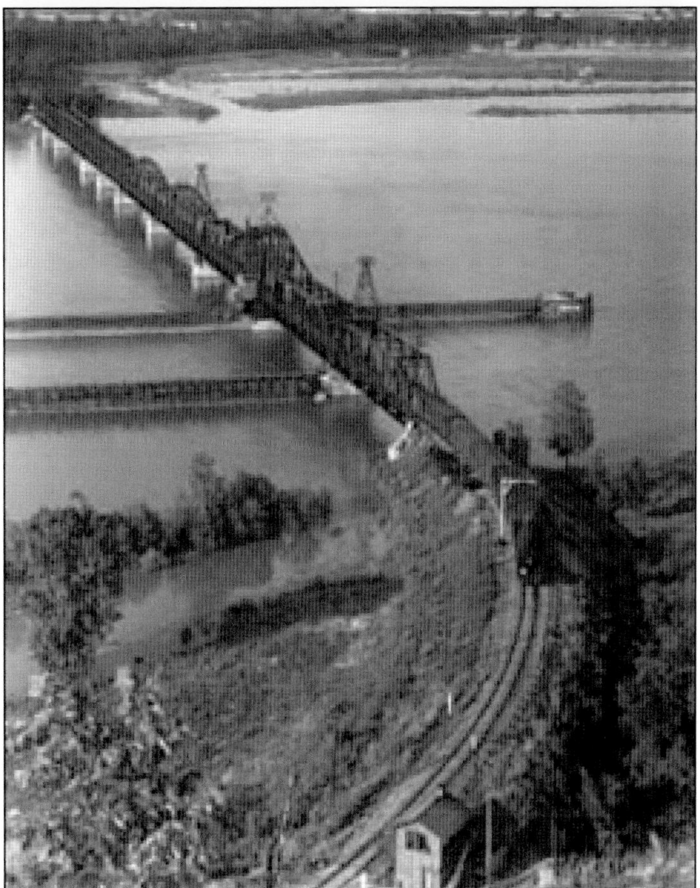

At right, a train enters the Missouri side of the railroad bridge. Note the man near the track (bottom) ready to hand off instructions to the engineer. (Courtesy John Wood.)

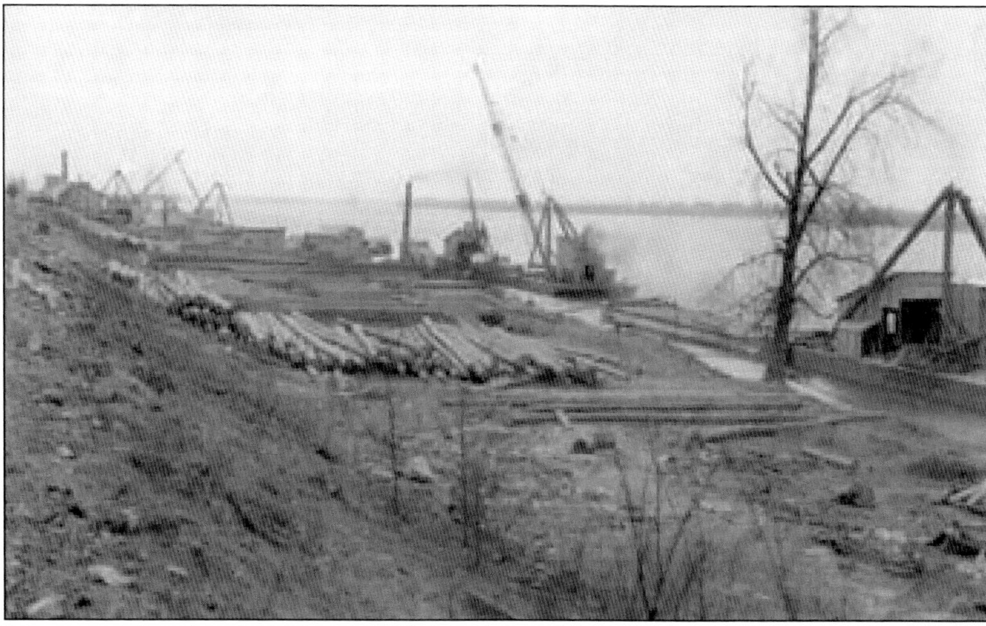

The material yard of the Missouri Valley Bridge and Iron Company shows the driving piling for the cofferdam at Pier 1 in 1927 for the Champ Clark Bridge. The bridge was completed and opened for traffic on May 12, 1928. (Courtesy John Wood.)

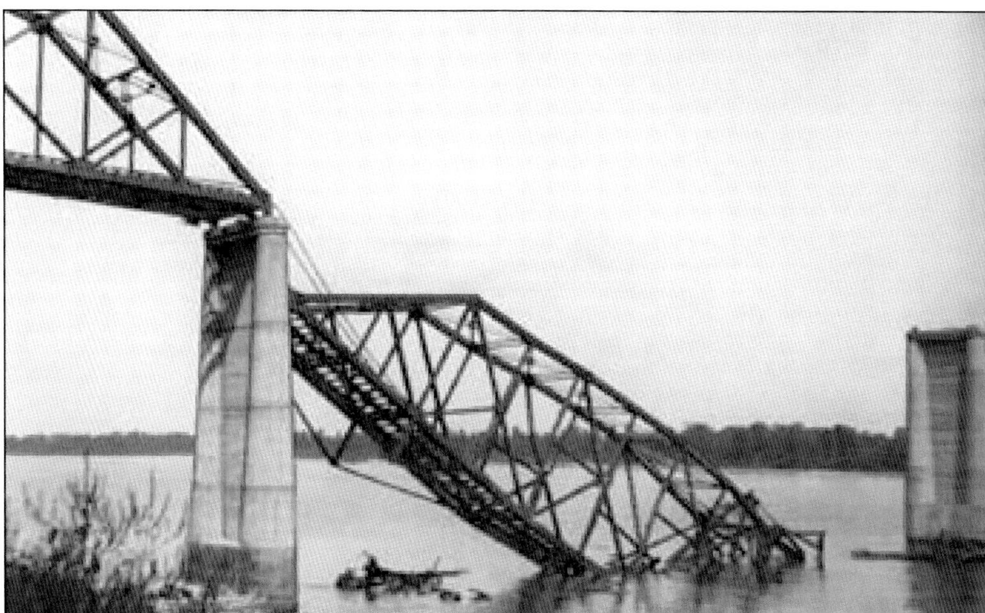

In May 1927, during construction of the Champ Clark Bridge, a 314-foot span toppled into the Mississippi River when the structure was almost completed, killing one workman. (Courtesy John Wood.)

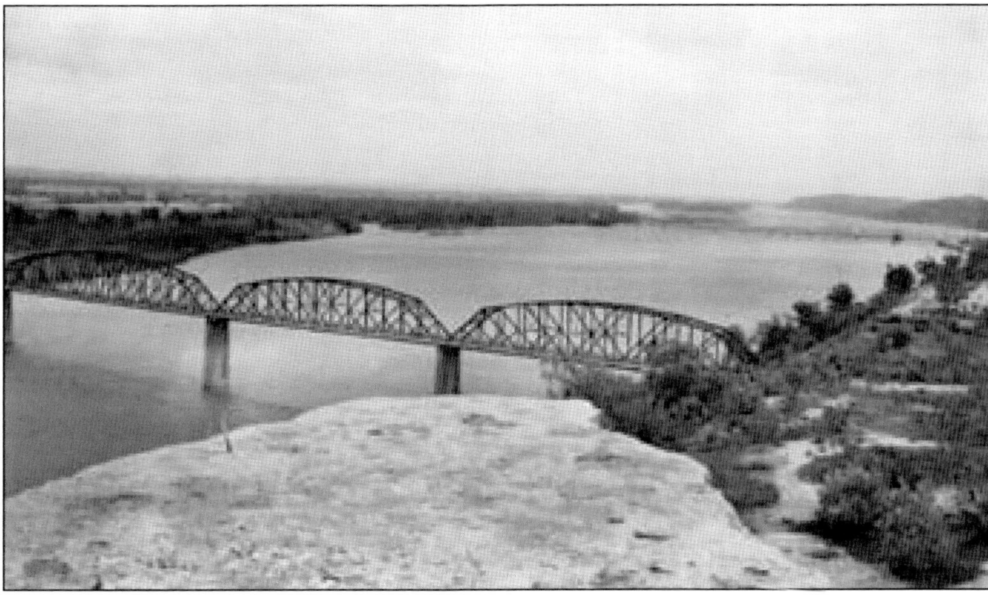

In the foreground is the Champ Clark Bridge spanning the beloved Mississippi River. On the right in the distance is the Railroad Bridge. (Courtesy John Wood.)

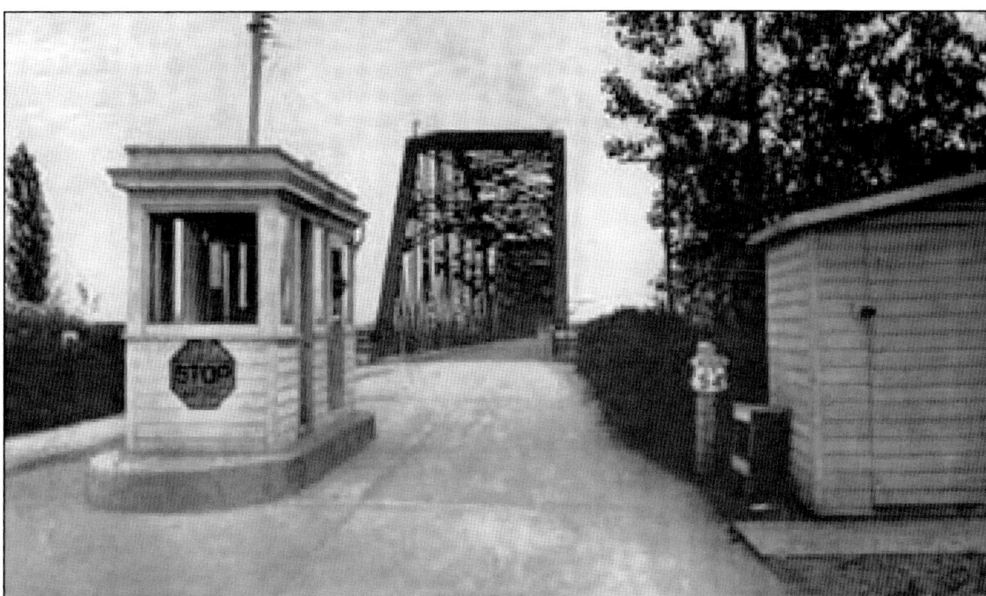

The Champ Clark Bridge's first toll-takers were Ernest Scott, Charles Billings, and George Burbach, each working eight-hour shifts. The last person to cross the toll bridge was Ray Dolbeare in June 1952, after a document was signed calling for the end of tolls on the bridge. (Courtesy Betty Jane Allen.)

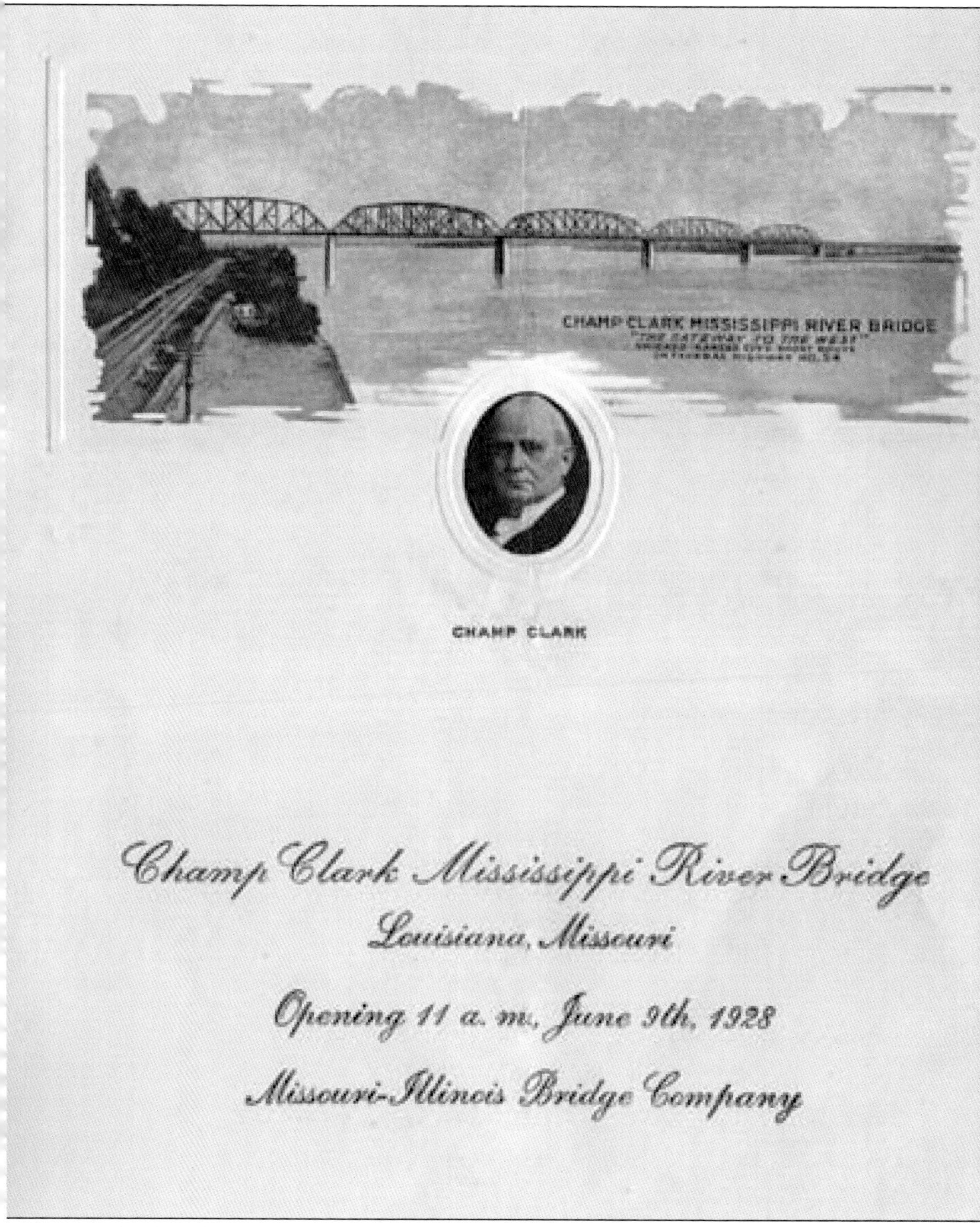

This formal, printed program was handed out at the dedication of the Champ Clark Bridge on June 9, 1928. Clark had died in 1921, but his family was in attendance. Clark was a congressman

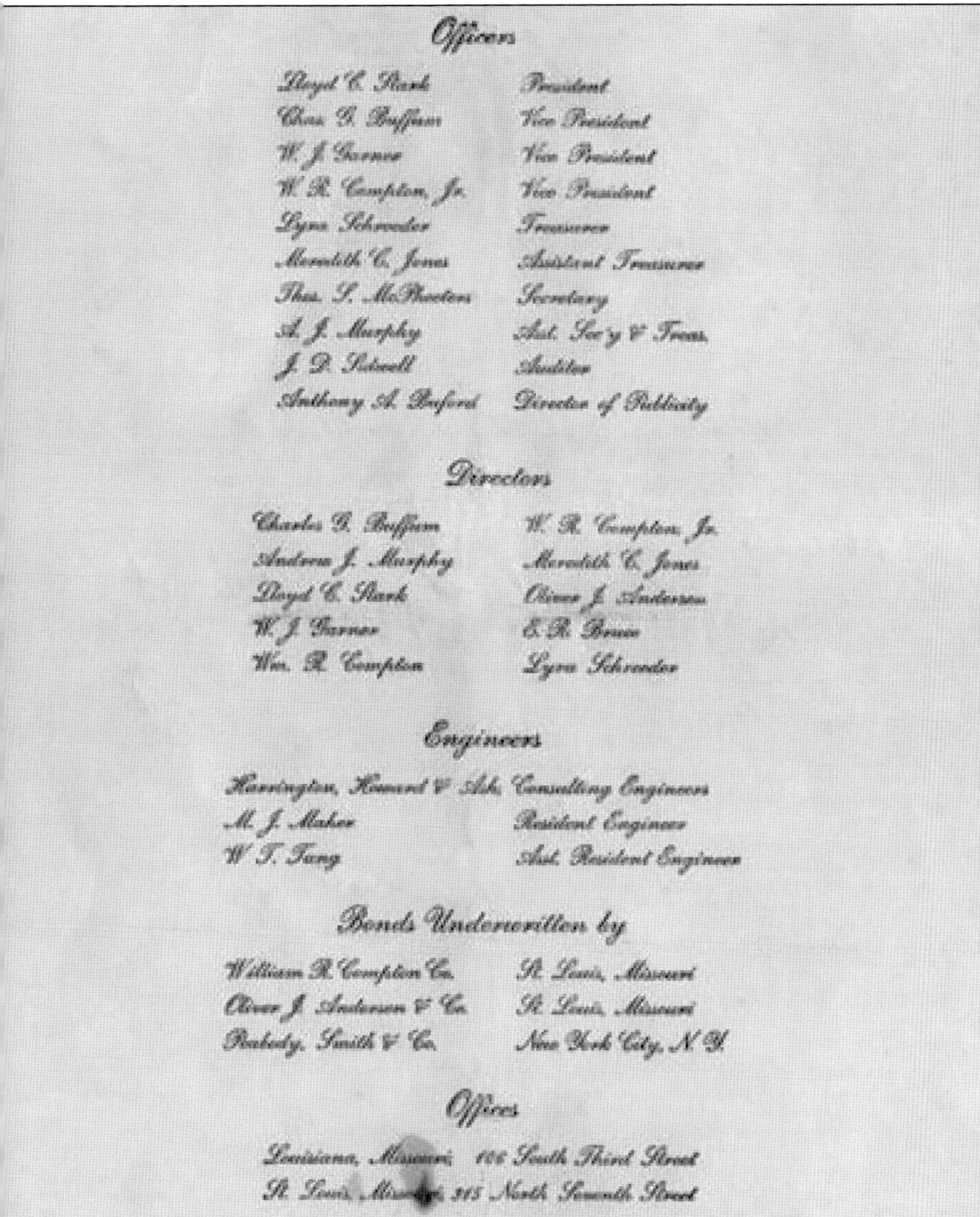

Officers

Lloyd C. Stark	President
Chas. G. Buffum	Vice President
W. J. Garner	Vice President
W. R. Compton, Jr.	Vice President
Lyra Schroeder	Treasurer
Meredith C. Jones	Assistant Treasurer
Thos. F. McPheeters	Secretary
A. J. Murphy	Asst. Sec'y & Treas.
J. D. Sidwell	Auditor
Anthony A. Buford	Director of Publicity

Directors

Charles G. Buffum	W. R. Compton, Jr.
Andrew J. Murphy	Meredith C. Jones
Lloyd C. Stark	Oliver J. Anderson
W. J. Garner	E. R. Bruce
Wm. R. Compton	Lyra Schroeder

Engineers

Harrington, Howard & Ash, Consulting Engineers

M. J. Maher	Resident Engineer
W. T. Tang	Asst. Resident Engineer

Bonds Underwritten by

William R. Compton Co.	St. Louis, Missouri
Oliver J. Anderson & Co.	St. Louis, Missouri
Peabody, Smith & Co.	New York City, N. Y.

Offices

Louisiana, Missouri; 106 South Third Street

St. Louis, Missouri, 315 North Seventh Street

for 26 years, including eight years as the Speaker of the House. (Courtesy Louisiana Area Historical Museum.)

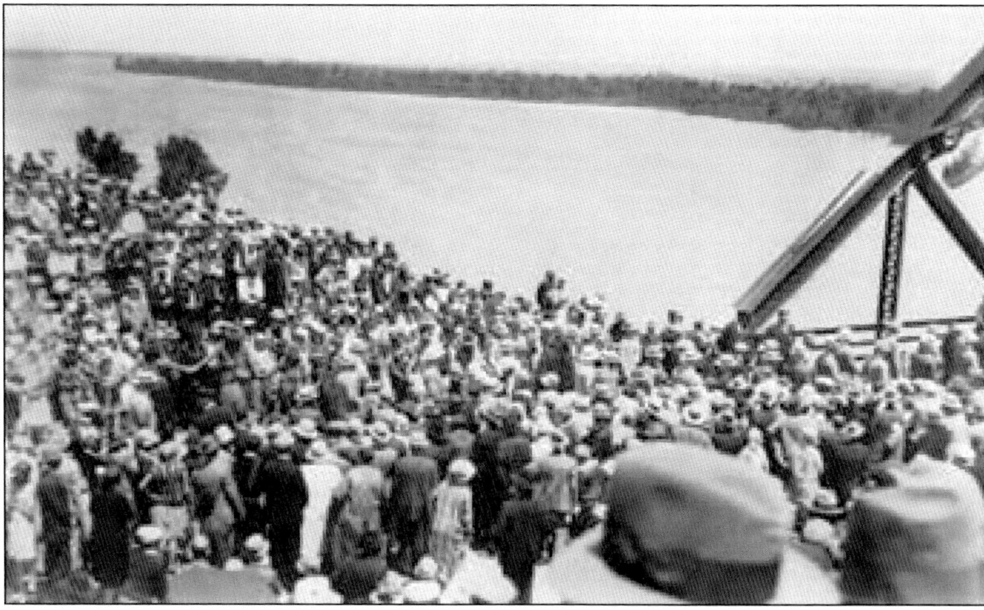

The Champ Clark Bridge opened for traffic on May 12, 1928, and was dedicated on June 9, with an estimated 30,000 people and 4,000 automobiles from 27 states in attendance. Tolls were charged to cross the bridge for 24 years until it became toll-free in 1952. (Courtesy Betty Jane Allen.)

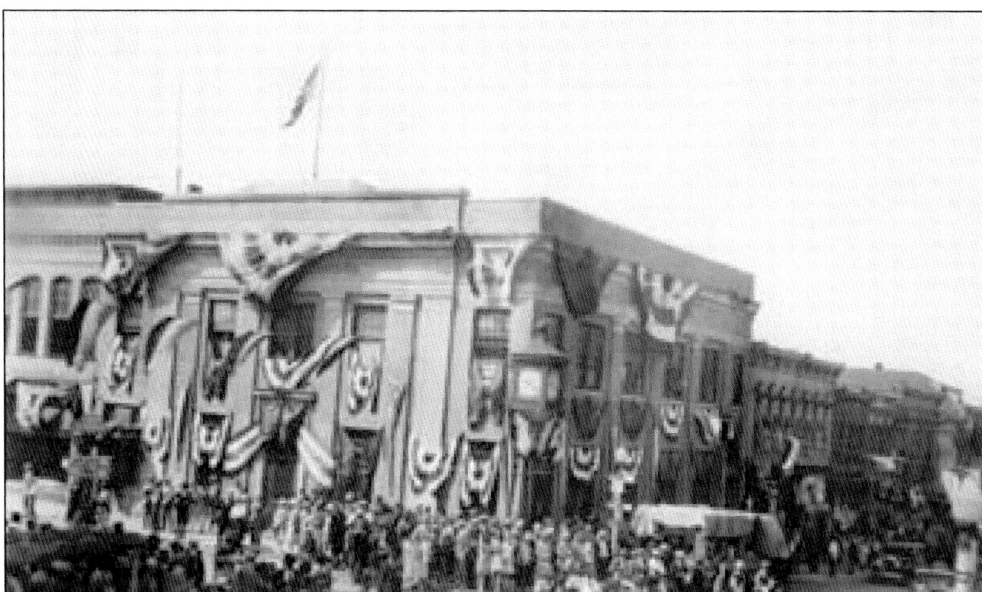

People celebrate the opening of the Champ Clark Bridge in front of the Bank of Louisiana. Buildings were decorated and the bridge dedication brought the largest crowd ever assembled in Louisiana. The name of the bridge was selected after 400 suggestions were made and a statewide vote was held. (Courtesy Betty Jane Allen.)

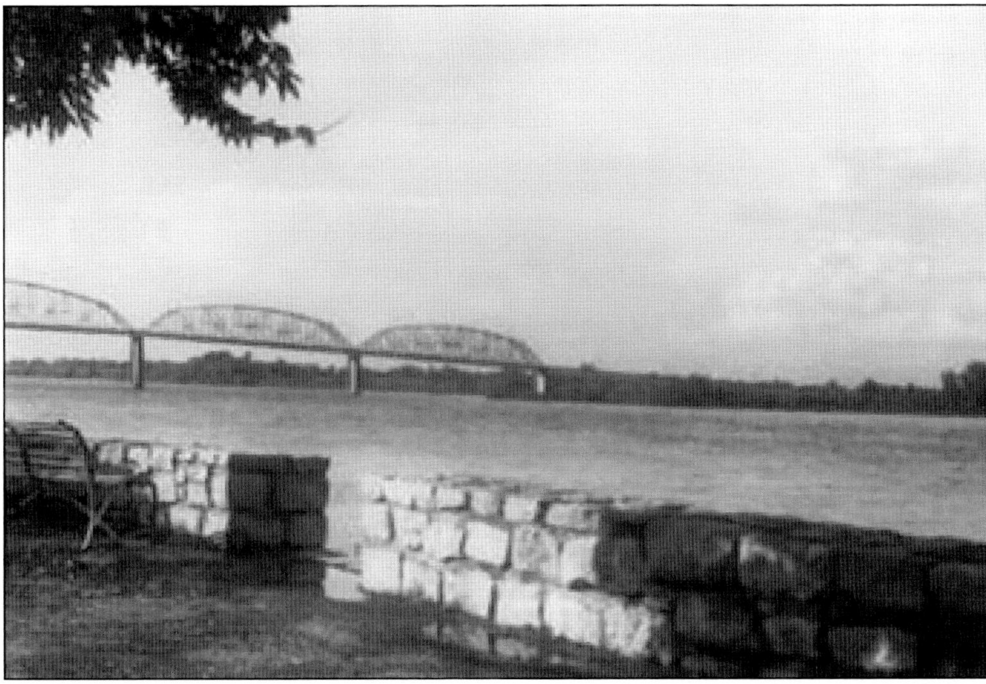

The Mississippi River front wall was built in 1933 by Works Progress Administration (WPA) workers. Pike County was allotted approximately 400 jobs for men to work on various civic projects for 45¢ an hour, $30 a week. The wall is still a favorite spot. The Champ Clark Bridge and the Illinois shore are part of the view from the wall. (Courtesy Betty Jane Allen.)

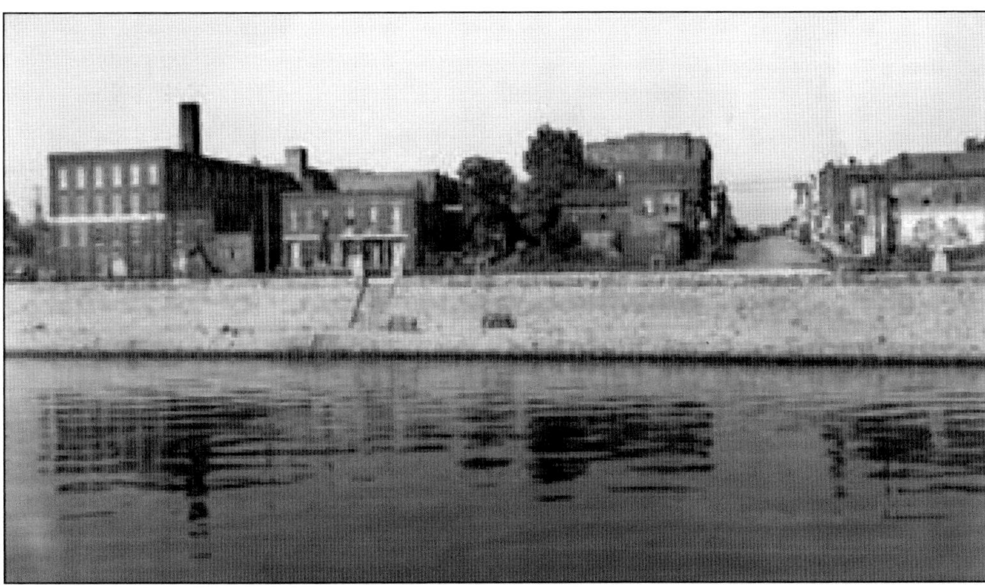

This photograph taken from the river provides a better view of the stone wall built by WPA workers. The street seen here leads straight to downtown Louisiana. (Courtesy Betty Jane Allen.)

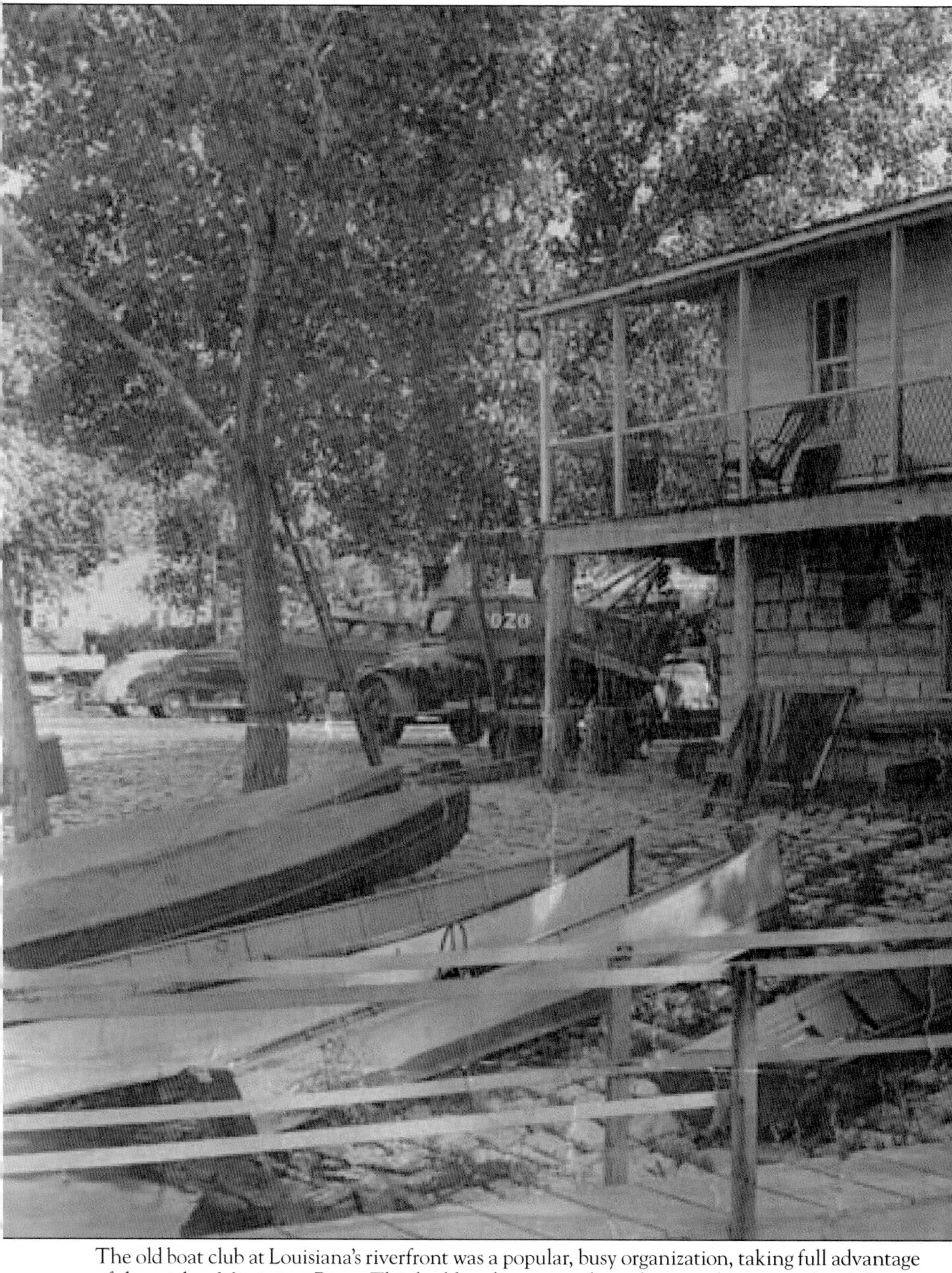

The old boat club at Louisiana's riverfront was a popular, busy organization, taking full advantage of the mighty Mississippi River. This building began as a houseboat, and it is speculated that in

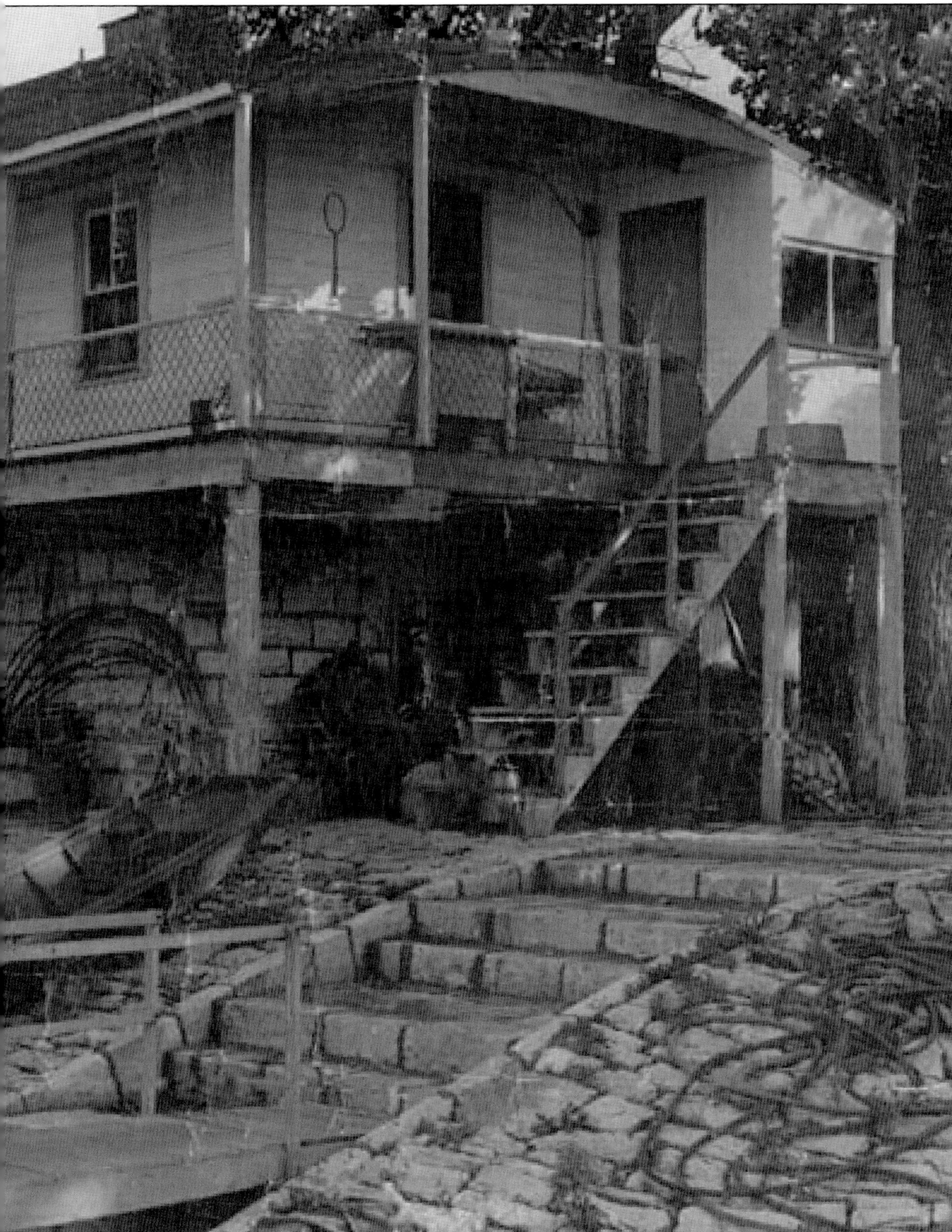

the 1930s, the rock foundation was built under the houseboat. The upstairs was enlarged in the early 1950s. The Louisiana Boat Club was incorporated in 1952. (Courtesy Larry White.)

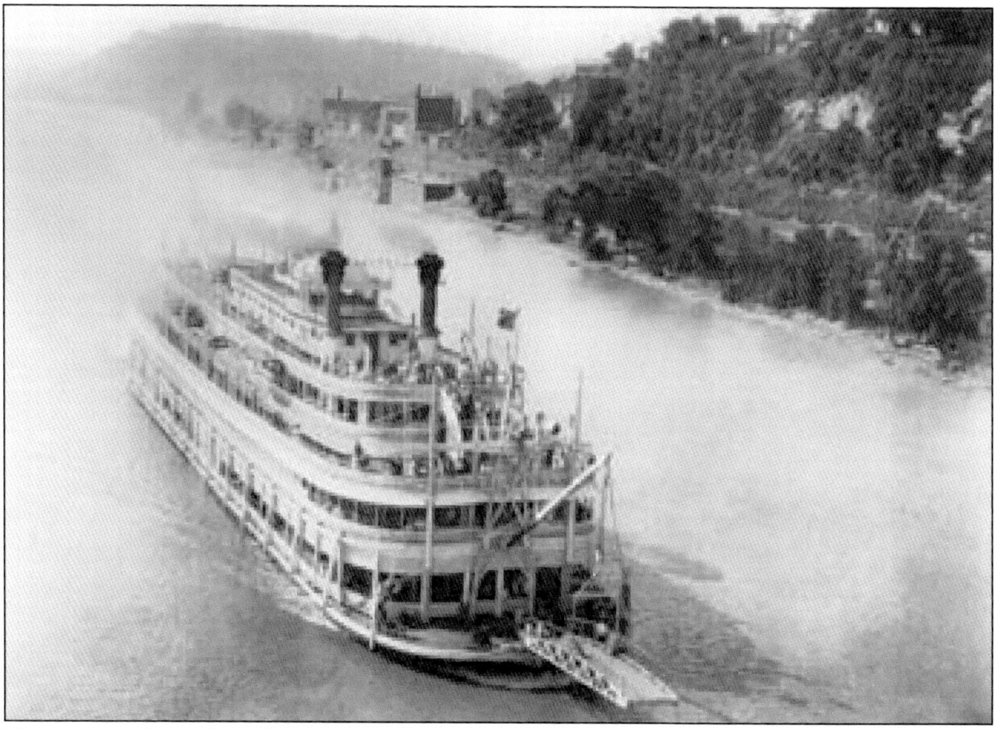

The steamer *Capitol*, of the Streckius line, departs from Louisiana's riverfront. Records of the Masonic Lodge on August 4, 1902, show a motion was approved and adopted to have a moonlight excursion on a riverboat. This evening cruise carried Masons and Eastern Star members. The photograph appeared in the Missouri pictorial supplement to the *St. Louis Post-Dispatch* on August 23, 1936. The road along the river's edge is still used today. (Courtesy John Wood.)

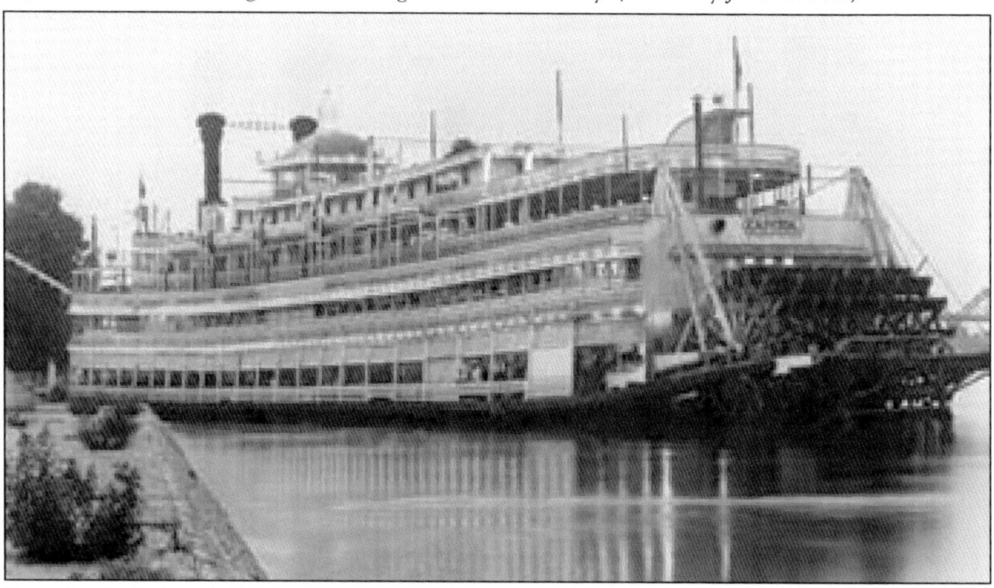

Capitol is docked at the Mississippi riverfront in Louisiana. There are surely many people waiting to board with picnic baskets and cameras in hand for a daytime cruise on the Mississippi. (Courtesy John Wood.)

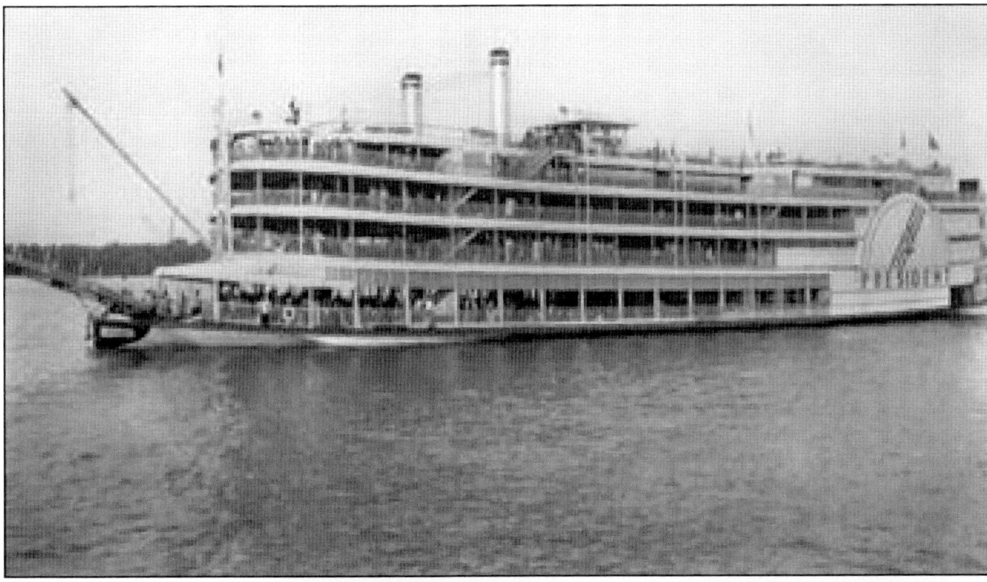

The *President* (above), a popular excursion boat, is filled with people on this afternoon cruise to Hannibal and back on August 24, 1940. The *President* scheduled a night cruise each time it booked a day cruise in Louisiana. Instant photographs could be made for 25¢ and were a cherished souvenir. (Courtesy Betty Jane Allen.)

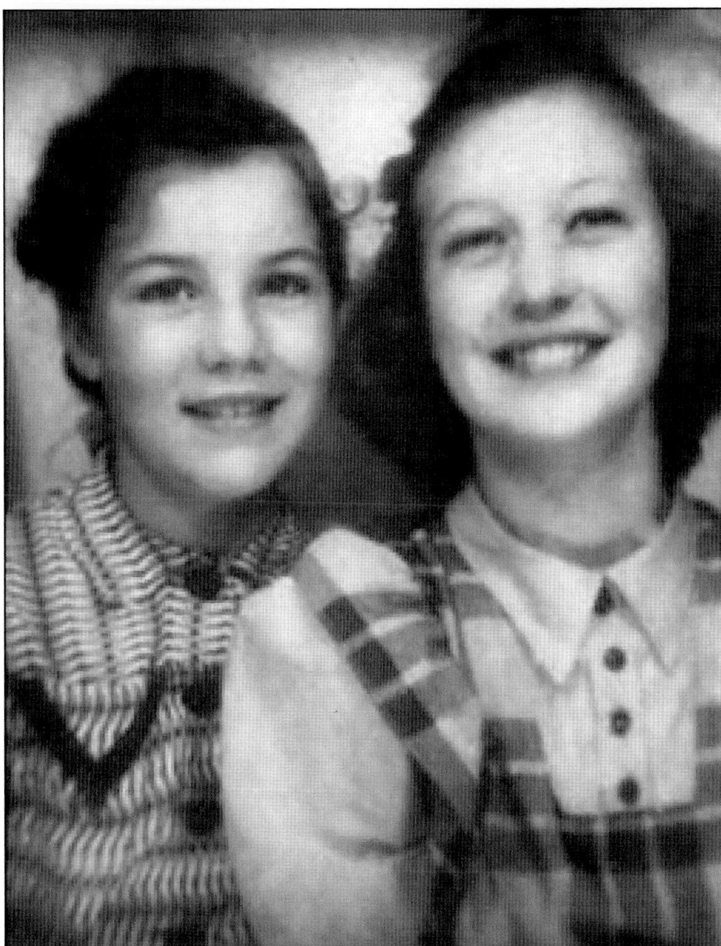

Grade school students Betty Jane Conrad (Allen), coauthor of this book (left), and Mary Alice Jaeger (Middleton) had this photograph taken while cruising. (Courtesy Betty Jane Allen.)

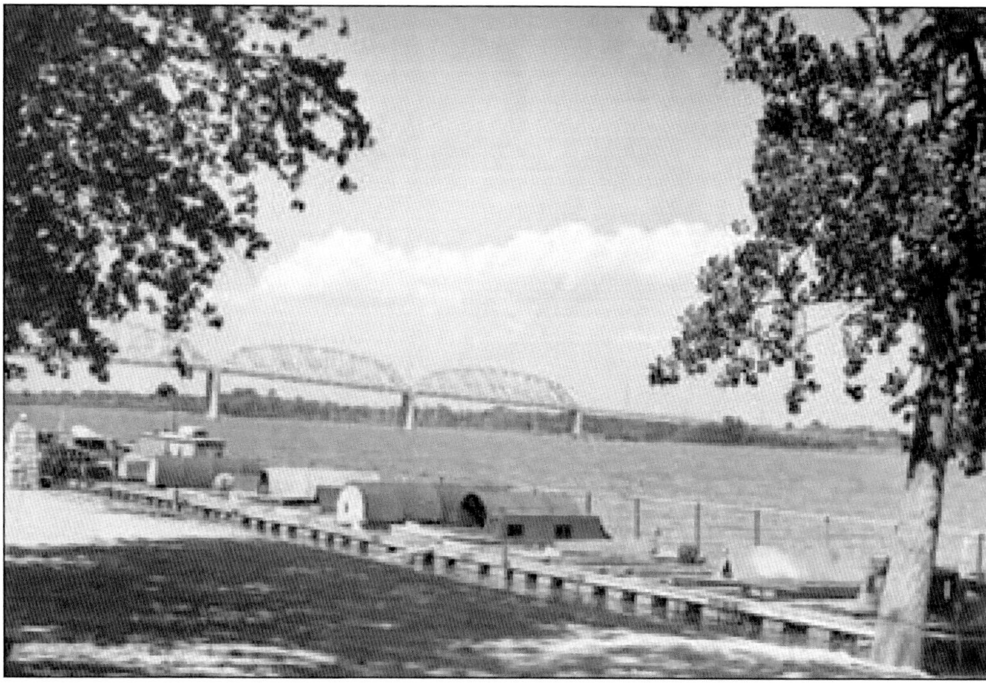

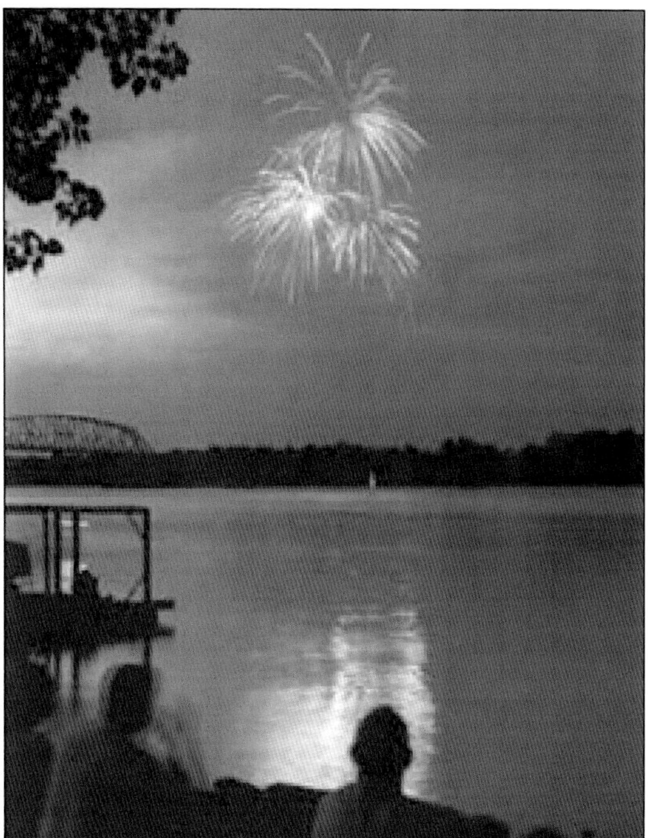

The boat dock in the foreground is not far from the Champ Clark Bridge and provided easy access for pleasure and business pursuits, which it continues to do today. (Courtesy Louisiana Area Historical Museum.)

The annual fireworks display at the Mississippi River draws large crowds every year. Fireworks are set off from a barge on the river and can be seen from miles away. Henderson Riverview Park near the bridge is a favorite viewing spot. The event is sponsored by the chamber of commerce, whose members work hard to make it better each year. (Courtesy Louisiana Area Historical Museum.)

Two

A Growing Downtown

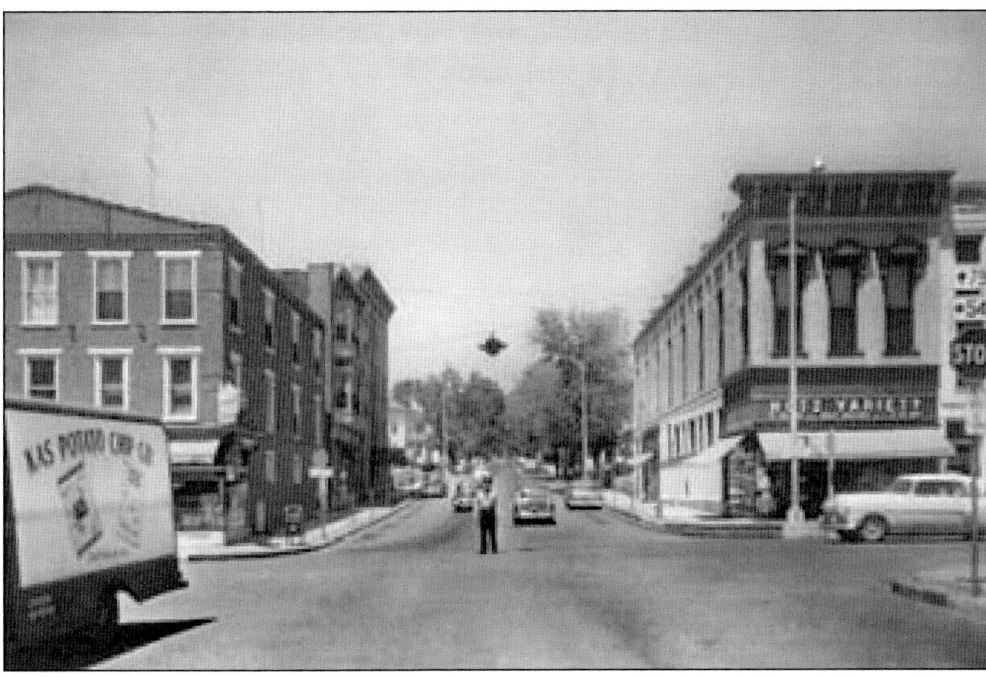

The downtown business hub of Louisiana is the intersection of Third and Georgia Streets (Routes 54 and 79), seen here in the 1950s. Today, the Eagles Nest has replaced Hotz Variety on the right. (Courtesy Sally Dinwiddie.)

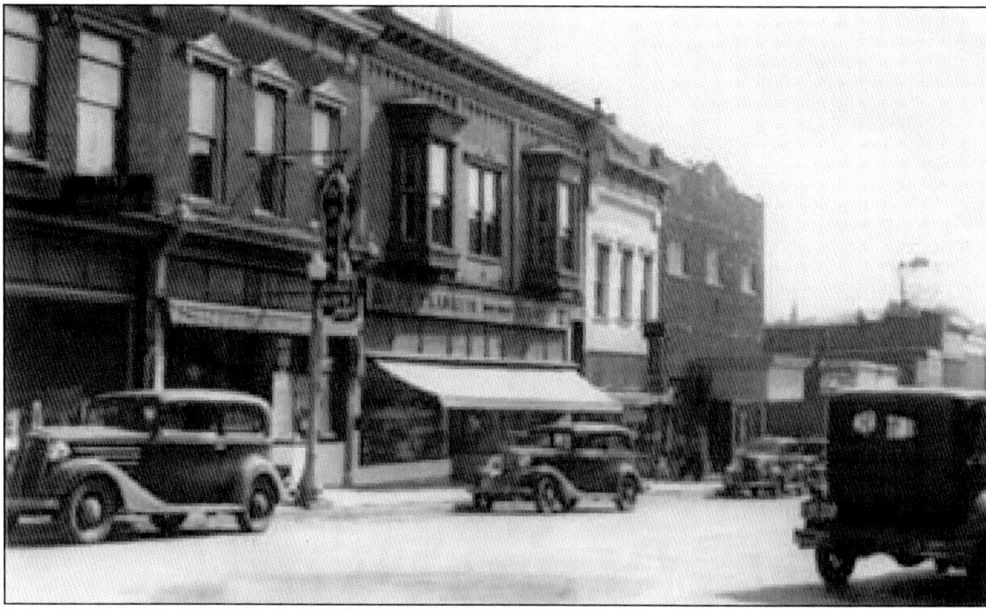

This mid-1930s image of the south side of the 300 block of the Georgia Street business district shows, from left to right, Schmidt Tailor, Pike Beauty Shop, Bray's Drugs, Ben Franklin Store, Nickle's Drugs, and Park's Music House. This block and six others on Georgia Street are now listed in the National Register of Historic Places. (Courtesy John Wood.)

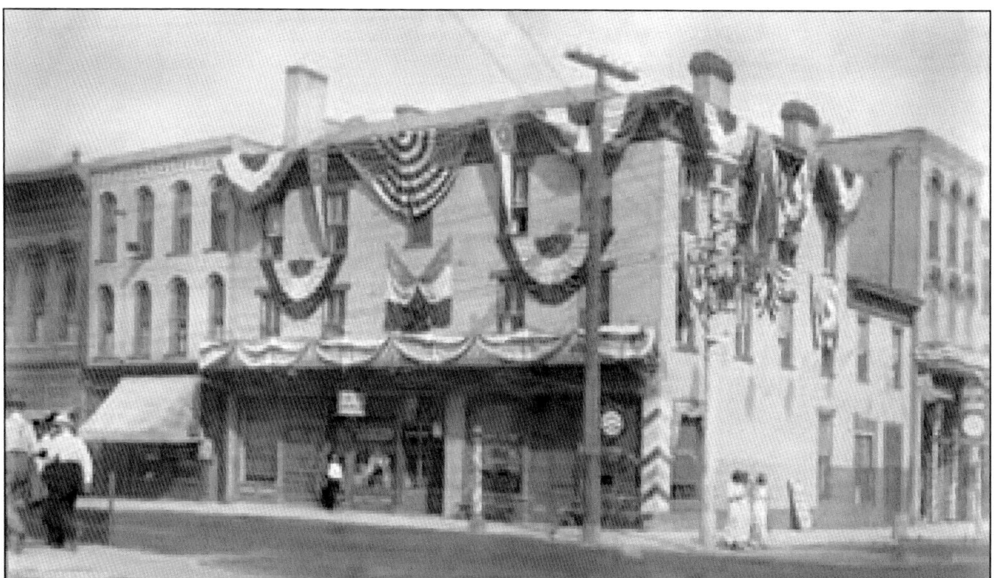

The Stichter Building, at Third and Georgia Streets, decorated patriotically in 1913, is still vital to downtown Louisiana today. This photograph notes that the second and third floors were occupied by Mrs. W.J. English, while dressmaking and millinery were on the first floor. An optician, a barbershop, and a Western Union were also in the building. Family Drug operates here today. (Courtesy John Wood.)

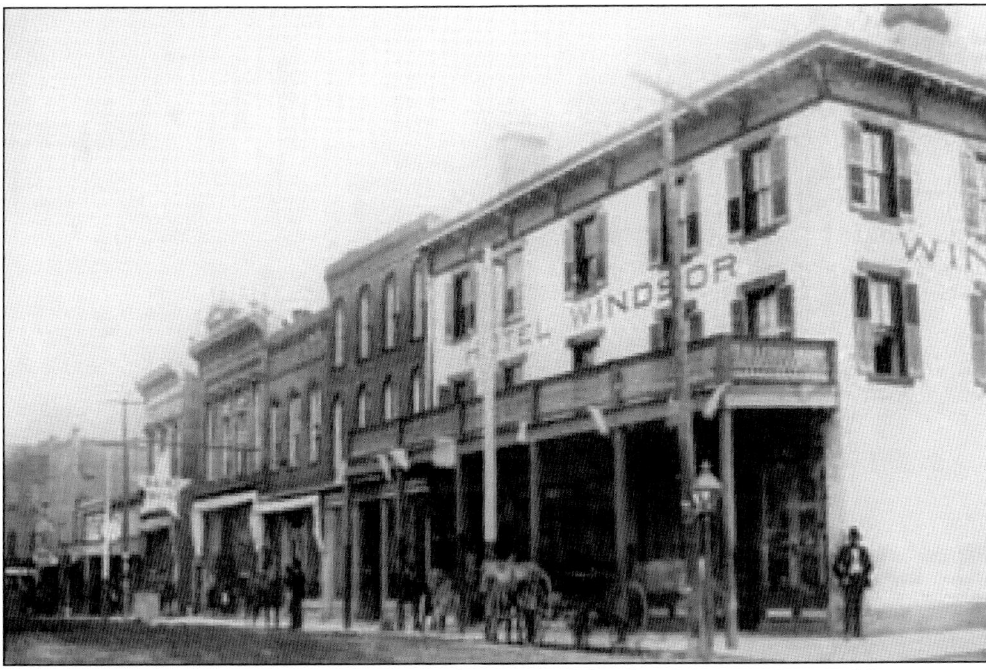

Thomas Jefferson Baird built the Baird Hotel in 1846 at Third and Georgia Streets. He instructed his wife, Catherine, to have it finished should he die before its completion, which she did, after his death that same year. It was later known as the Hotel Windsor. The Mercantile Bank is located there today. (Courtesy Betty Jane Allen.)

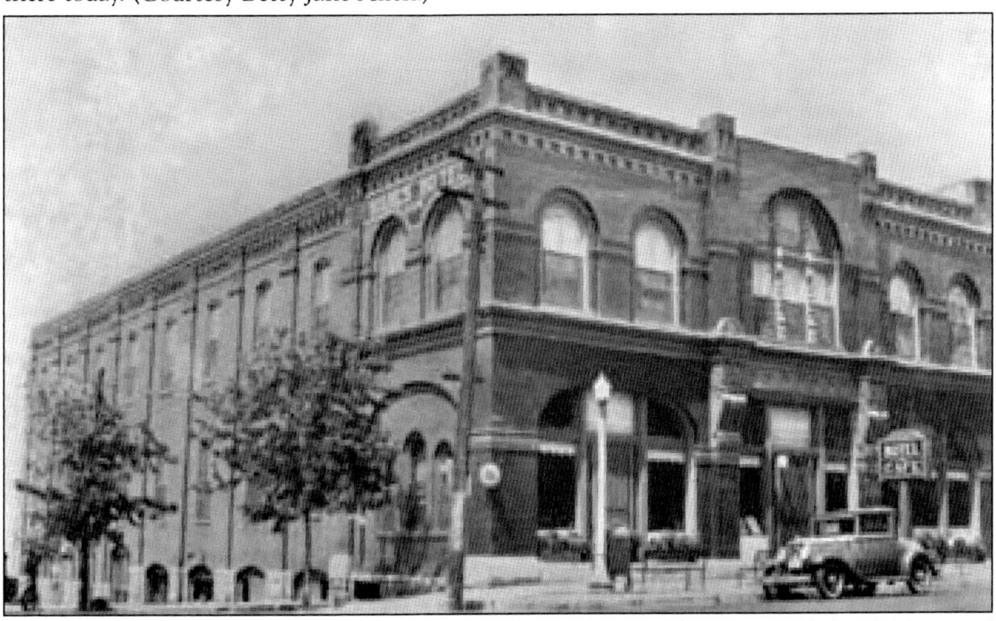

The Grand Hotel, on Third and South Carolina Streets, was sold to Arnold C.G. Wahl around 1918. He renamed it the Wahl Hotel. With his wife, Ruth Bramlett, they operated an excellent restaurant. It was also a busy bus stop with several bus lines, and later was exclusively used by Greyhound. Today, the ASL Pewter Shop occupies the renovated first floor and several upstairs apartments have been completed and are rented. (Courtesy Linda Ince Beer.)

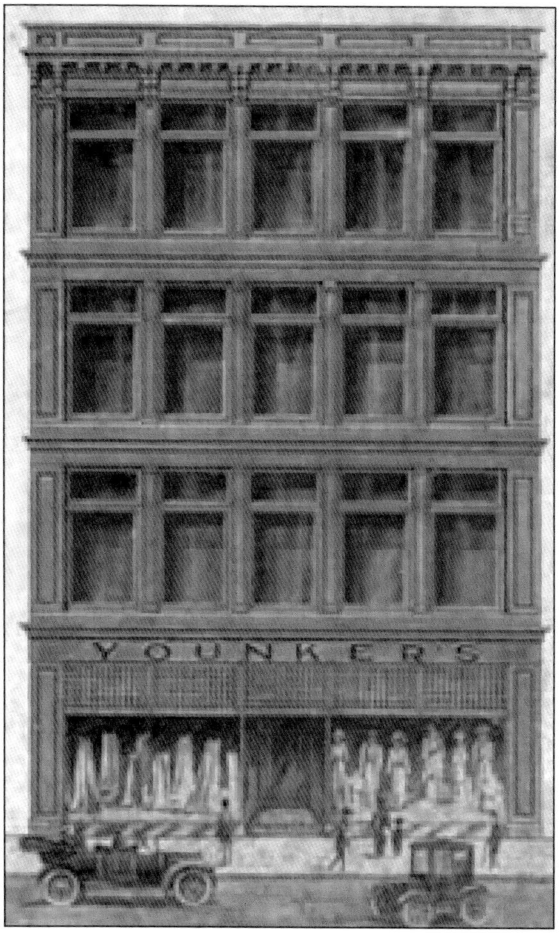

The Younker's Building, the only four-story building in Louisiana, featured the Younker's dry goods store, which was popular in the mid- to late 1800s. Seen here on a postcard dated December 24, 1914, it was next to the Stichter Building on Georgia Street and had a fancy elevator. The Younker family established a chain of dry goods stores in the Midwest. The Younkers were civic-minded, serving the community capably. Although most of the Younkers married, none had children. High winds destroyed the building in 2004. (Courtesy John Wood.)

The Wald brothers—Louis, Adam, and David—had an emporium on the corner of Third and Main Streets in 1874 (below). David managed the dry goods, and Louis and Adam sold clothing. In 1878, the store relocated to Third and Georgia Streets. The brothers and their wives built three stone houses side by side on Third Street, just two blocks from their business. A carriage barn was behind Louis's house for a horse and cow. (Courtesy John Wood.)

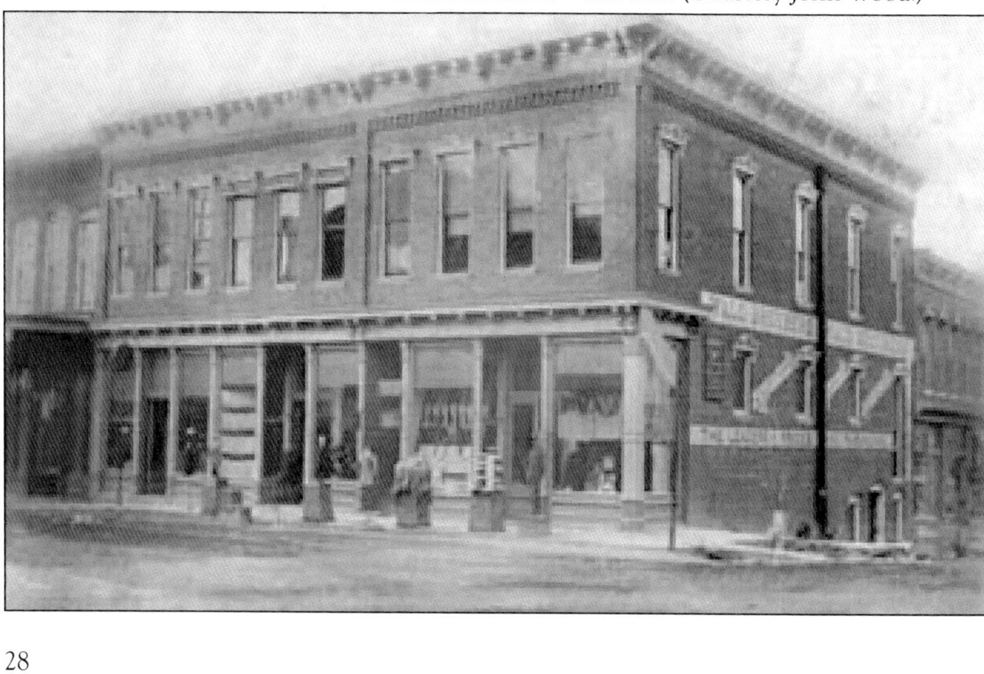

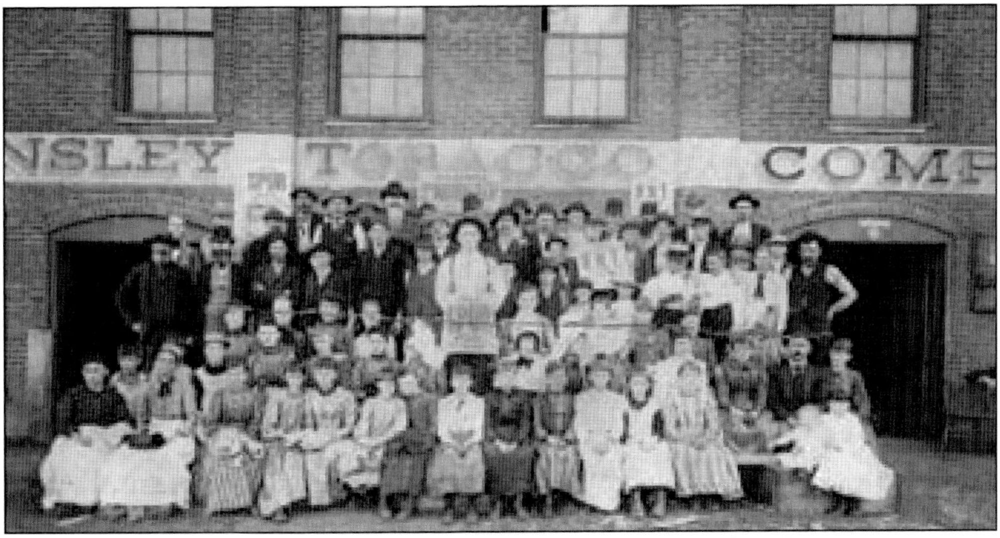

Four tobacco companies were located in this building, starting with the John Myers Company; followed by McCune, Palmer, and Knight; L. Tinsley Tobacco Company (seen here); and the American Tobacco Company. Later, the building housed the Buffum Tool Company. After the tool company closed in 1902, the Nord-Buffum Pearl Button Factory was founded. In the 1930s, it employed 100 people and produced 72,000 pearl buttons annually. It closed in August 1976. (Courtesy Betty Jane Allen.)

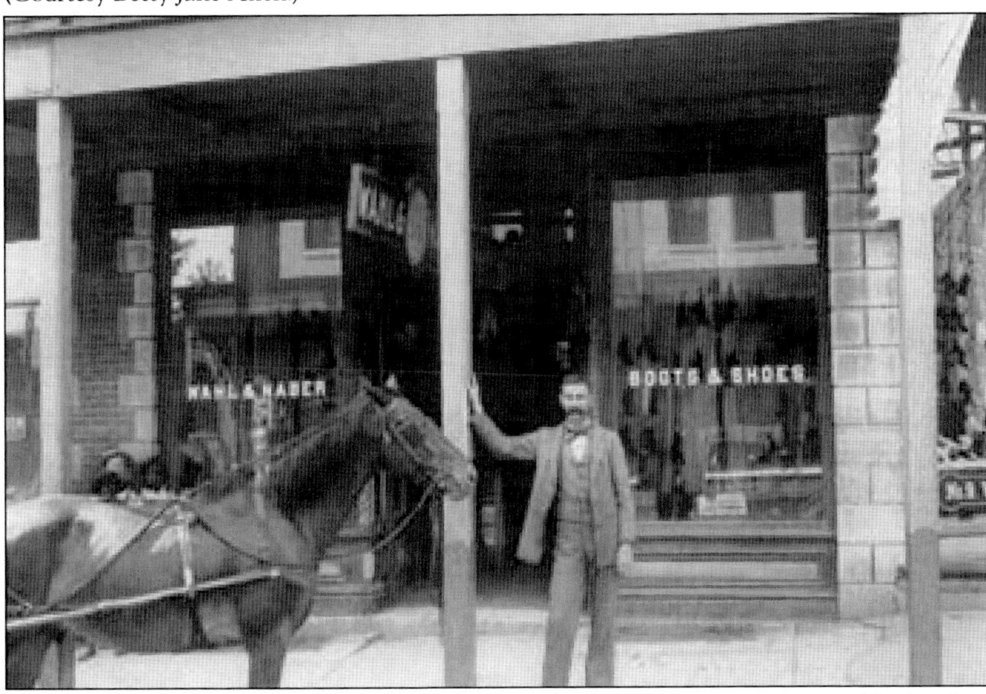

Wahl & Naber, on the north corner of Fourth and Georgia Streets, was owned by brothers Charles and George Wahl. In 1862, they had this three-story brick building built, with the first floor divided in two sections. Henry G. Naber was an associate of the brothers in their shoe manufacturing business, which was in one of the sections. In the other section, Charles sold beer that he brewed on North Seventh Street. (Courtesy John Wood.)

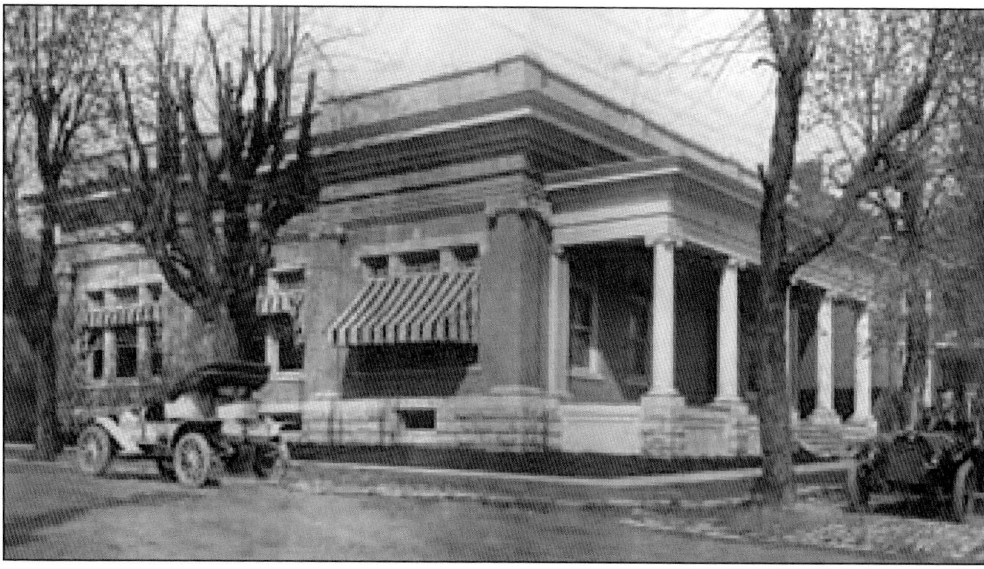

LaCrosse Lumber Company was established by Gov. Cadwallader C. Washburn of LaCrosse, Wisconsin, in 1873. Lumber was Louisiana's first chief industry, and the river was active in wholesale shipping. Besides LaCrosse, seven other lumber companies were recorded in town before 1875. In 1910, LaCrosse built corporate headquarters at 200 North Main Street, where it is still located today. (Courtesy LaCrosse Lumber Co.)

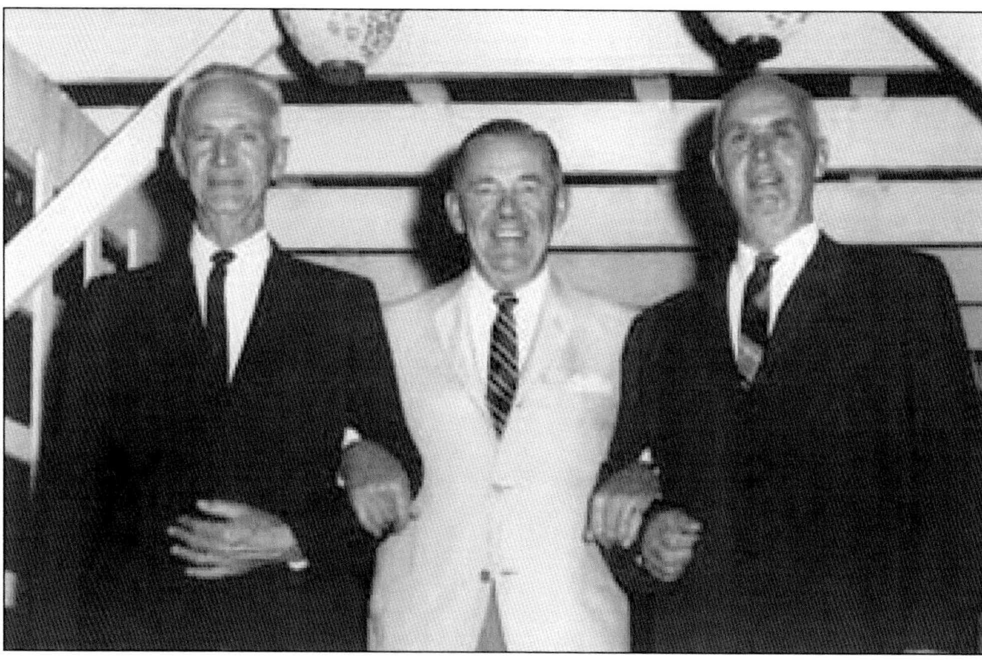

From left to right, Evan Angle, Charles Buffum Jr., and Rufus Angle seem to be enjoying a gala evening. On January 1, 1949, an addition to the Pike County Hospital was proposed by Buffum, who was the president of the hospital's board of trustees, and E.E. Angle, the secretary. Well respected in this community, these men were also officers at the LaCrosse Lumber Company. (Courtesy Louisiana Area Historical Museum.)

Isaac Newton Bryson Jr., born on December 13, 1852, called himself the "Filosoefer" and had quite a way with words. For 50 years, he wrote, edited, and published the *Louisiana Press Journal*, which he purchased in 1877, when it was known as the *Louisiana Press*. He died on November 7, 1938, after he was hit by a car at Third and Georgia Streets returning to work in the rain after supper. He is buried in Riverview Cemetery. (Courtesy Betty Jane Allen.)

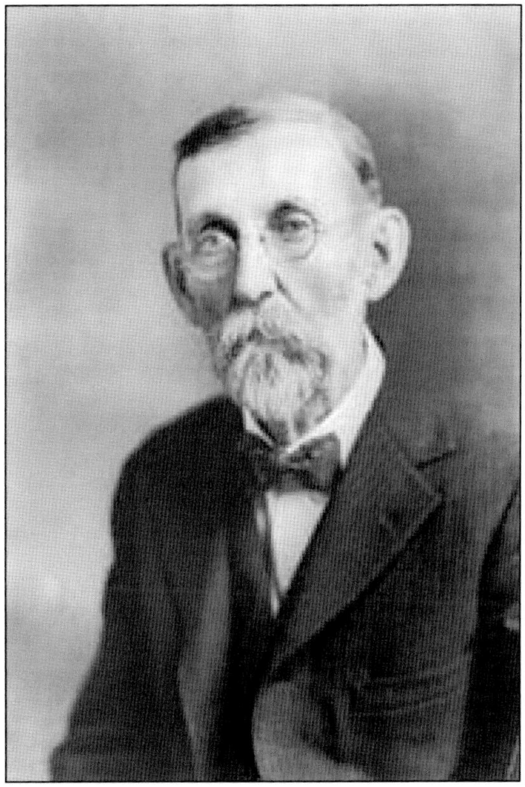

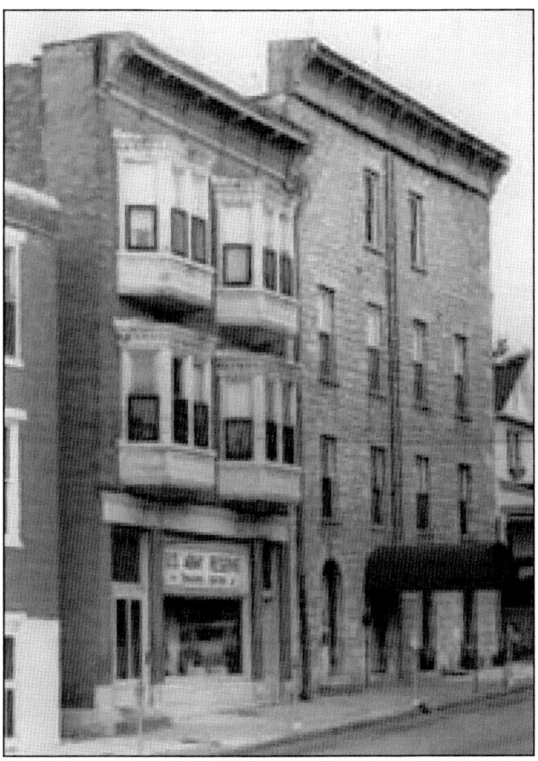

William Alexander built this large stone mill at 106 North Third Street and operated a milling business with his brother James for three years, before it failed in 1875. In 1881, the building was purchased by Samuel Reid and equipped for the manufacturing of tobacco, with a daily production capacity of 3,000 pounds of tobacco. The Joe Bowers brand was a favorite tobacco and was shipped to 12 states. The factory burned in 1883. Insurance paid for rebuilding and W.F. Suda, who had a funeral business at another location, purchased it. Following Suda's death, J.B. Sterne, an employee of Suda's, took over and moved the business to 106 North Third Street on May 23, 1941. After Sterne's death in 1995, his son David took over. Sterne Mortuary closed in 2011. (Courtesy Betty Jane Allen.)

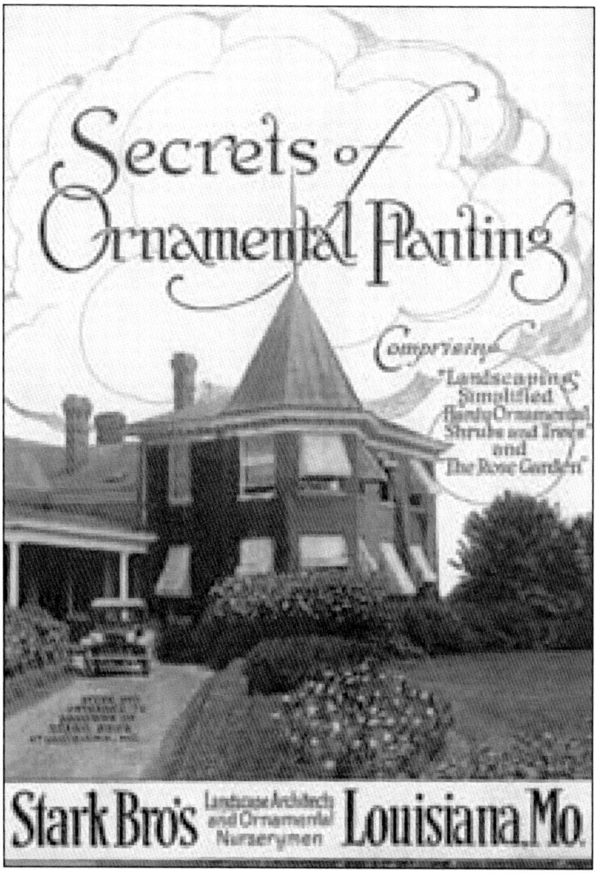

Luther Burbank chose Stark Bro's Nurseries & Orchards Co. to take over his seed stock and breeding programs before he died in 1926. James Hart Stark started Stark Bro's Nurseries & Orchards Co. in 1816, and the company eventually laid claim to being America's oldest, and the world's largest, nursery business. (Courtesy The Stark Story.)

Below, 30 members of the Louisiana Garden Club pose in front of the Stark Cabin Museum in 1951, after John Hart Stark's log home was moved from its country location. Some of the ladies included Lula Beth Giffith, Willella Unsell, Girlie Wyman, Lucy Green, Ada Dorwood, and Lucille Creamer. The garden club has done many beautification projects through the years. (Courtesy Louisiana Area Historical Museum.)

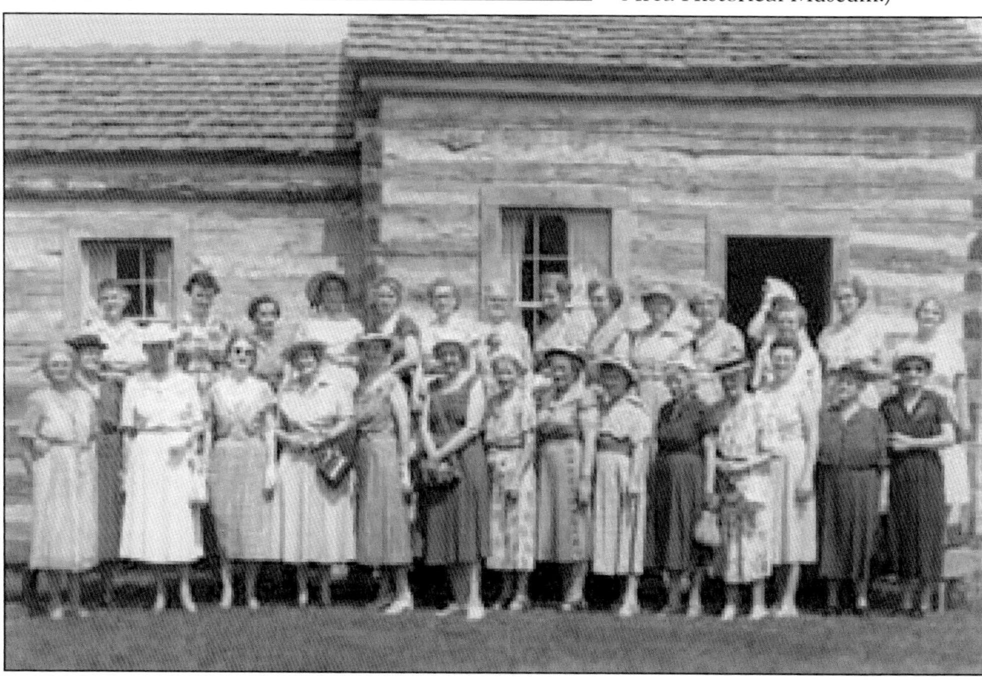

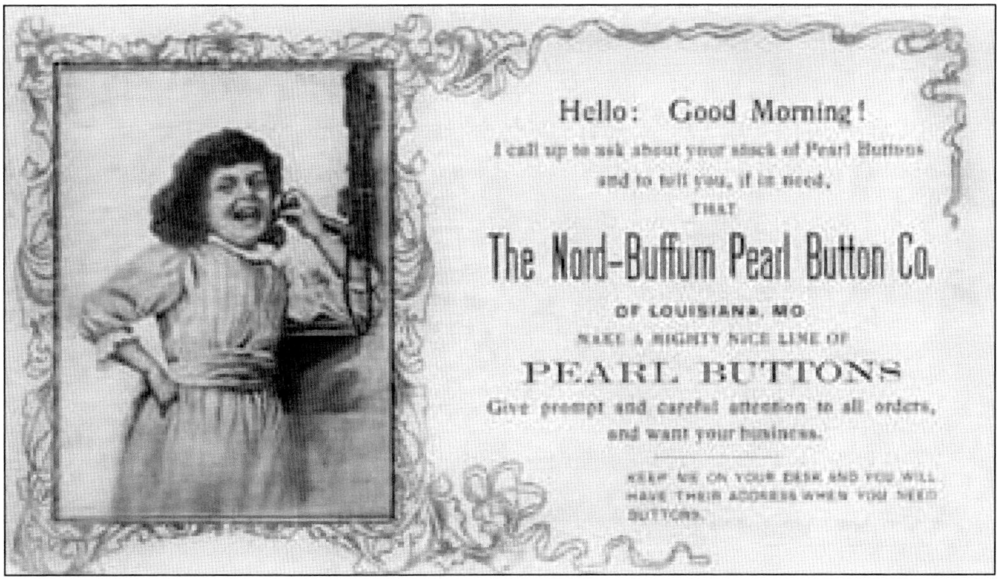

This is a unique advertisement for the beautiful mother-of-pearl buttons made from the shells of mussels gathered from the Mississippi River, which was across Water Street from the Nord-Buffum Pearl Button Company. (Courtesy Betty Jane Allen.)

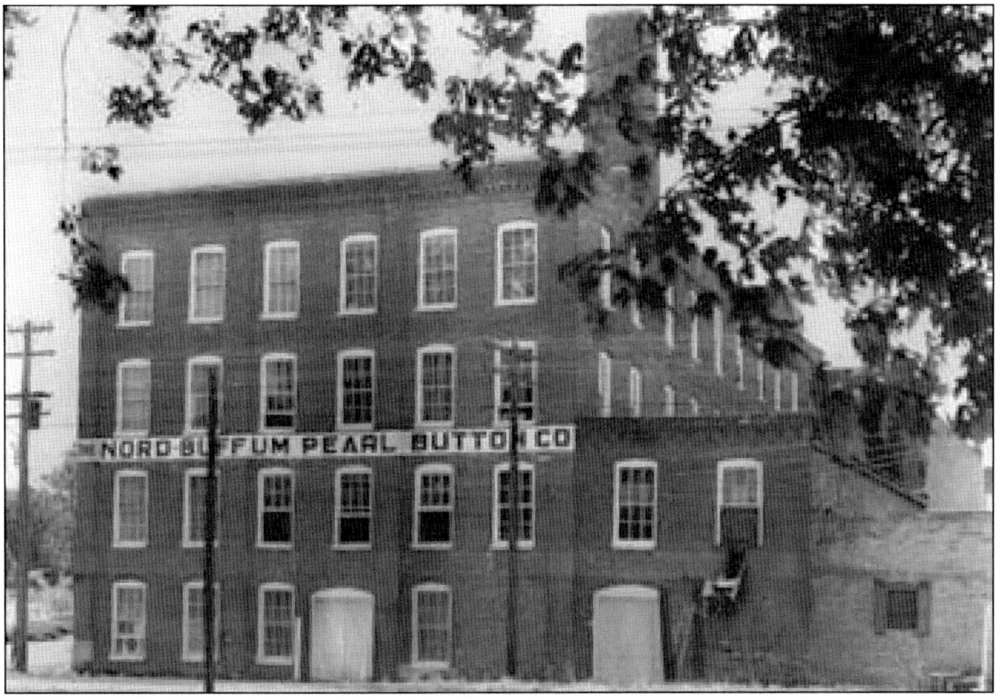

In 1902, P.F. Nord, with the assistance of Charles and Frank Buffum, founded the Nord-Buffum Pearl Button Company. In the 1930s, the Company produced about 72 million pearl buttons annually. Charles F. Nord Sr. purchased the partnership in 1951, becoming sole owner. Because of the influx of plastic buttons, the market for the expensive mother-of-pearl buttons declined, so the company joined the trend to plastics. One of Louisiana's oldest industries, the Nord-Buffum Pearl Button Company closed its doors in August 1976. (Courtesy Betty Jane Allen.)

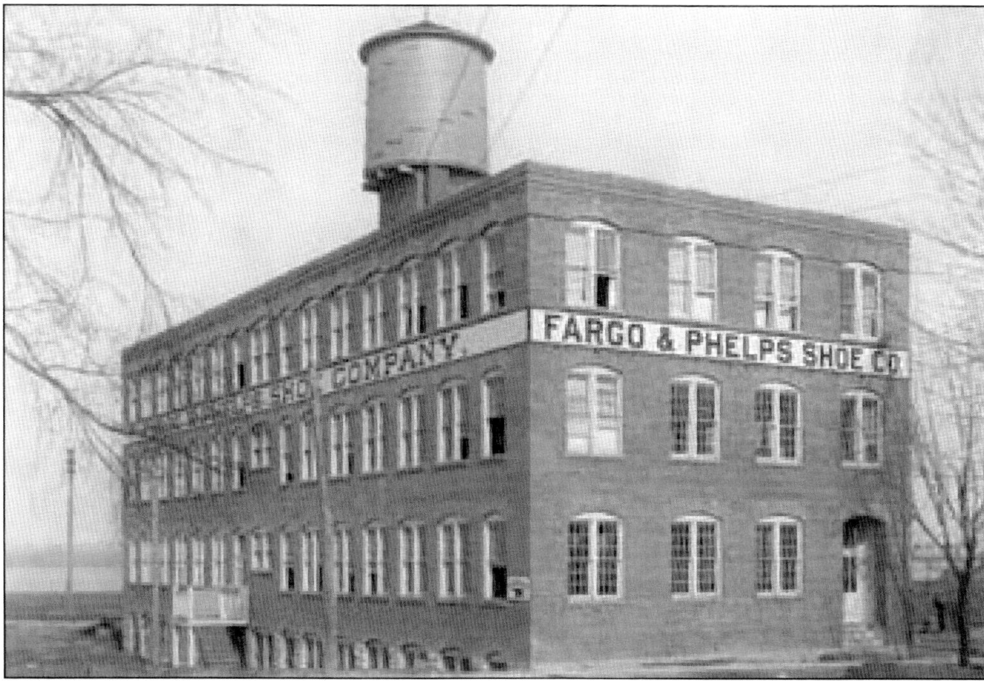

The Fargo & Phelps Shoe Company first occupied this building. Later, the building housed the McElroy-Sloan Shoe Company, the Wells-Lamont glove factory, the Tallman Conduit Company, and finally, the Whittle Toy Train Company. In April 1917, the McElroy-Sloan Shoe Company was given a contract for 100,000 Army shoes. (Courtesy John Wood.)

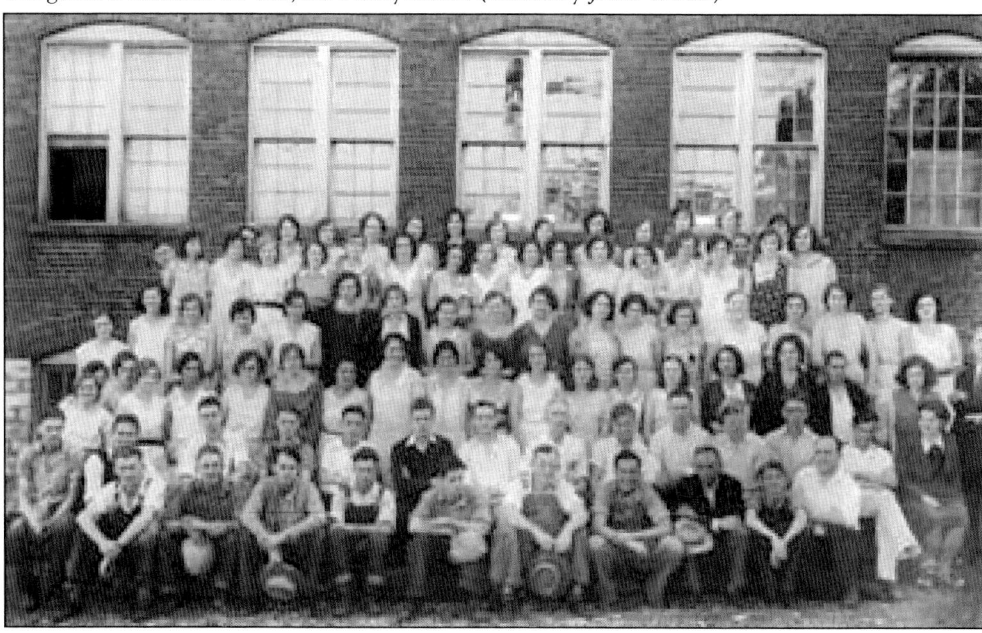

The Wells-Lamont glove factory served many purposes. It brought new industry to Louisiana. It employed approximately 115 men, boys, women, and girls, helping with the unemployment problems of the Great Depression in 1936. The building was eventually purchased by the chamber of commerce. (Courtesy John Wood.)

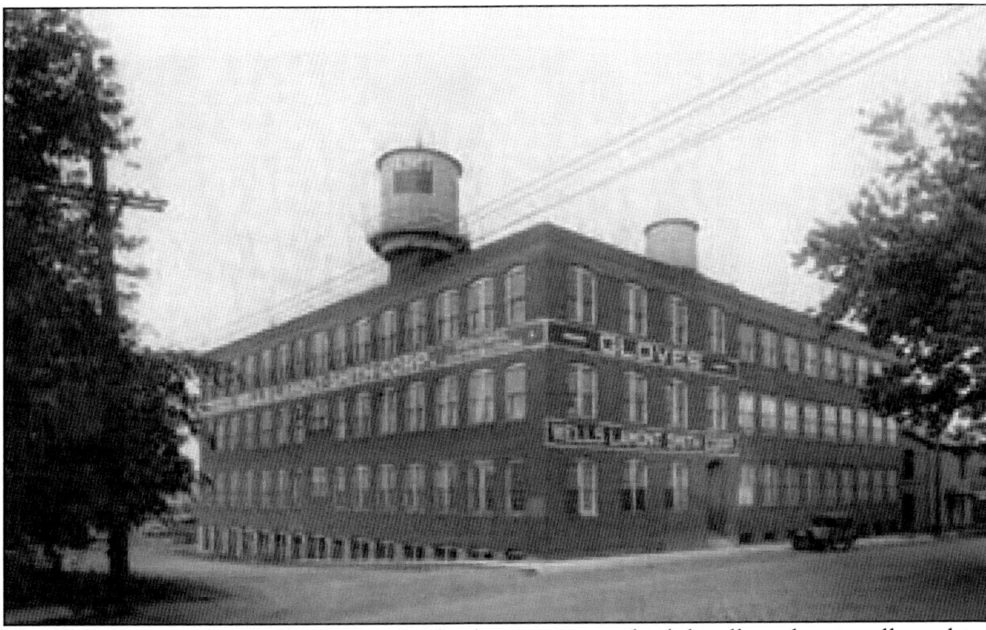

The Wells-Lamont-Smith Corporation had a thriving impact both locally and nationally, making gloves for distribution all over the country. (Courtesy John Wood.)

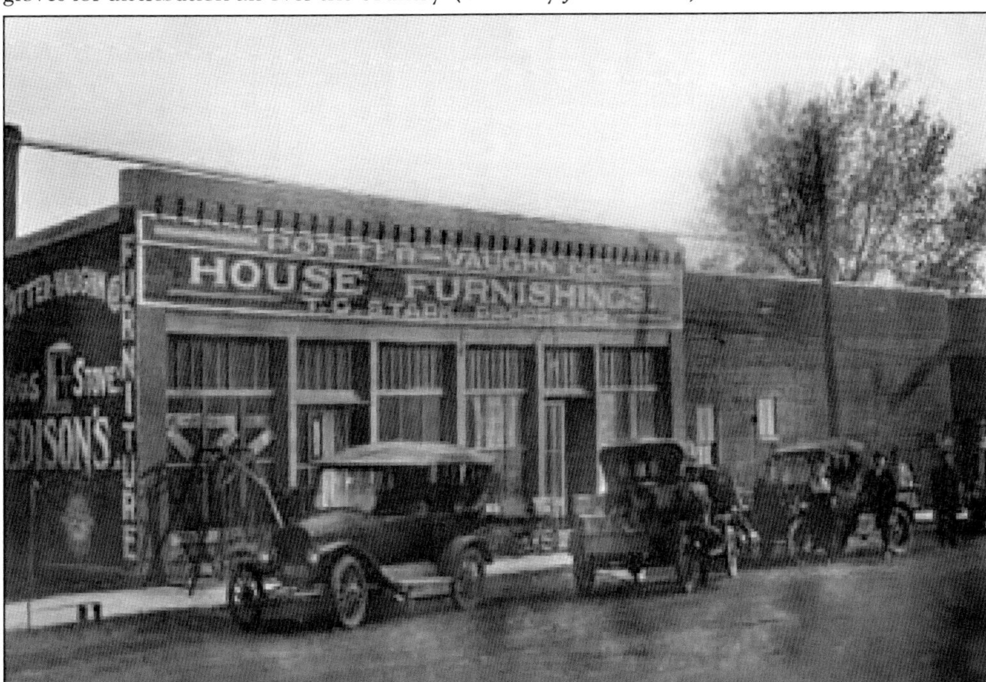

The Potter and Vaughn Company, located in the 300 block of South Carolina Street, advertised "house furnishings, cash or credit" and called itself "the store where quality and economy meet. We have everything but eatables and wearables." T.G. Stark was the proprietor and the phone extension was 349. On May 29, 1930, a fire destroyed the building and Southwestern Bell Company purchased the lot and built on it. (Courtesy John Wood.)

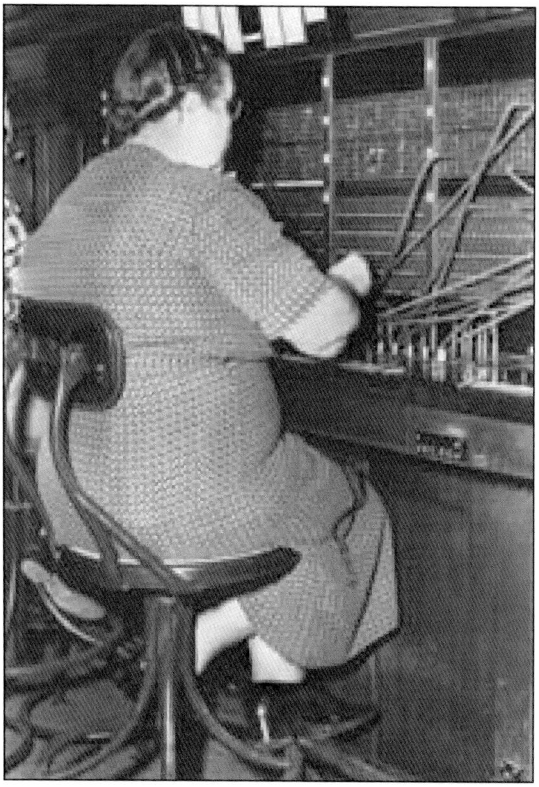

The Buffum Telephone Company was organized in 1901 when Frank Washburn Buffum left the family business he ran with his father and brother, LaCrosse Lumber Company, and founded the telephone company. Hallie Richardson (left) was one of several telephone operators working for Buffum's successful business. (Courtesy Betty Jane Allen.)

Ab's Café was a popular family-owned restaurant in the early 1940s. Pictured seated at the counter are Buddy Martin (left) and Richard "Tippy" Asquith. Standing are Phyllis Wood (left) and Roberta Meyers. Woods later married Martin. Albia Steer's wife, Irene, and daughters Hazel, Joyce, and Iola often helped. Ab's was located at 111 South Third Street, which is now part of the Bank of Louisiana parking lot. (Courtesy Betty Asquith.)

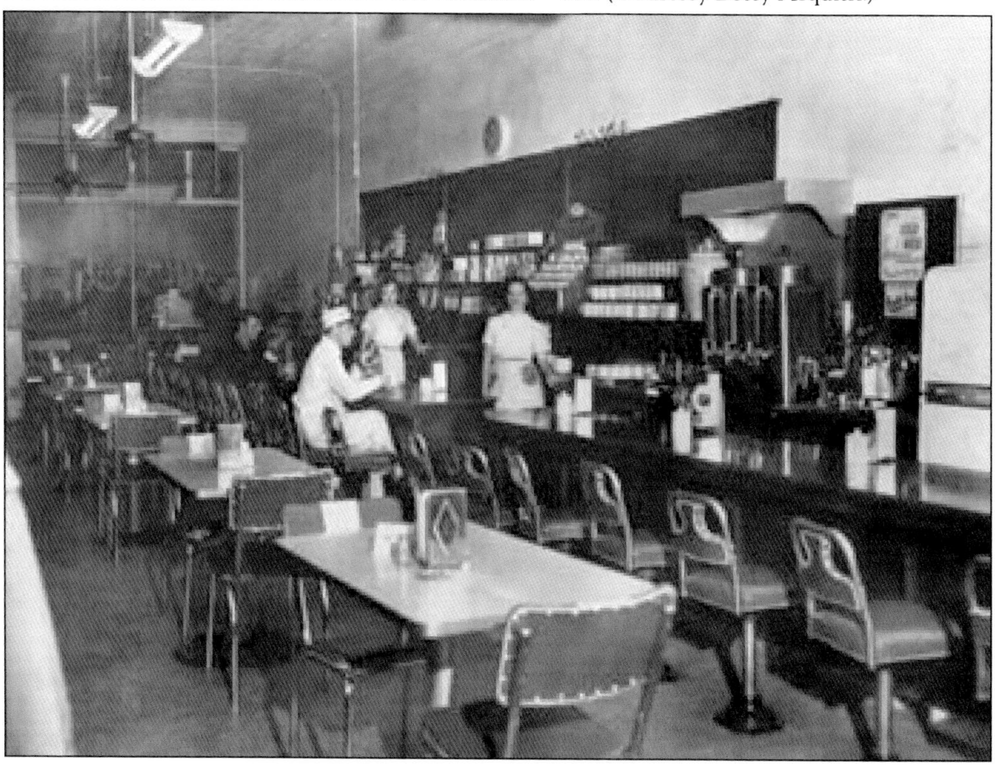

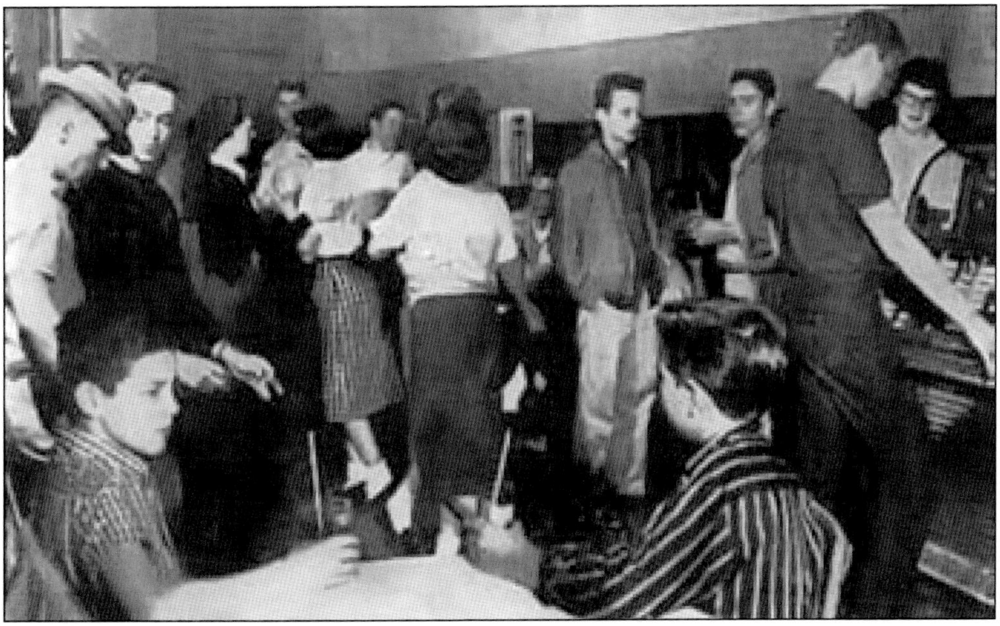

Zook's Nook was the place to be after school in the 1950s. Jitterbug was the exercise for kids, and a jukebox, a soft drink, and maybe a hamburger were in order. Sue Zook, owner and manager, would ask the kids for the magic word when ordering: please! Some of the cool kids in this photograph are, in no particular order, Bob Shields, John Casteel, Wendel Brown, Margie Branstetter, Jerry VanStrien, Jeff Pennock, Clay Taliferro, Mack Jennings, Steve Bokor, Paula Bruce, Ireland Allensworth, Sudy York, and Barbara Thomas. (Courtesy Jeff Guay.)

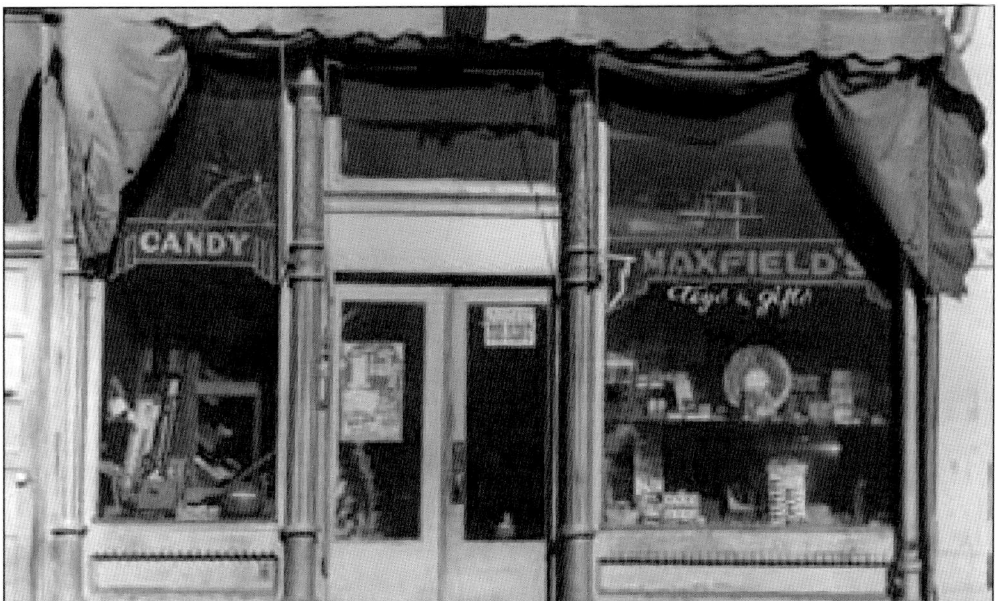

Maxfield's was a favorite mom-and-pop store in town. Penny candy and comic books were major attractions for kids. Maxfield's was at Fourth and Georgia Streets, catty-cornered across from the Clark Theatre. Among many other products, Maxfield's sold little paraffin bottles that, after the "lid" was bitten off, had something sweet to drink inside. (Courtesy Betty Jane Allen.)

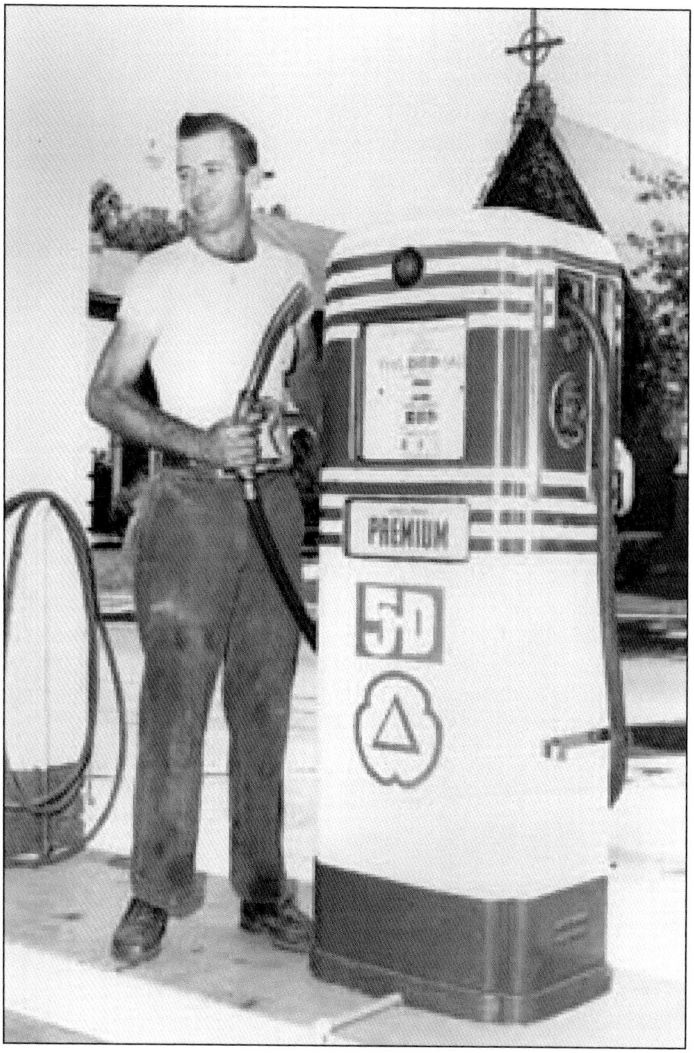

Bill Poor came from Shelbyville in 1953 and opened a Cities Service filling station at 711 Georgia Street, which is now the Dairy Queen. In 1962, he moved to 201 South Third Street for Standard Oil, where he stayed for 29 years until he retired in 1991. Bill and his wife, Dodie, raised and educated four girls: Debra, Dawne, Diana, and Deidre. (Courtesy Irene Steers.)

Best Quali-T-Shoes was at 304 Georgia Street, which is now the Louisiana Area Historical Museum. In the 1940s and 1950s, the shoe store was owned by Earl and Bonnie Best. It was well stocked and people from neighboring towns came here for new shoes. Note the parking meters that were in use at the time. (Courtesy Louisiana Area Historical Museum.)

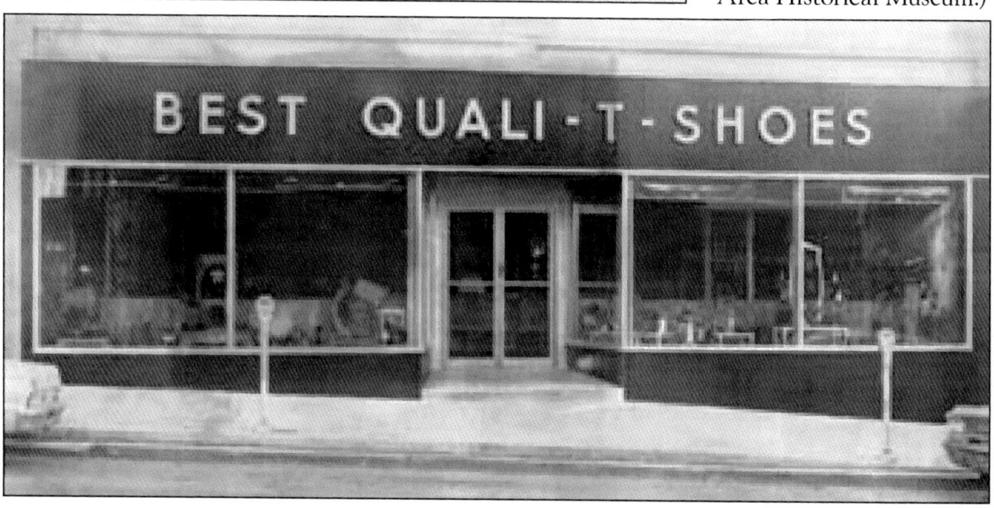

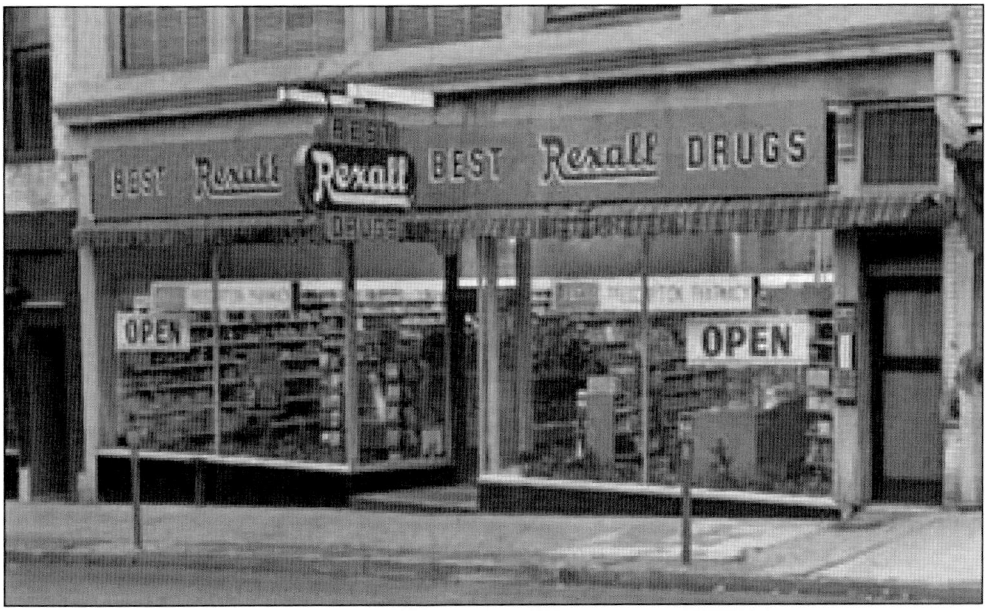

Best Rexall Drugs was located at 307–309 Georgia Street. In 1959, when Lawrence Nickles, the pharmacist who owned the building, died, pharmacist Earl Best purchased it and moved his drugstore there from the 400 block of Georgia Street. This four-story building suffered major wind damage on May 25, 2004, and was razed for safety in June 2004. (Courtesy Louisiana Area Historical Museum.)

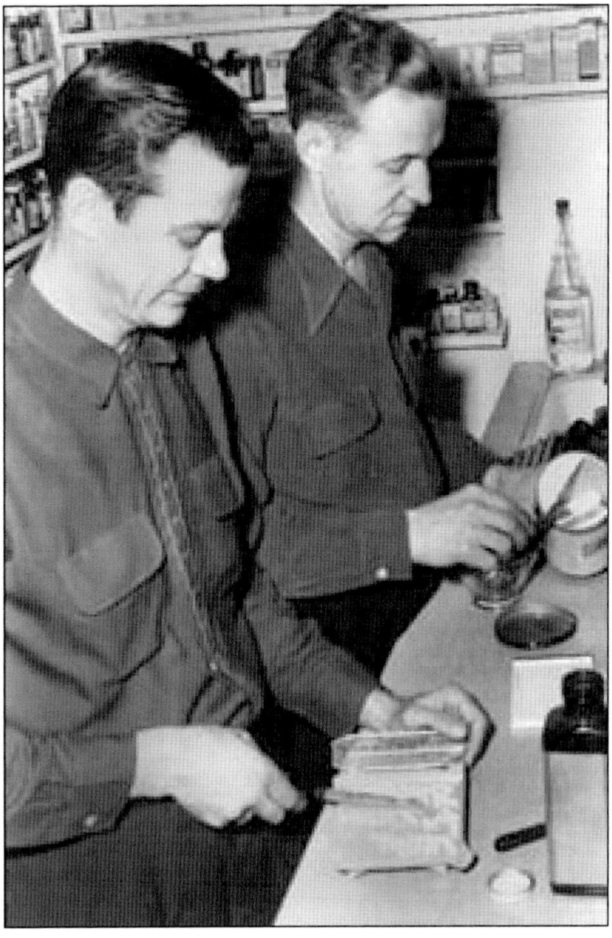

Pharmacists Earl Best (left) and Carl Littrell work at Best Rexall Drugs. Littrell and his family came to Louisiana in 1953 from St. Louis and the men worked together for 15 years. The drugstore was a popular business with trusted, caring pharmacists. Littrell was a Scoutmaster, and he and his wife, Mary, had four sons and a daughter. (Courtesy Louisiana Area Historical Museum.)

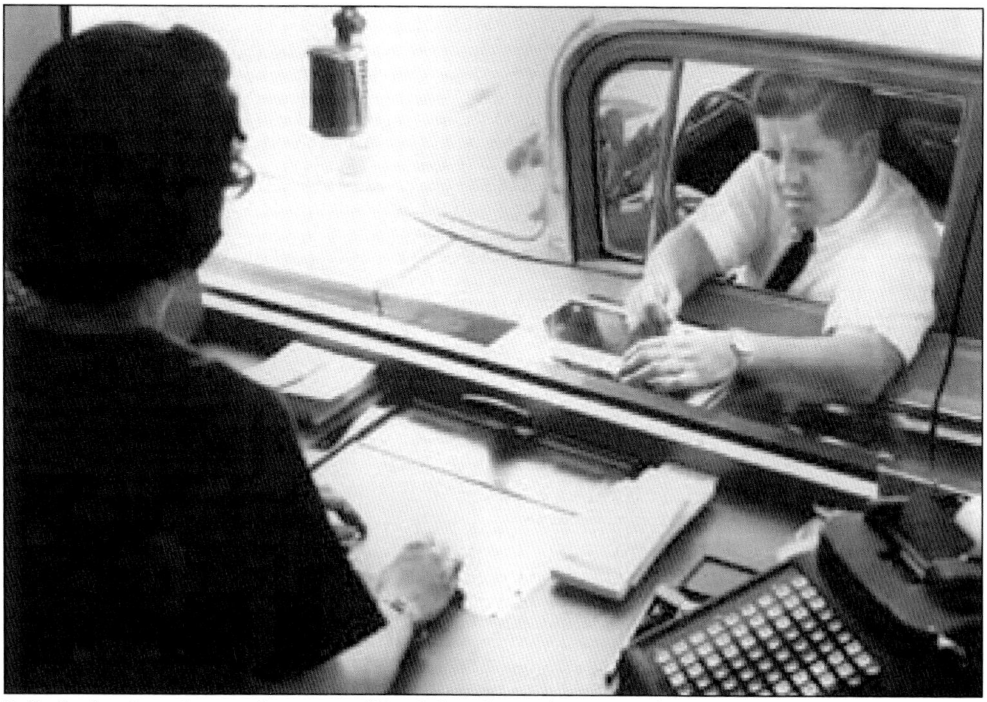

Billy Jordan Jr., who was known as "Duck," makes a deposit at the Mercantile Bank. His father, W.A. Jordan Sr., and Francis Murphy opened the J&M Market on Main Street just around the corner from the bank. Duck, who graduated from Louisiana High School in 1949, managed the market after his father's death. (Courtesy Louisiana Area Historical Museum.)

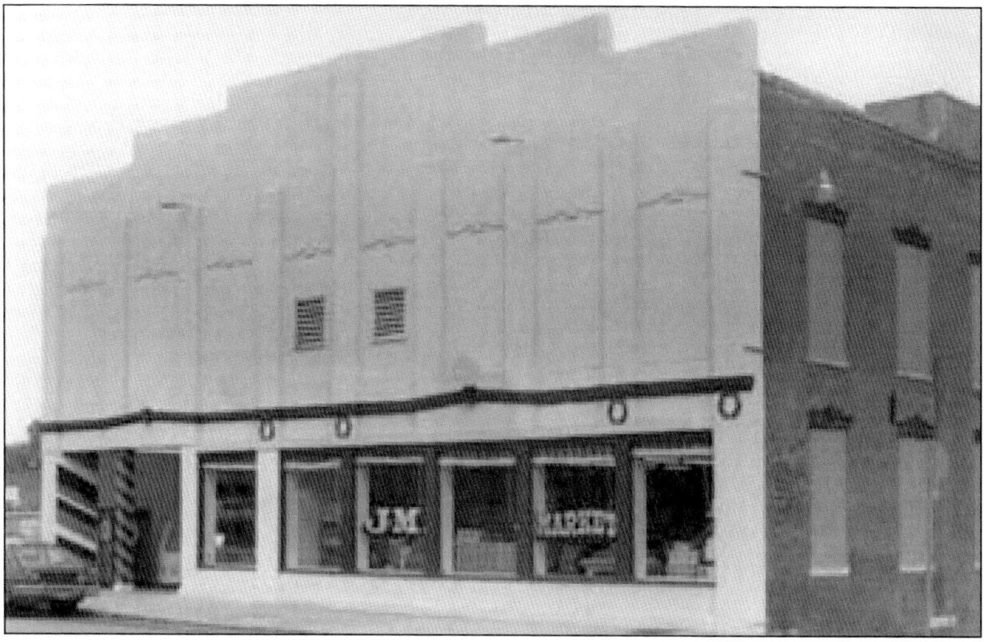

The J&M Market was an important grocery store with locker facilities across the street for customers who did butchering. Jordan and Murphy provided friendly service and chose high-quality foods. (Courtesy Betty Jane Allen.)

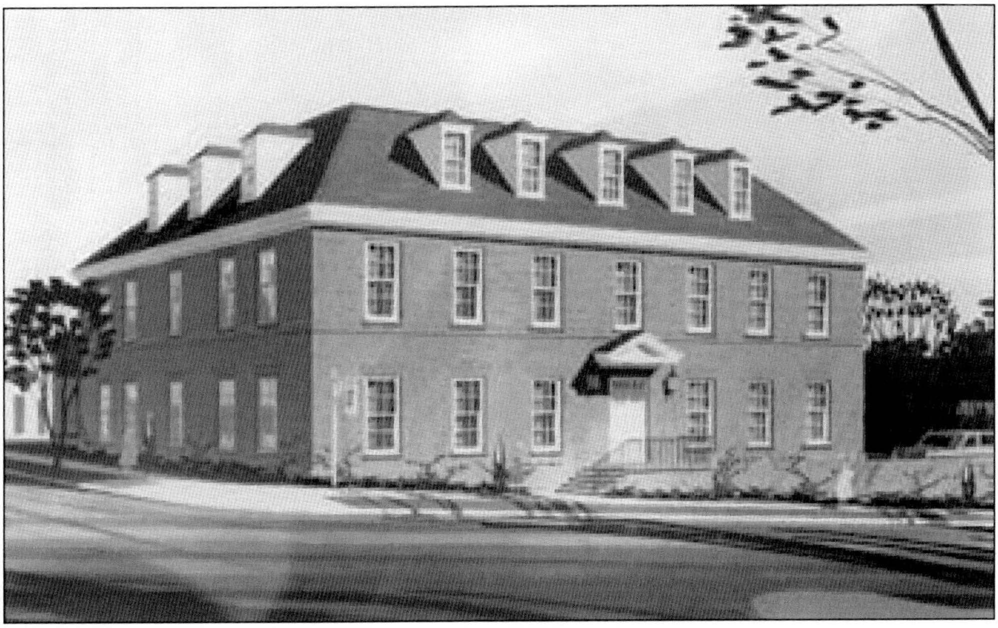

Missouri Edison Company built this structure in 1966 for general office headquarters. A subsidiary of Union Electric Company, Missouri Edison Company merged with it in 1984. The unoccupied building was leased to local attorney Philip G. Smith from 1984 to 1998. In 1999, the city purchased the building and it became the city administration building, also housing the chamber of commerce. The Lynott house once stood on this site. (Courtesy Louisiana Area Historical Museum.)

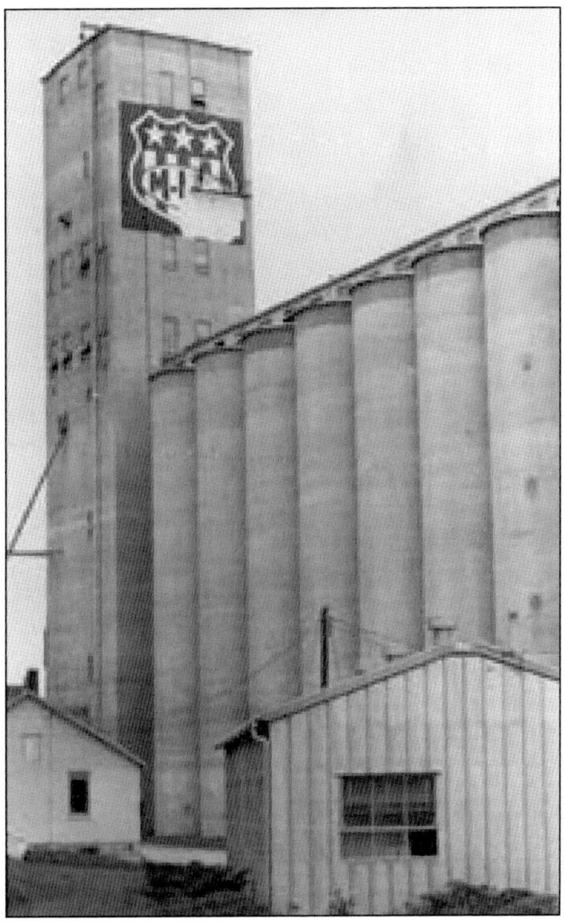

The Missouri Farmers Association (MFA) first expressed interest in acquiring river frontage for a grain terminal with barge-loading facilities in 1952. In February 1957, the company loaded its first barge with 42,000 bushels of soybeans. It became one of the busiest grain terminals on the Mississippi River, with trucks coming from as far as 100 miles. It was later sold to the Bunge Corporation, which continues business there today. (Courtesy Louisiana Area Historical Museum.)

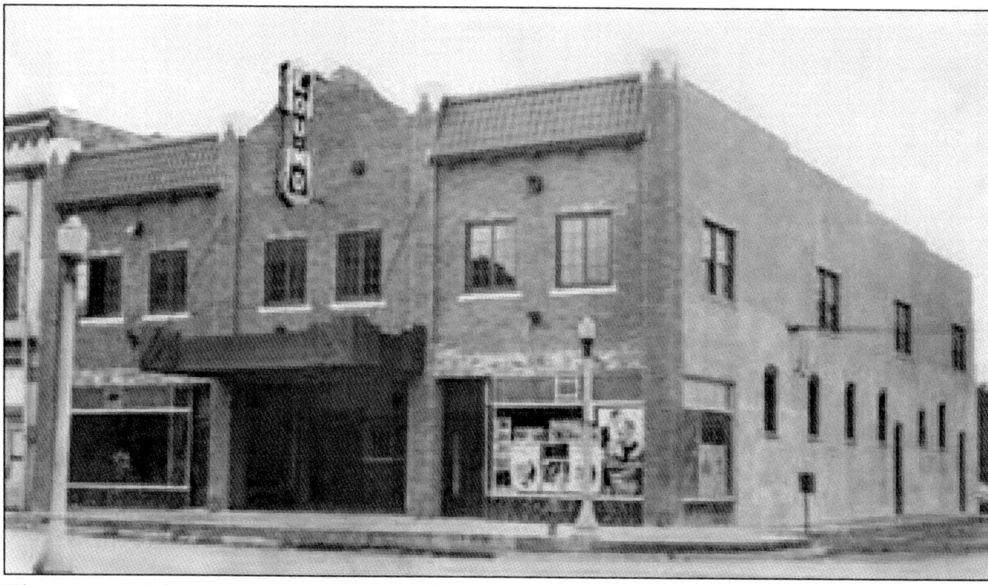

The Lou-Mo Theatre at the corner of Fifth and Georgia Streets, was opened on May 7, 1931, by Glenn "Junior" Boyd, a year after the Star Theatre was destroyed by fire. The Lou-Mo did not fare well and was out of business within a year. Pikers Restaurant occupies the site today. (Courtesy John Wood.)

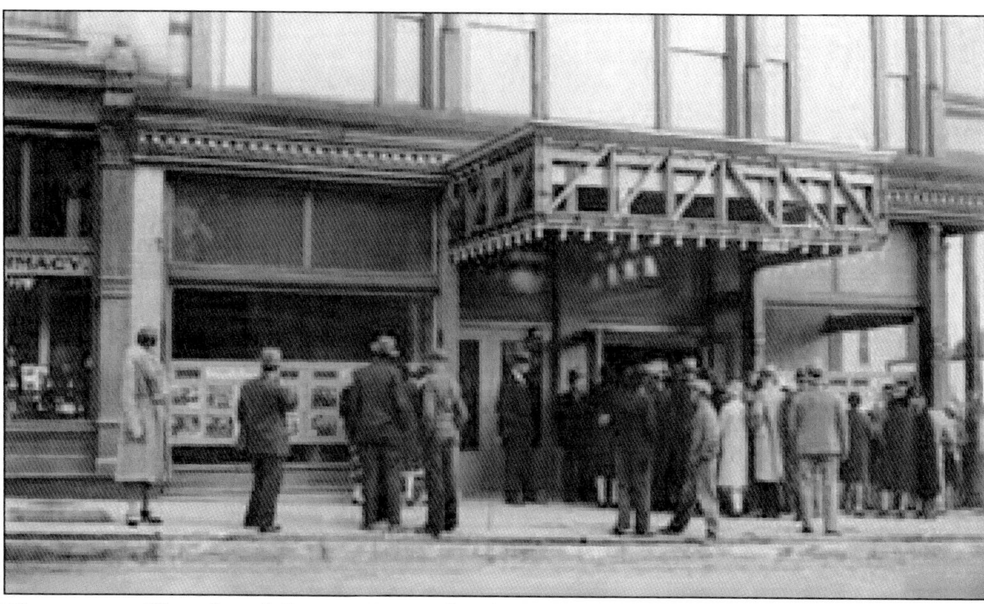

The corner of Fourth and Georgia Streets has been a busy place over the years. In 1891, Edgar Alonzo Parks Sr. built the Parks Music House. In 1931, Clark Armentrout and his son Russell converted it to a movie theater. The Louisiana Area Historical Museum is now home to two pianos made at the Parks. Both are playable, and one is older and more ornate. The first movie shown at the Clark Theatre was *Cracked Nuts*, starring Bert Wheeler and Robert Woolsey. (Courtesy Betty Jane Allen.)

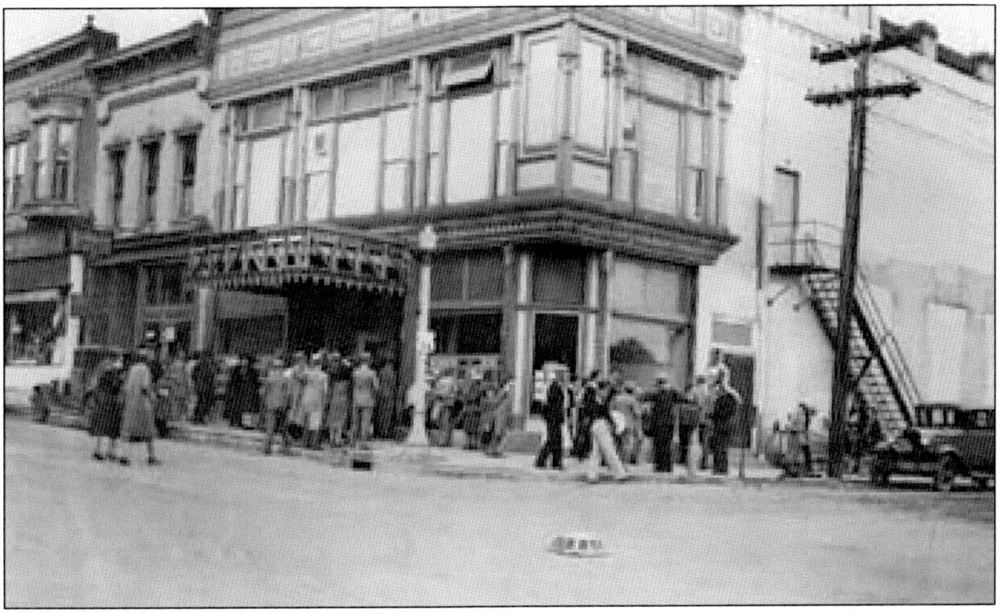

This crowd enters the Clark Theatre on May 22, 1931, for its opening night. (Courtesy John Wood.)

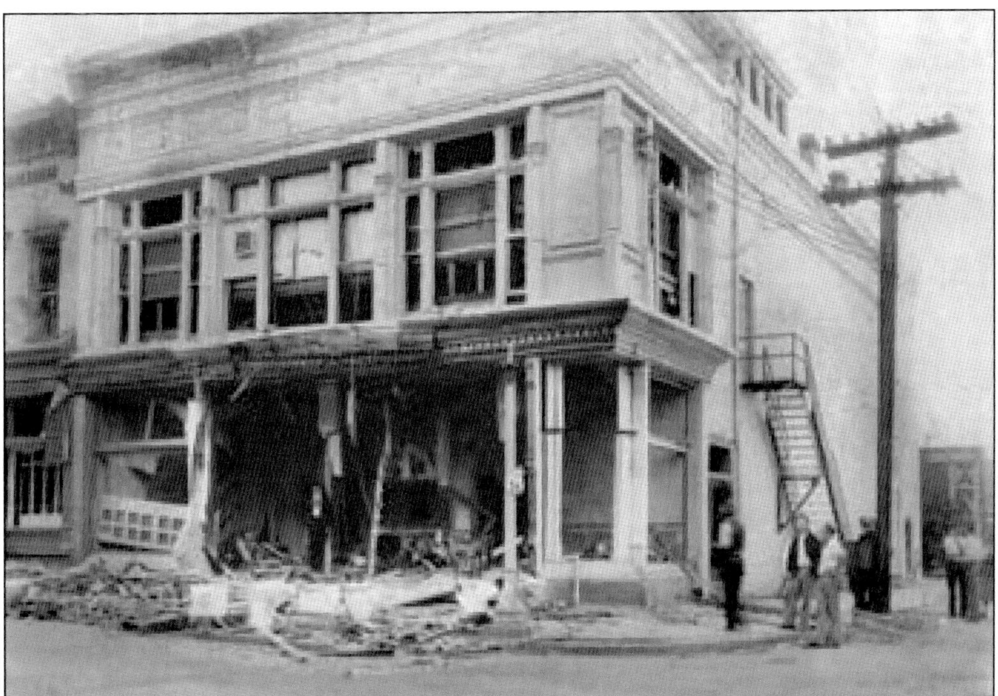

On May 28, 1931, a bomb exploded on the sidewalk in front of the Clark Theatre. Although damaged, the theater was repaired and reopened on June 6. The mystery of the bombing was never solved. In 1987, the theater burned and was subsequently torn down. (Courtesy *Louisiana Press Journal*.)

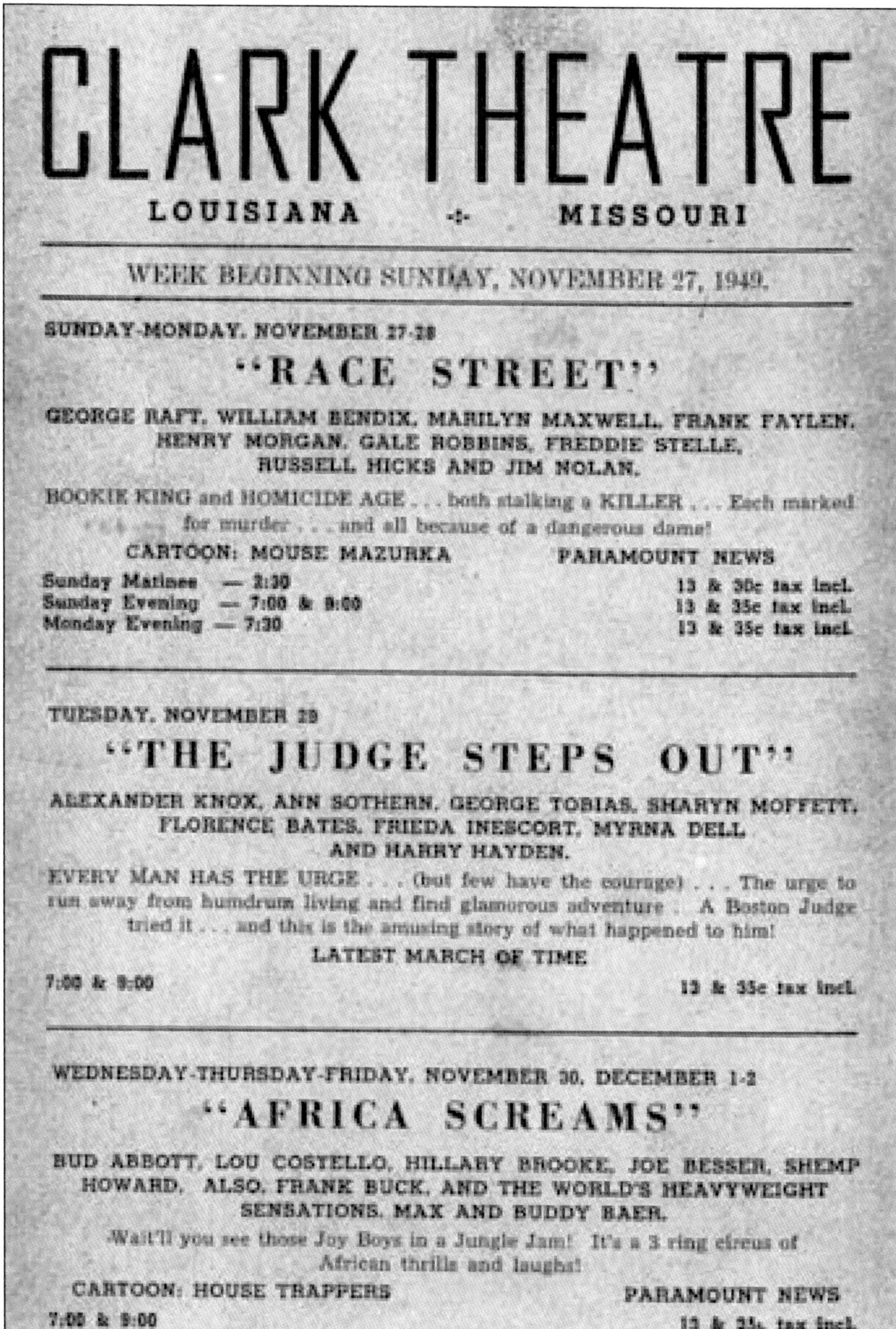

CLARK THEATRE

LOUISIANA — MISSOURI

WEEK BEGINNING SUNDAY, NOVEMBER 27, 1949.

SUNDAY-MONDAY, NOVEMBER 27-28

"RACE STREET"

GEORGE RAFT, WILLIAM BENDIX, MARILYN MAXWELL, FRANK FAYLEN, HENRY MORGAN, GALE ROBBINS, FREDDIE STELLE, RUSSELL HICKS AND JIM NOLAN.

BOOKIE KING and HOMICIDE AGE . . . both stalking a KILLER . . . Each marked for murder . . . and all because of a dangerous dame!

CARTOON: MOUSE MAZURKA — **PARAMOUNT NEWS**

Sunday Matinee — 2:30	13 & 30c tax incl.
Sunday Evening — 7:00 & 9:00	13 & 35c tax incl.
Monday Evening — 7:30	13 & 35c tax incl.

TUESDAY, NOVEMBER 29

"THE JUDGE STEPS OUT"

ALEXANDER KNOX, ANN SOTHERN, GEORGE TOBIAS, SHARYN MOFFETT, FLORENCE BATES, FRIEDA INESCORT, MYRNA DELL AND HARRY HAYDEN.

EVERY MAN HAS THE URGE . . . (but few have the courage) . . . The urge to run away from humdrum living and find glamorous adventure . A Boston Judge tried it . . . and this is the amusing story of what happened to him!

LATEST MARCH OF TIME

7:00 & 9:00 — 13 & 35c tax incl.

WEDNESDAY-THURSDAY-FRIDAY, NOVEMBER 30, DECEMBER 1-2

"AFRICA SCREAMS"

BUD ABBOTT, LOU COSTELLO, HILLARY BROOKE, JOE BESSER, SHEMP HOWARD, ALSO, FRANK BUCK, AND THE WORLD'S HEAVYWEIGHT SENSATIONS, MAX AND BUDDY BAER.

Wait'll you see those Joy Boys in a Jungle Jam! It's a 3 ring circus of African thrills and laughs!

CARTOON: HOUSE TRAPPERS — **PARAMOUNT NEWS**

7:00 & 9:00 — 13 & 35c tax incl.

In 1949, the Press Journal Publishing Company announced the new movies playing every week on these bulletins. (Courtesy Betty Jane Allen.)

This 1958 booklet is an introduction from Hercules Missouri Ordnance Works to Louisiana. When the company arrived in 1941, the town population was 4,600. Hercules brought with it 275 "Herculites." (Courtesy Louisiana Area Historical Museum.)

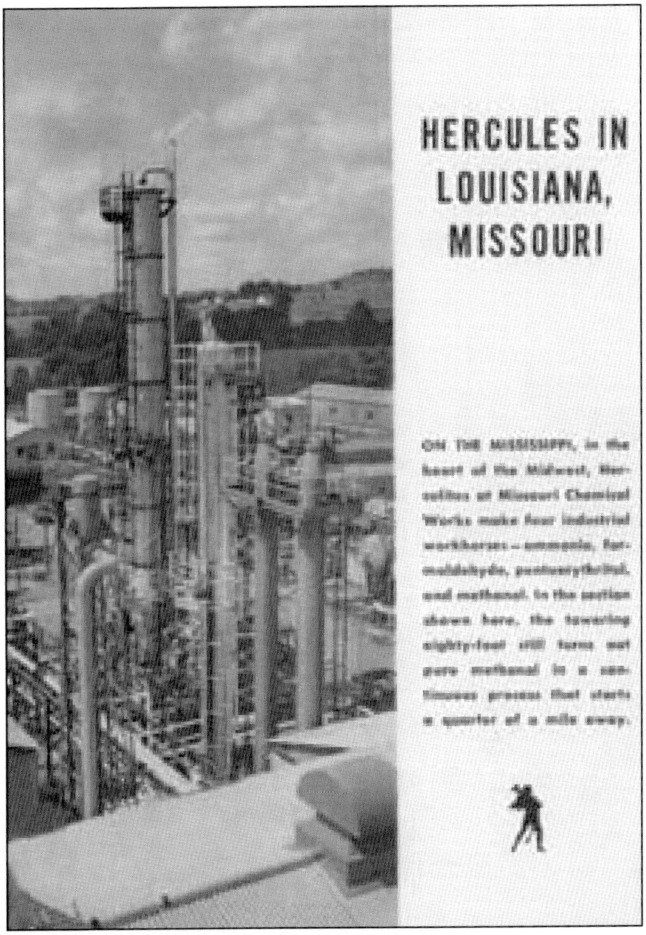

The housing project below was known as Little Ordonia, and the adjacent two-story houses were called Big Ordonia. They were built for plant officials and employees of Hercules Missouri Ordnance Works when the US government chose Louisiana for an ordnance works facility in 1941. The houses were directly across from the plant. The Little Ordonia houses were sold and moved from the plant location when they were no longer needed. Today, the houses are gone and the lots are grass. (Courtesy John Wood.)

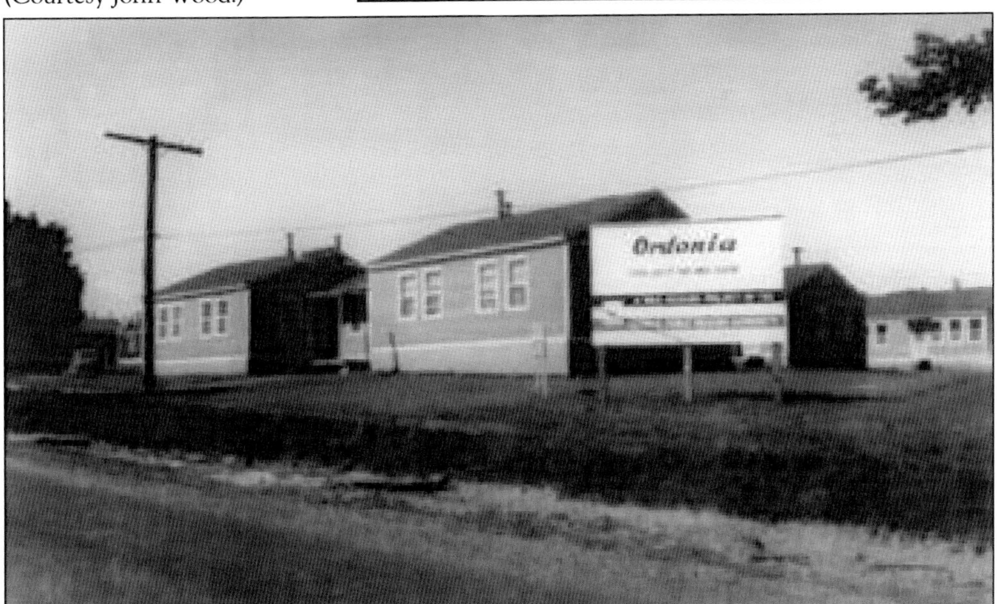

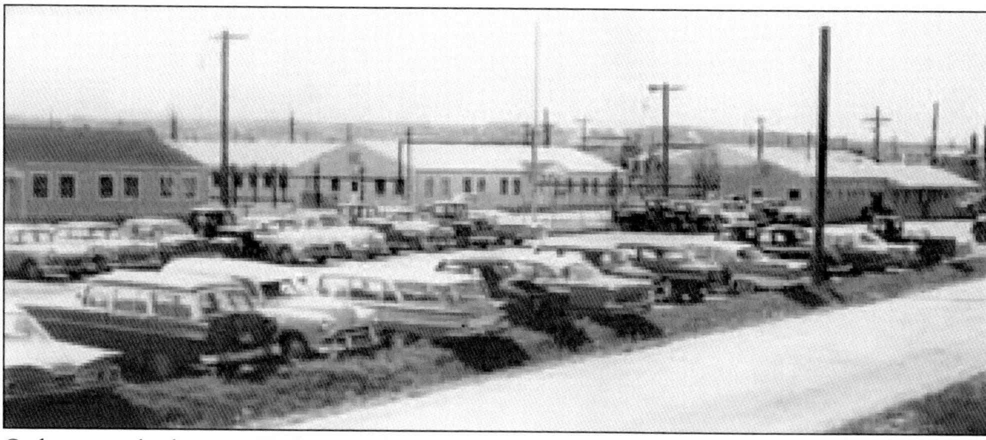

Ordonia was built across Highway D from the Hercules Missouri Ordnance Works (MOW). This view from Ordonia faced the plant. (Courtesy Louisiana Area Historical Museum.)

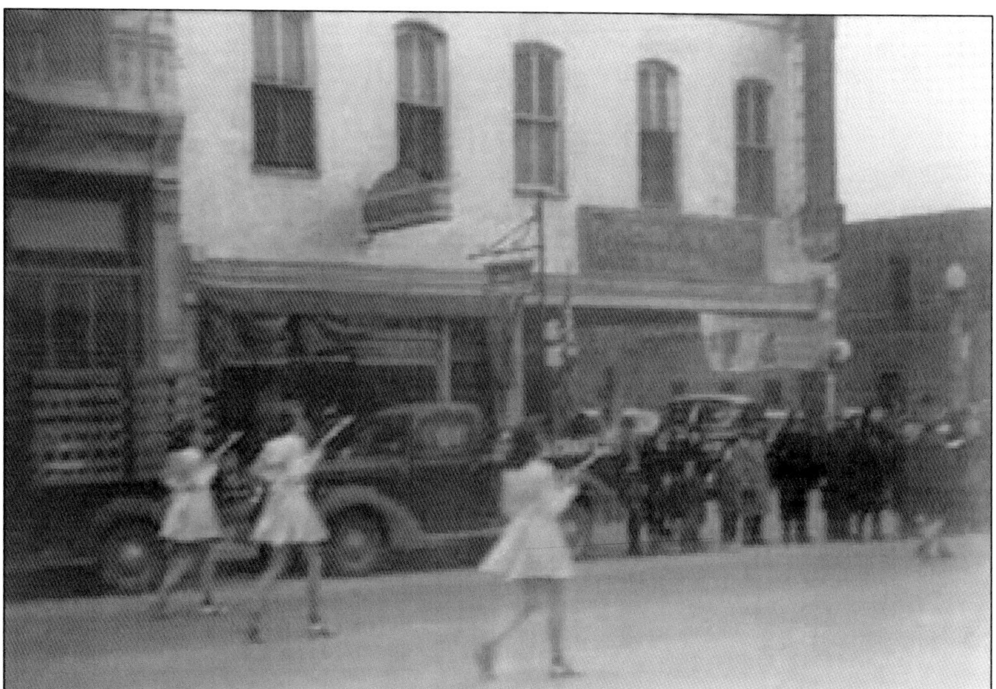

The Hercules MOW plant was dedicated on November 9, 1941. The Louisiana High School majorettes led the band and the rest of the dedication parade as they marched from Louisiana to the plant site, just under two miles away, on a very cold day. (Courtesy Louisiana Area Historical Museum.)

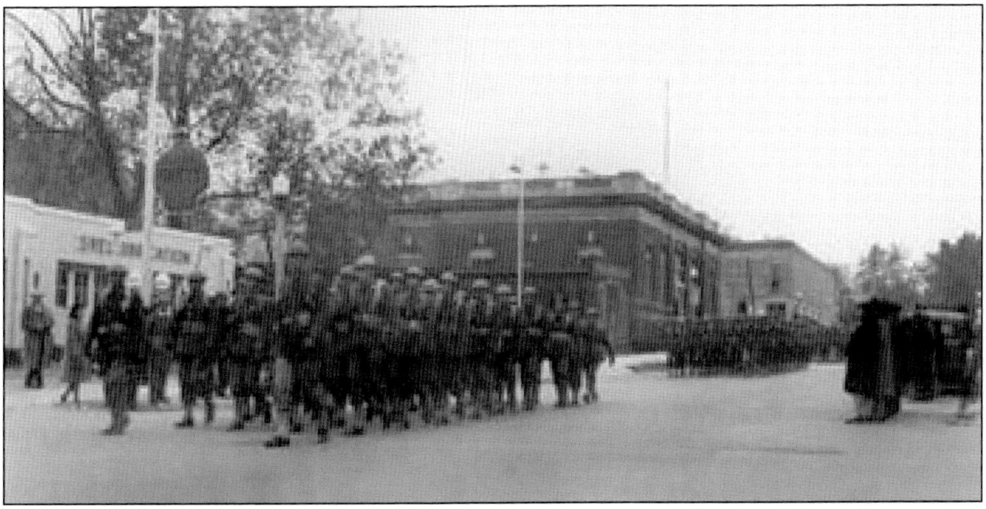

Since the plant was under the jurisdiction of the War Department, a number of soldiers and officers were assigned to it. The post office is in the background of this photograph of the dedication parade. (Courtesy Louisiana Area Historical Museum.)

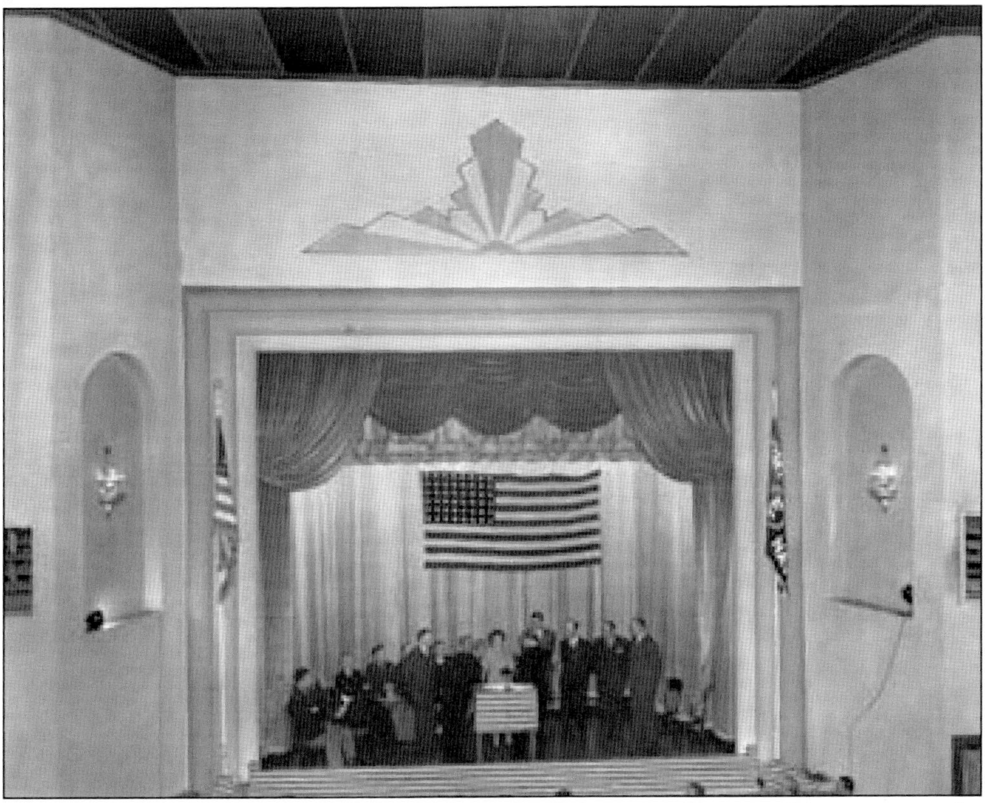

This photograph was taken inside Clark Theatre. An "E" commendation medal was given to the Hercules MOW plant for its war effort in the 1940s. It was one of the first cost-plus construction jobs by the government's War Department. "This was done to expedite completion of jobs during wartime. Jobs (construction) were whatever they cost, plus a 10-percent fee," according to historian and MOW plant chemist Miller Waugh. (Courtesy Louisiana Area Historical Museum.)

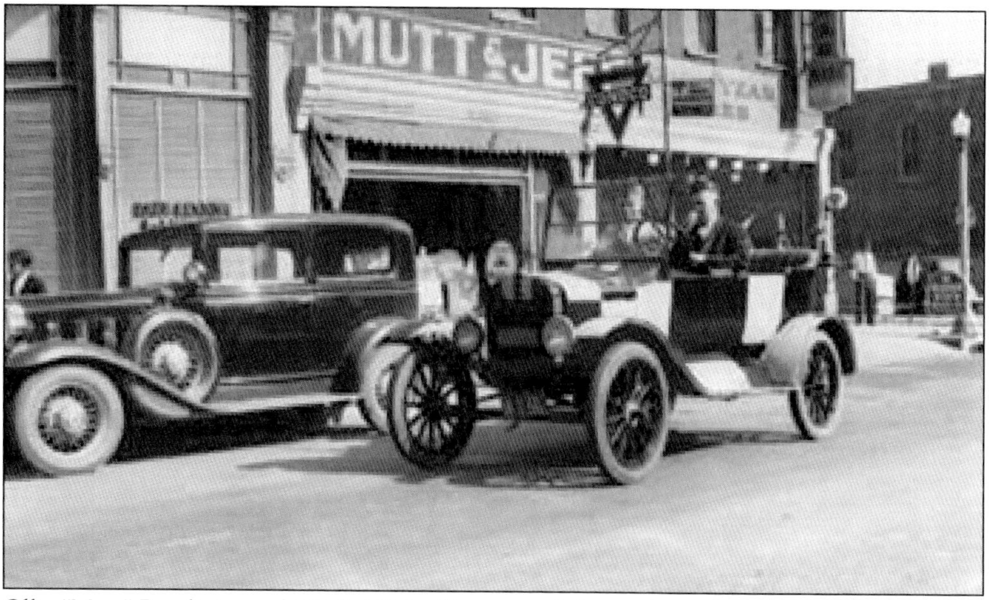

Ollie "Mutt" Boudinier and Bill "Jeff" Shaffner owned this appliance store at Fifth and Georgia Streets. Boudinier was very short and Shaffner was very tall. The store sold gasoline and Goodyear tires, and patrons could have their tires vulcanized during World War II. Also available at the store were Frigidaire refrigerators and stoves. (Courtesy John Wood.)

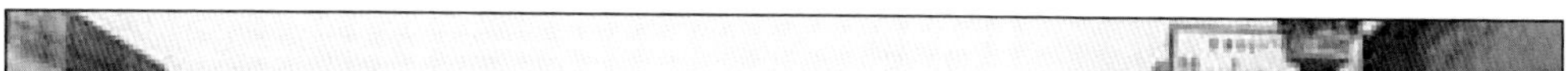

Water and sewer lines were dug by hand in 1939, when this photograph was taken on Fifth Street looking north. Cody Long's 500 Tire Company is on the left, and there are gas tanks on the right. (Courtesy John Wood.)

Three
READIN', WRITIN', AND RELIGION

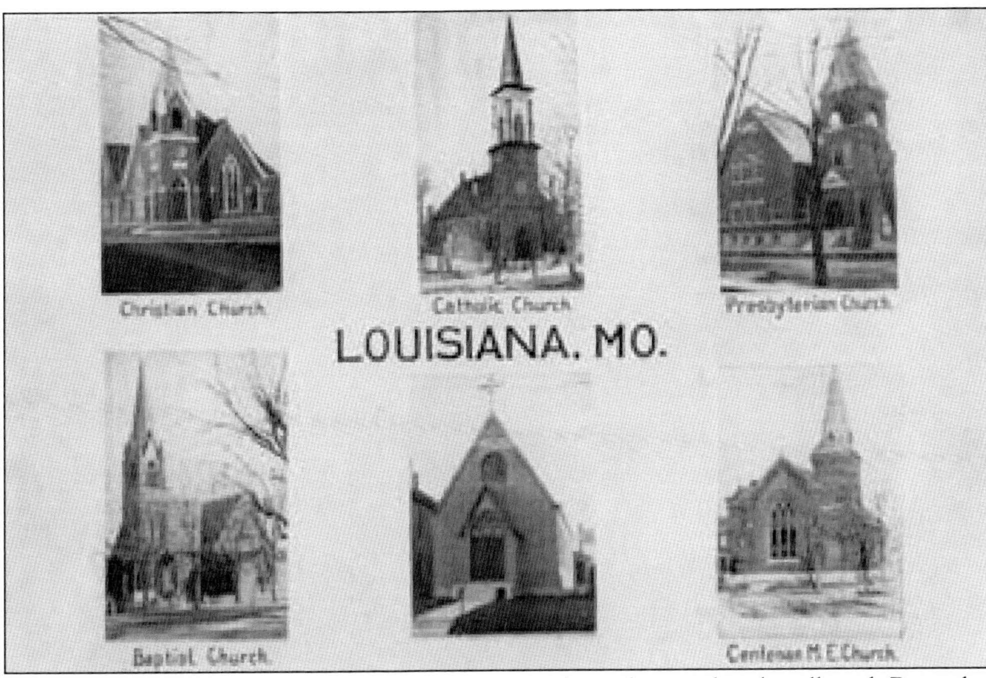

The Louisiana Area Historical Museum has presented a mid-town church walk each December since 1995. Six mid-town churches are visited and a short program is presented at each church. The six churches are all within walking distance of each other and a group of approximately 50 to 125 folks usually attend the walk. The churches are Bethel Chapel AME Church, First Christian Church, First Baptist Church, Centenary United Methodist Church, Calvary Episcopal Church, and First Presbyterian Church. In 1995, Bethel Chapel AME Church was placed in the National Register of Historic Places. A mural of churches was done by artist Cindy Logan and is located on Sixth and Tennessee Streets. (Courtesy Betty Jane Allen.)

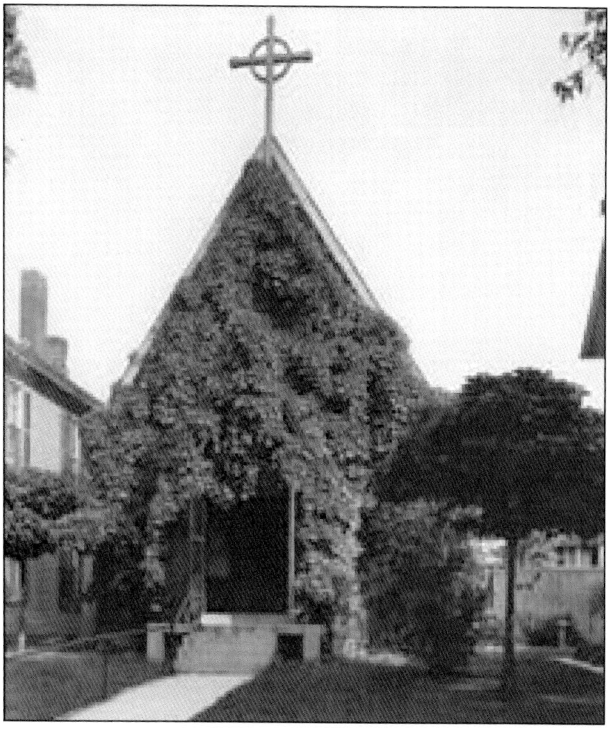

The Calvary Episcopal Church was organized in 1854, and congregants worshipped in various places. Their first church was erected in 1872 at the corner of Fifth and Virginia Streets. The wooden structure was moved in 1878 to its present location at 704 Georgia Street. The church was faced with red brick. Now more than 125 years old, the church is still used. This photograph was taken on June 15, 1926. (Courtesy Louisiana Area Historical Museum.)

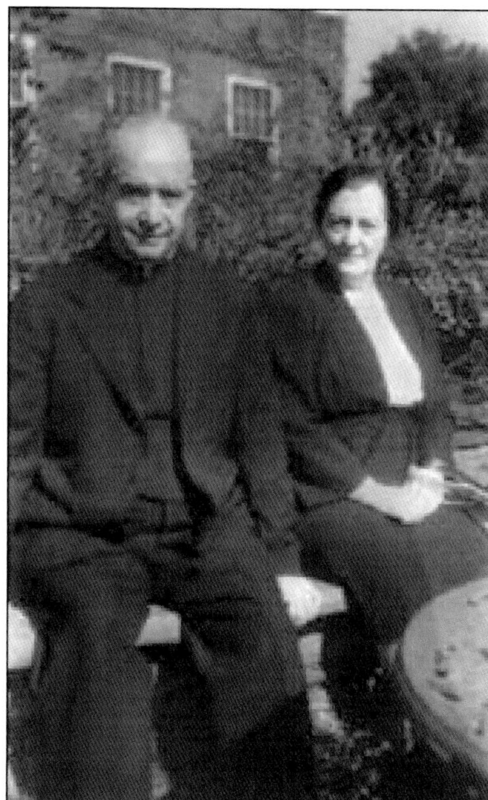

From 1923 to 1958, Rev. David Coombs served as rector of Calvary Episcopal Church. During his ministry, a great deal of mission work was done on behalf of the poor and the beautiful stained-glass windows were added to the church. The large stained-glass window over the altar depicting the Last Supper was donated by Reverend Coombs and his wife, Ethyl Meek Irish Coombs, in memory of their son David Irish Coombs. (Courtesy Reverend Pat Glenn.)

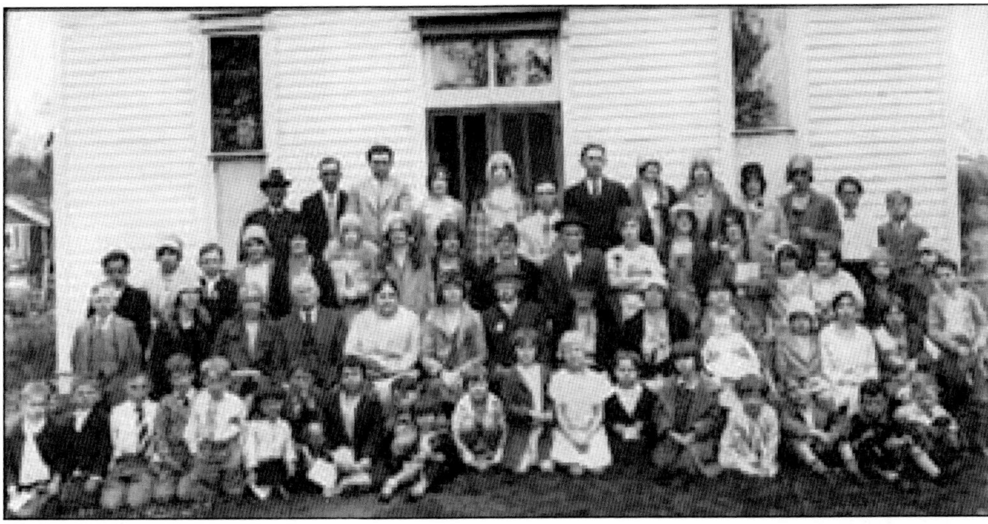

The Elmwood Presbyterian Church's Sunday school classes pose for a group photograph on April 20, 1930. The Baldy Chapel Methodist church building—which was originally one of the three rural Grassy Creek churches—was purchased from Robert May by Elmwood Presbyterian Church, and each board of the former Baldy Chapel Methodist building was removed, marked, and transported on November 30, 1913, to where it stands now at Thirtieth and South Carolina Streets as Elmwood Presbyterian Church. The structure was rebuilt in its original form. Elmwood Presbyterian Church, established in 1910, held services in the Fritz Tavern next door until acquiring the rebuilt structure. (Courtesy Linda Ince Beer.)

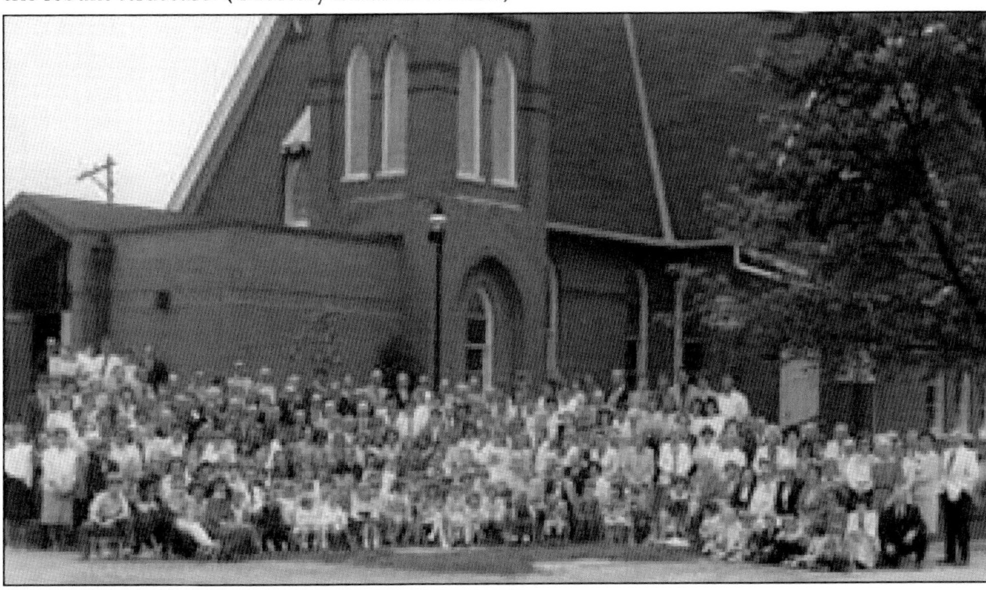

The congregation at the First Baptist Church is seen here after the sanctuary underwent remodeling and refurbishing in 1963. The church was organized on March 26, 1853. There were 36 charter members. From 1854 until 1891, the church was located at the southeast corner of Seventh and Georgia Streets. In 1891, a new home, the present building, was constructed at the southeast corner of Seventh and South Carolina Streets. The new church building was dedicated on November 15, 1891. In November 1913, thanks to a gift from the Carnegie Foundation, a Kilgen-built pipe organ was purchased and installed. (Courtesy Louisiana Area Historical Museum.)

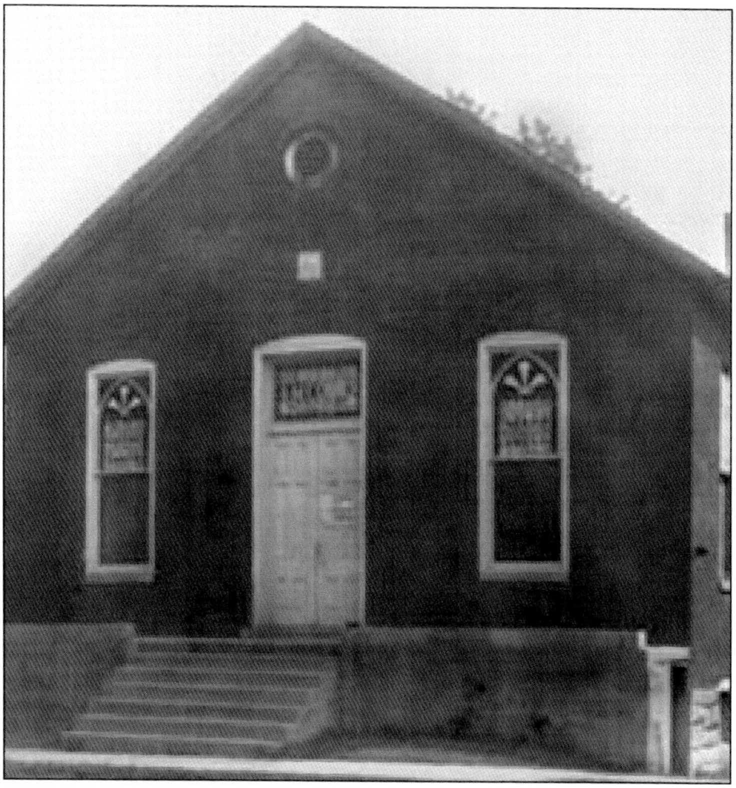

The Bethel Chapel AME Church enjoyed a role as the "mother church" for various congregations in the area. In 1856, no black churches were established west of St. Louis, but, following the emancipation in 1865, it is likely the Bethel Chapel AME Church was built in 1869, probably about five years after the congregation was organized. The Bethel Chapel AME Church has endured to this day and was officially entered in the National Register of Historic Places on July 28, 1995. (Courtesy Sally Cropp.)

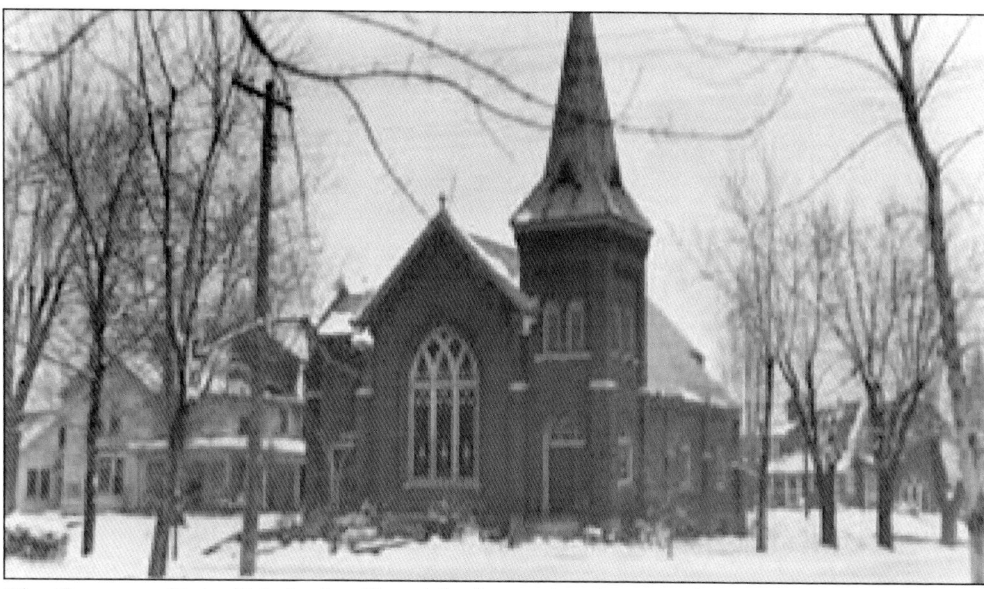

The Centenary United Methodist Church had several unfortunate happenings in its beginnings in the mid-1800s. However, determination won out, and the third attempt to build a church was successful. In 1884, Jane Byers deeded a house and a lot on the corner of Seventh and South Carolina Streets, where the church stands today. On November 13, 1887, the bishop preached the dedicatory sermons. The pipe organ still in use today was installed in 1929. (Courtesy Betty Jane Allen.)

The First Christian Church did not have a permanent place of worship until 1859, when a building was erected on Third Street. A Reuter pipe organ was purchased in 1929. Louisiana natives Glenn Rose and William Bass were ordained from this congregation. On August 13, 1994, lightning struck the roof of the church, destroying the sanctuary and narthex. Efforts were made to salvage the 65-year-old organ, but the damage was too extensive. An electric organ was donated by the Troy Christian Church and is now in use. The dedication of the rebuilt sanctuary and narthex was held in October 1996. (Courtesy Linda Ince Beer.)

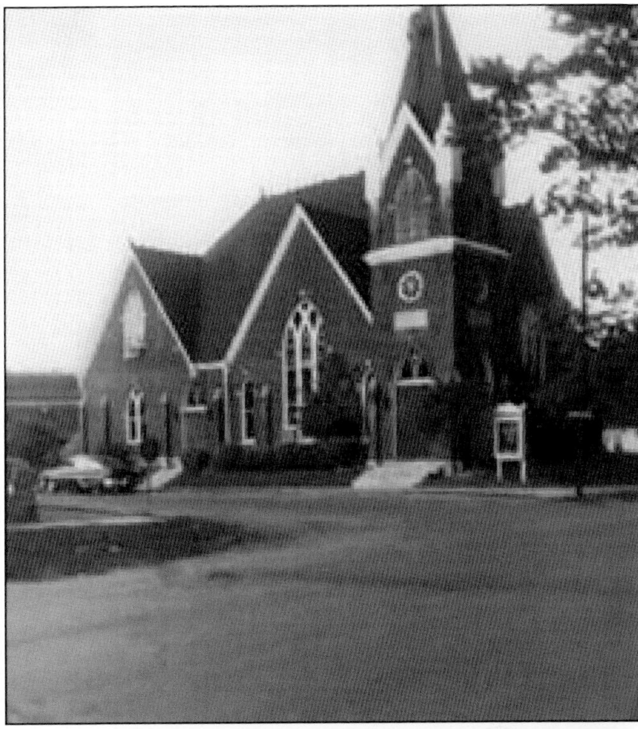

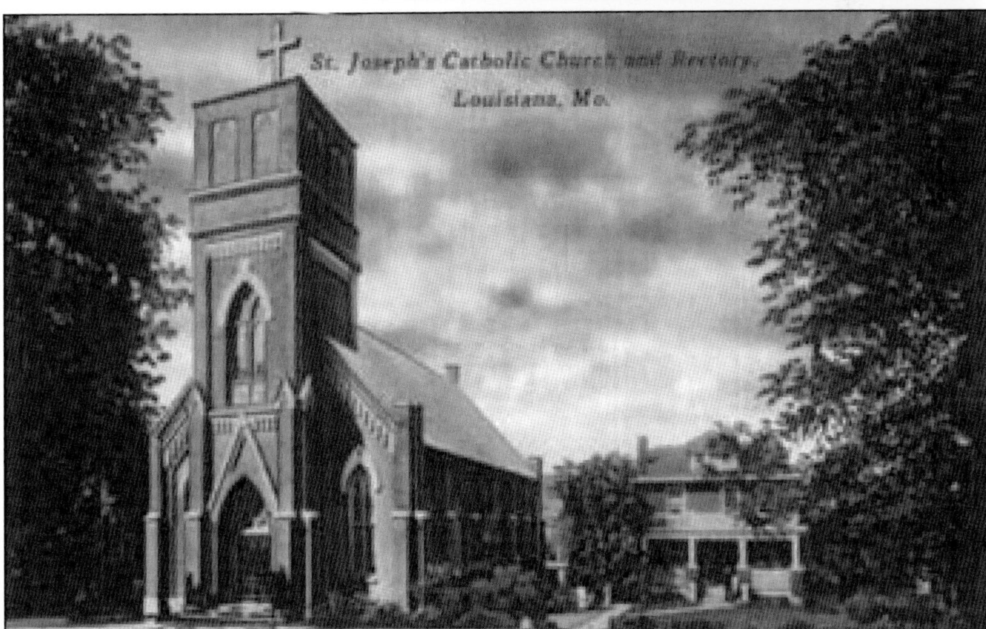

A few Catholics erected a small church on Noyes Street in 1850. Rev. John A. Cummings, the first resident pastor, came in 1864. St. Joseph's Parish was founded in 1865. After Reverend Cummings refused to take the Ironclad Oath of loyalty to the Union after the Civil War, the US Supreme Court ruled the oath unconstitutional. Today's church was dedicated in 1874. The Catholic cemetery was established in 1878. In 1881, the church opened a parochial school with more than 100 pupils, but it did not survive. (Courtesy Bill & Anne Keller.)

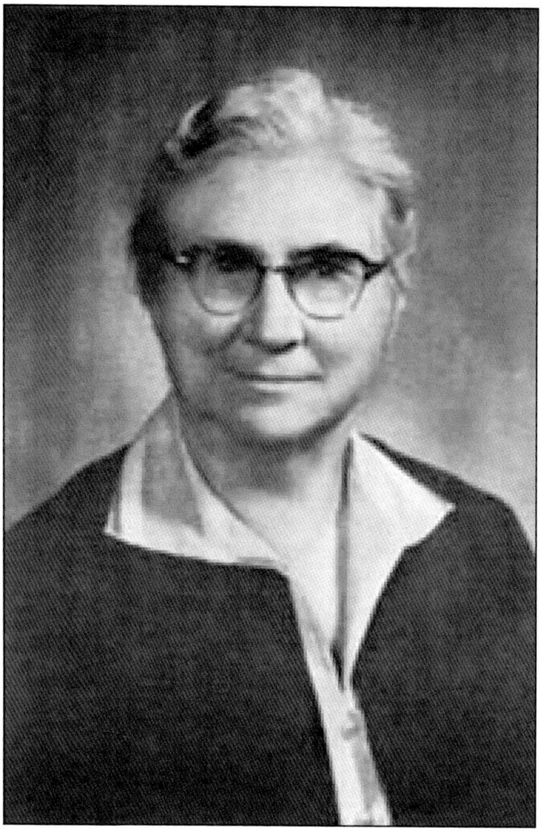

Lois Elizabeth Hastings (June 3, 1906–August 25, 1996) was Louisiana's only 50-year teacher. In 1924, she began teaching second grade, and from 1935 to 1994, she taught business education courses in Louisiana High School. Her mission was to give "on-the-job training," which she implemented with great success. She attended 10 summer school programs to obtain a bachelor's degree in education. (Courtesy Betty Jane Allen.)

In 1869, the J. Sam Brown School was built at Fifth and Jackson Streets. It later became the Central School (below). The first class was held on September 9, 1870, and there were 412 graduates over the next 38 years. On July 13, 1913, J. Sam Brown School was torn down and the Central School was built on the same site. Ray and Son, Inc., built the Central School and the Robert Russell Rowley Annex. (Courtesy John Wood.)

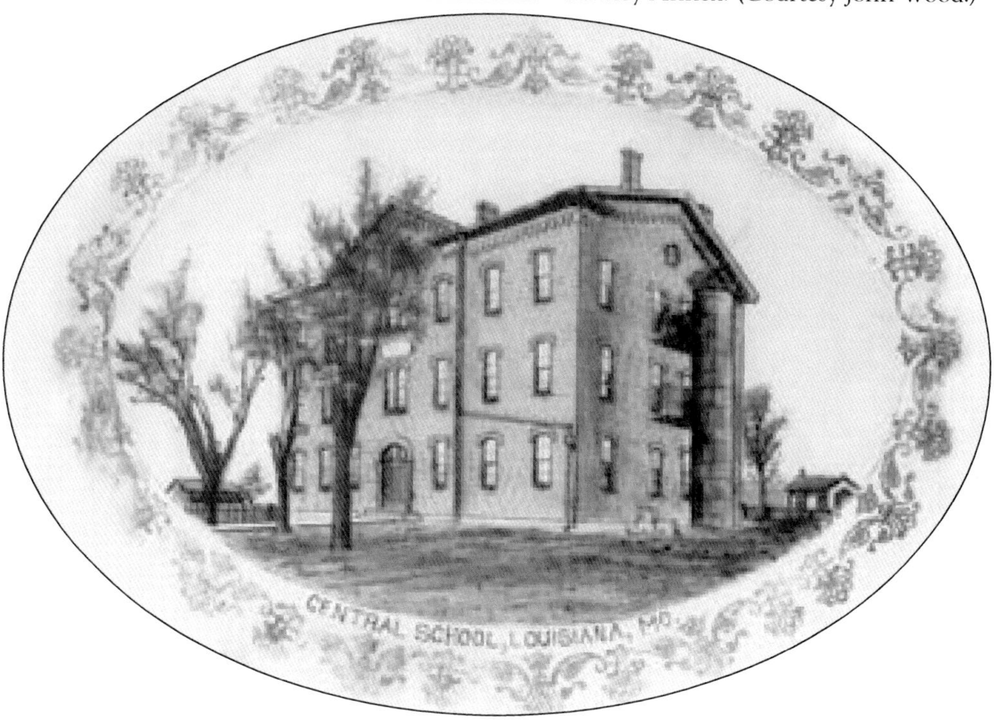

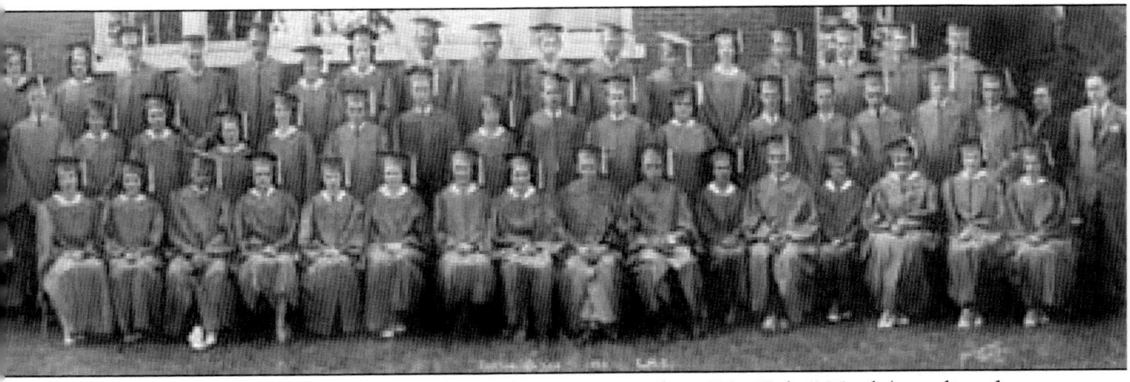

The Louisiana High School class of 1939, under superintendent T.L. "Jake" Noel (standing far right, second row), included these students listed alphabetically: James R. Baker, Bobby Bankhead, Wilbur Beckenholdt, Charles Bentley, Fred Berry, Ethel Bolomey, Charles Brimer, Maggie M. Burbridge, J.D. Burns, Clarence Campbell, Dorothy Lou Carroll, Gertrude Carroll, Clara Frances Caverly, Margaret Ann Cordle, Lillian Culwell, Maxine Dewey, Jack Dillender, Viola May Dreon, Leonard Elliott, Ruth England, John Henderson, Leonard Hess, Evelyn Holderness, Jess Hoover, Kenneth Hufford, Richard Hughart, Sara Lee Huston, Walter Jeffries, Pat Kitson, Bill Lohmeier, Jack Martin, George Mitchell, Alex Oliver, Ranny Pappenfort, Sarah Jane Pitzer, Marie Pollak, J.W. Pollard, Roger Shannon, Virginia Shields, Garnelle Sizemore, Sarah Smith, Emma Lou Sterne, Haley Stewart, Esther Stumbaugh, Maxine Trower, Dorothy Walkley, Elizabeth Wheatley, and Danny Wilkins. (Courtesy John Wood.)

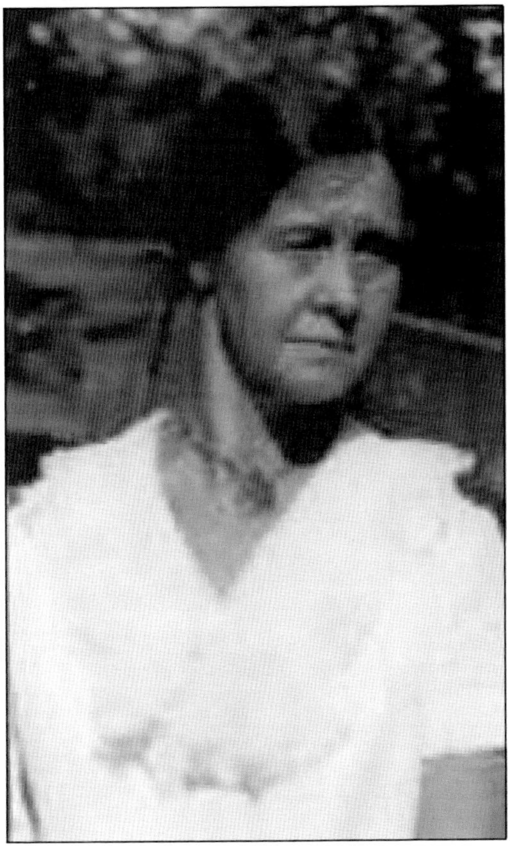

Grace Matilda Berry graduated from the University of Missouri in 1925. She taught 30 years in Louisiana High School and was involved in multiple facets of the school, participating in many civic activities. She was active in the Centenary United Methodist Church. She died at a young age of cancer (1891–1947). (Courtesy Grace Jane Catlett.)

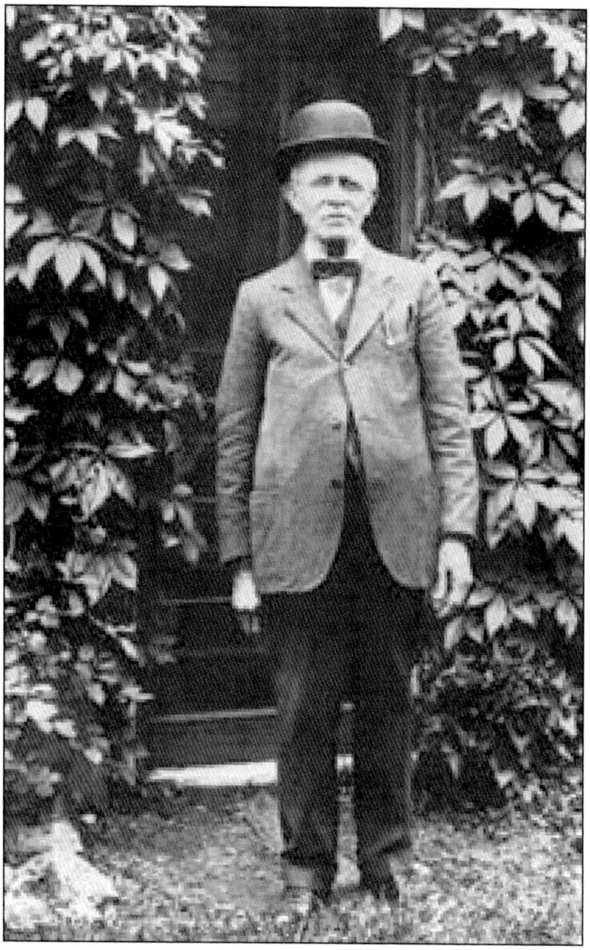

Robert Russell Rowley (January 4, 1854–January 26, 1935) had a national reputation among scientists for his research in entomology and paleontology. His collection of 60,000 fossils was the largest collection by an individual in the United States. He served for 39 years as a teacher and superintendent in the Louisiana School system. (Courtesy Betty Jane Allen.)

On November 8, 1934, the Masons and citizens formed in procession and marched together to lay the cornerstone of the Robert Russell Rowley Annex at Louisiana High School. It was laid according to Masonic custom, with the grand master delivering an address afterward. (Courtesy John Wood.)

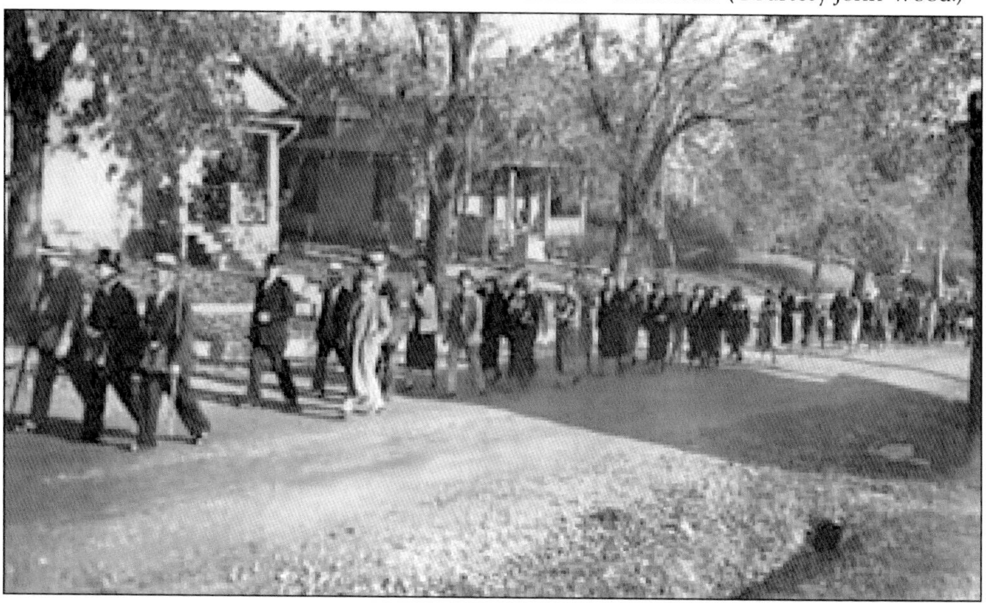

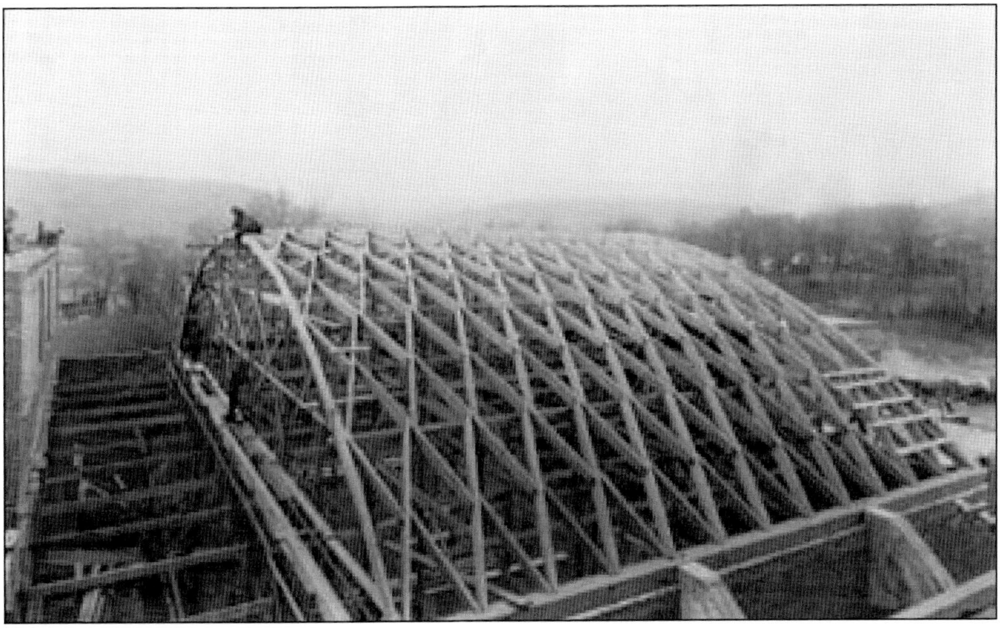

Construction for a gymnasium began on January 15, 1935, at Fifth and Jackson Streets as part of the Rowley Annex. Professor Rowley had been valedictorian of his class in 1875 and served the school for 39 years. His namesake school opened in the fall of 1935, only eight months after his death. (Courtesy Linda Ince Beer.)

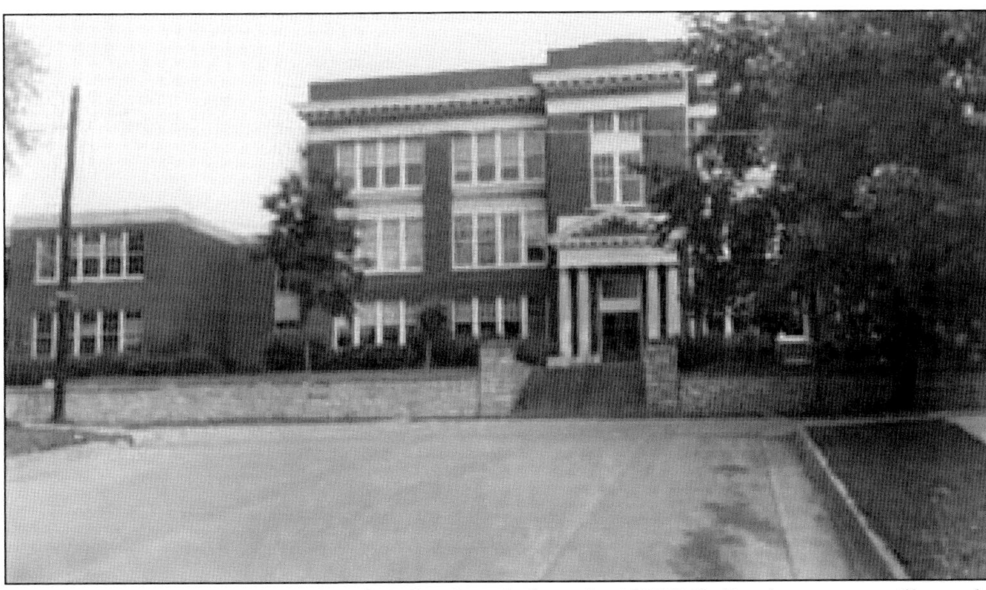

The Central Public Grade and High School, including the 1935 R.R. Rowley annex, still stands; its hallowed halls are filled with memories of students, teachers, principals, and superintendents. The attractive stone wall in front of the school was built by the Pike County Chapter of the Daughters of the American Revolution in 1916. (Courtesy Louisiana Area Historical Museum.)

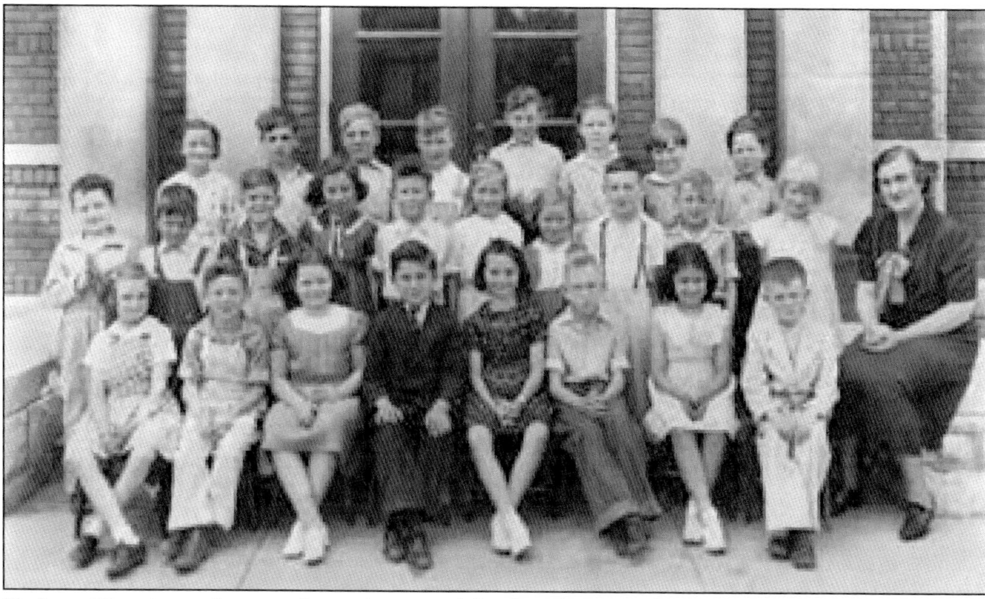

Kathryn Huntington's room-three class posed for this photograph outside Central School in 1938. (Courtesy Louisiana Area Historical Museum.)

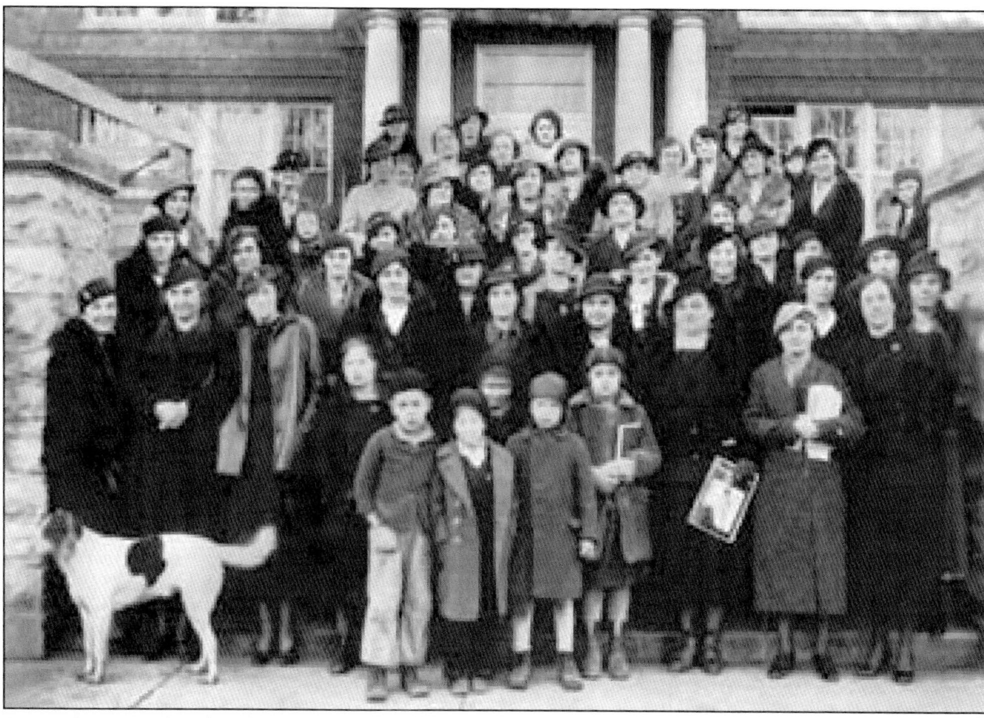

Several Central School seventh-graders (first row) pose at their school with members of the Parent Teacher Association in 1935. Marie Meriwether (first row, third from right, holding a file) founded the Central School PTA. Meriwether Elementary School was named in her honor and was dedicated in September 1954. She was active in many civic projects and encouraged the beginnings of the Louisiana Girl Scouts. She married Dr. Charles Louis Meriwether and had a son, Charles Meriwether Jr. (Courtesy Louisiana Area Historical Museum and Sesquicentennial.)

From 1929 to 1945, T.L. "Jake" Noel (right) spent 16 years as a teacher, coach, and administrator in the Louisiana school system. He taught math and coached track, basketball, and the football program that he began. In 1948, he was named the first executive director of the Missouri Athletic Association. In 2000, the Louisiana High School gymnasium was dedicated as Jake Noel Gymnasium. Noel died in 1979 at the age of 76. (Courtesy Betty Jane Allen.)

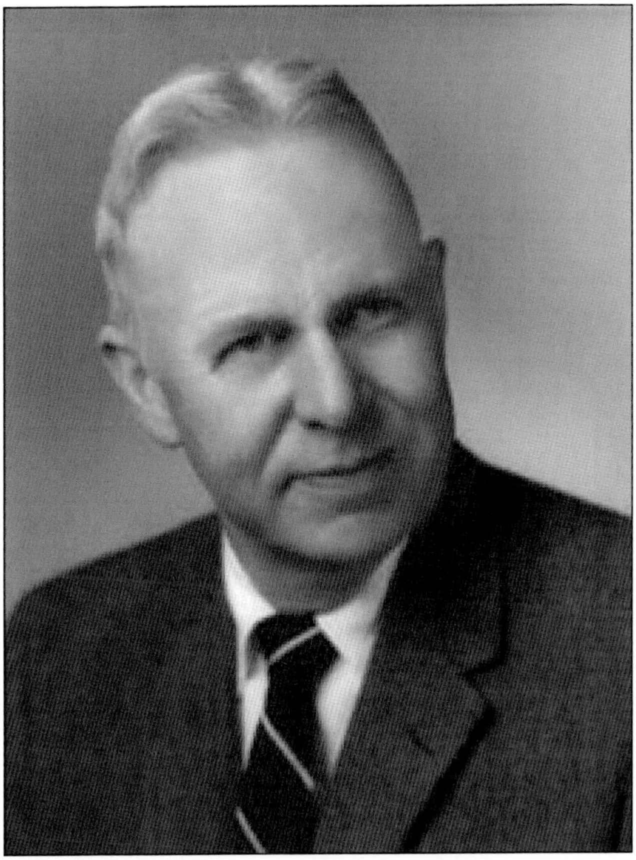

In 1932, the Louisiana High School Bulldog "Griddlers" were improving at football. They won four games, lost three, and tied two. They also outscored their opponents for the first time. Coach T.L. "Jake" Noel (standing, far right) began the football program in 1929. (Courtesy Betty Jane Allen.)

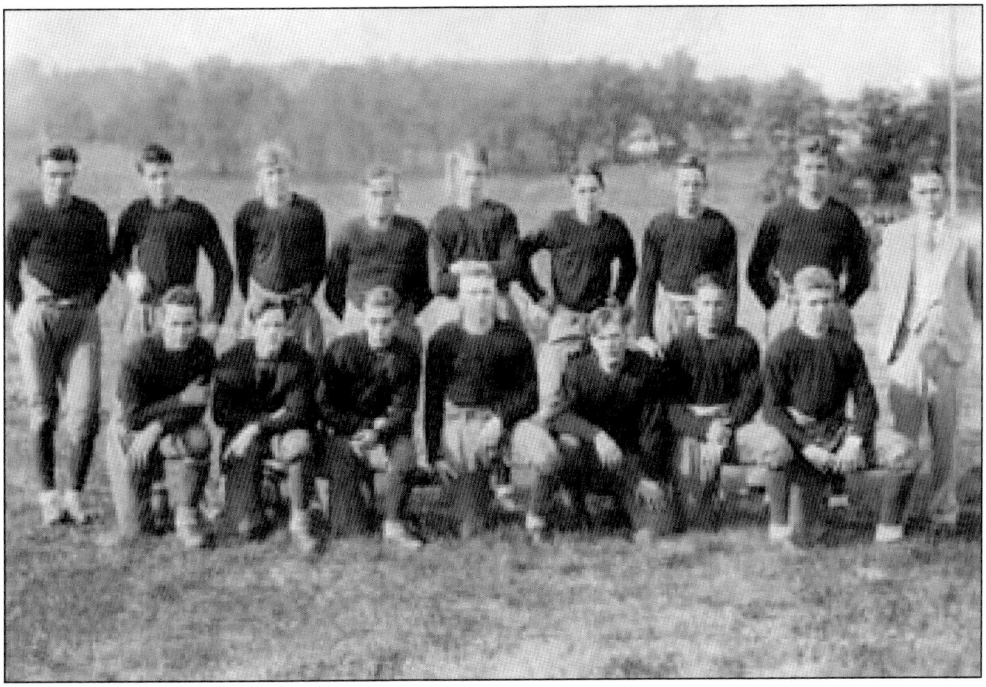

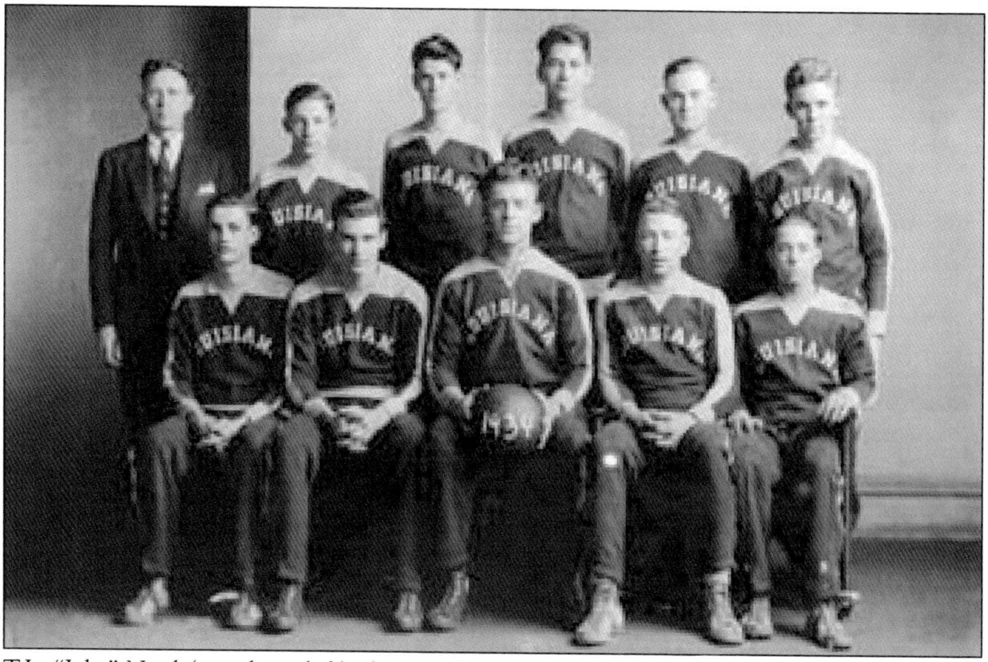

T.L. "Jake" Noel (standing, left) also coached the Louisiana High School basketball team. (Courtesy Betty Jane Allen.)

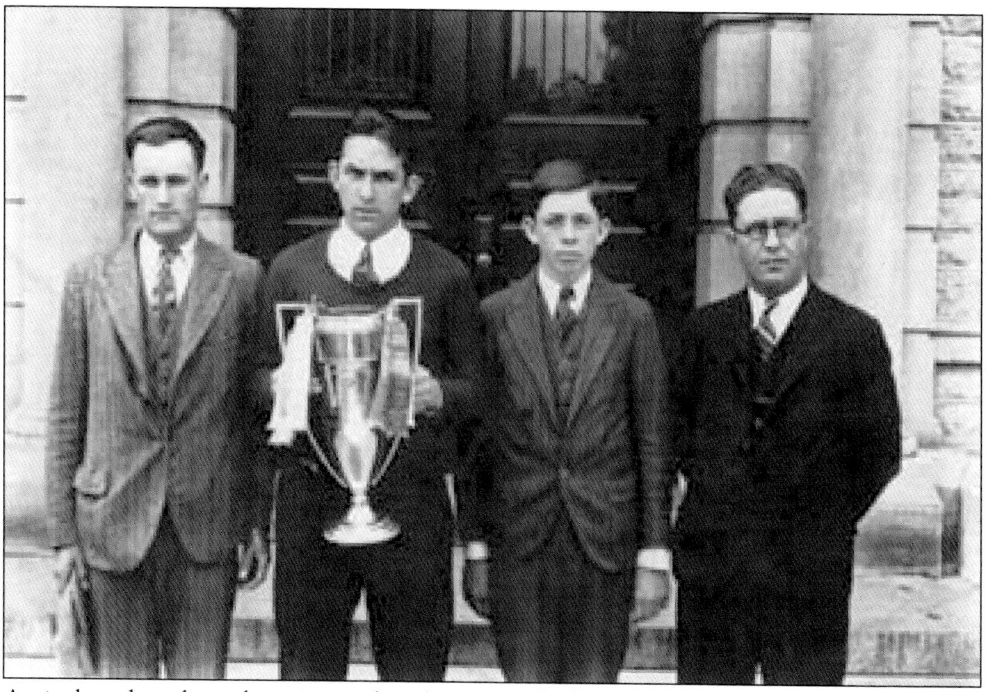

Agriculture has always been integral to the area and taken seriously. Children, particularly the boys, were expected to help with summer farming chores. Luther DeMoss (far right) was the agriculture teacher at Louisiana High School, and his 1930 dairy team won the state championship. The team included, from left to right, Steve Jeffries, King Edwards, and Lloyd Slater. (Courtesy Betty Jane Allen.)

On Tuesday, December 21, 1944, a service flag dedication, "World War II Roster of Louisiana High School Alumni," was held at Louisiana High School at 2:30 p.m. The honor roll board contained 236 names and was made by former student Walter Shepherd. The board, the service flag, and a beautiful American flag were all gifts from the class of 1943. (Courtesy Grace Jane Catlett.)

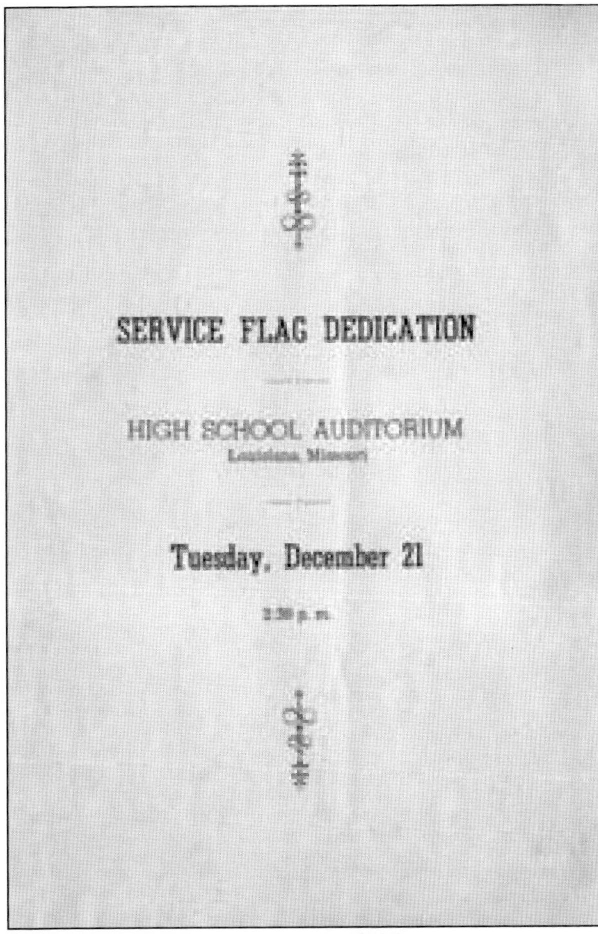
SERVICE FLAG DEDICATION

HIGH SCHOOL AUDITORIUM
Louisiana, Missouri

Tuesday, December 21

2:30 p.m.

The first Cottage School in Missouri, at Fifth and Jackson Streets, is seen below. For a time, it was used as a private residence, but in the 1920s, it was used for home economic classes for the high school across the street. It later became a private residence again and was eventually renovated into three apartments. (Courtesy John Wood.)

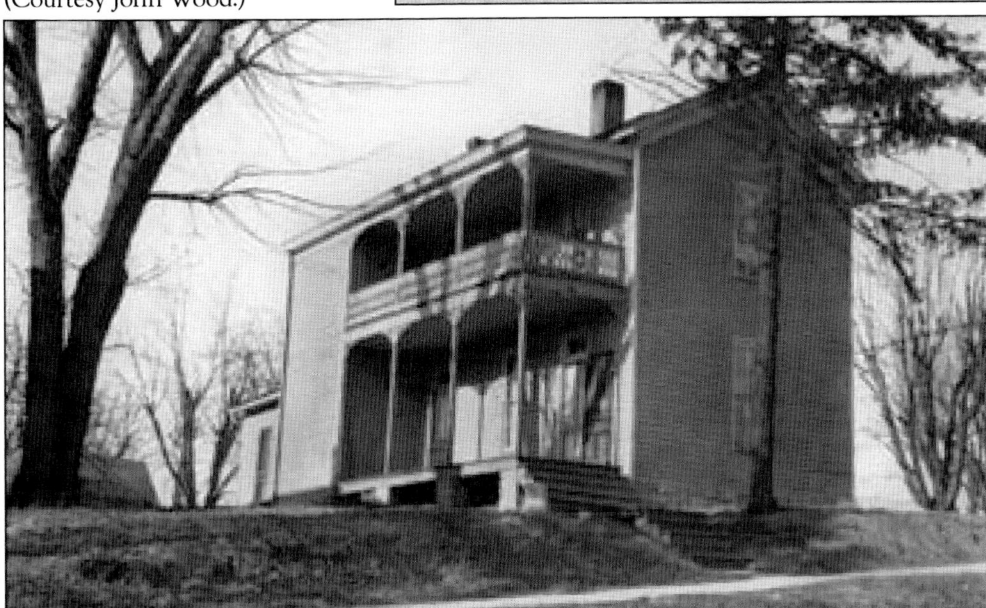

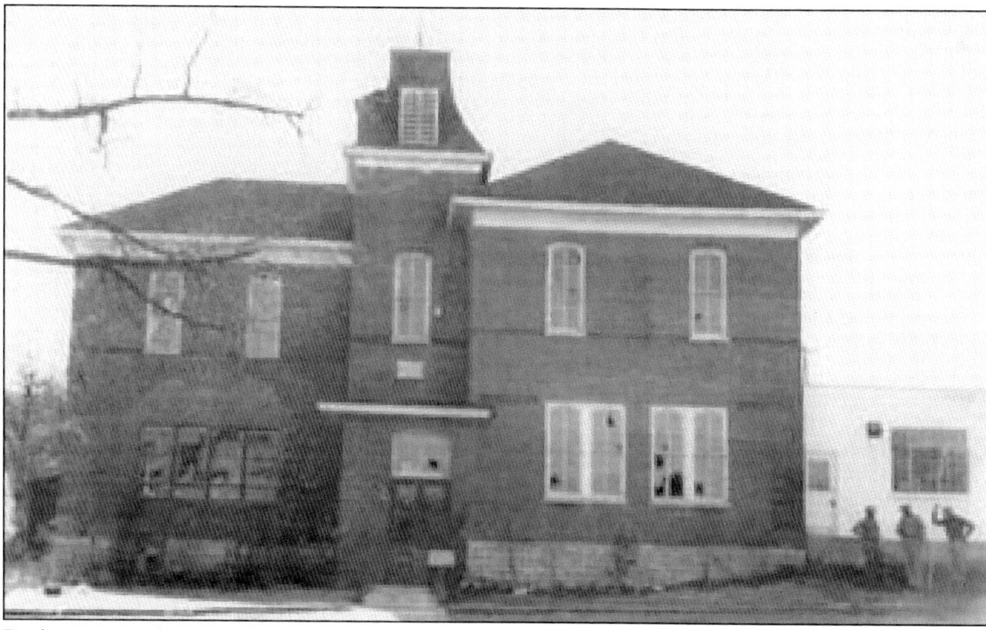

Built in 1900, the Lincoln School served black children from grades one through 12 in Louisiana until 1955. Elementary grades were integrated in the 1961–1962 school year. The city purchased the school and its multipurpose additional room at auction in 1961 for storage. Lincoln High School was the only state-accredited black high school in Pike County and its adjoining counties. (Courtesy Sally Cropp.)

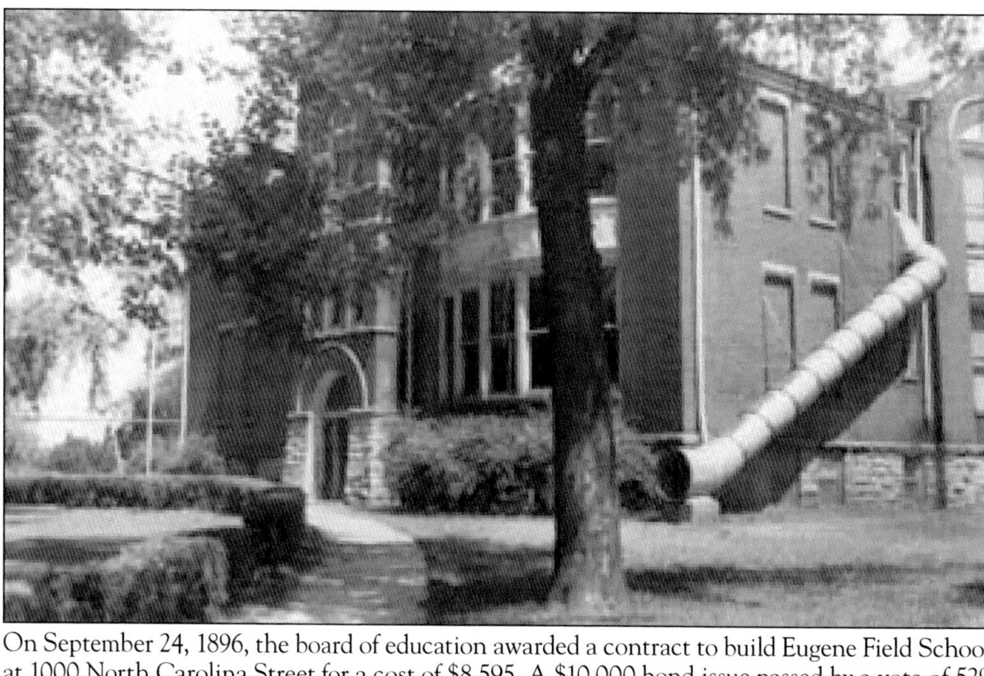

On September 24, 1896, the board of education awarded a contract to build Eugene Field School at 1000 North Carolina Street for a cost of $8,595. A $10,000 bond issue passed by a vote of 529 to 165. This school served grades one through eight until 1953, when Meriwether Elementary School was completed. Note the fire escape on the right side of the building. Field Village, a senior citizen's facility, now occupies the school and playground lots. (Courtesy Linda Ince Beer.)

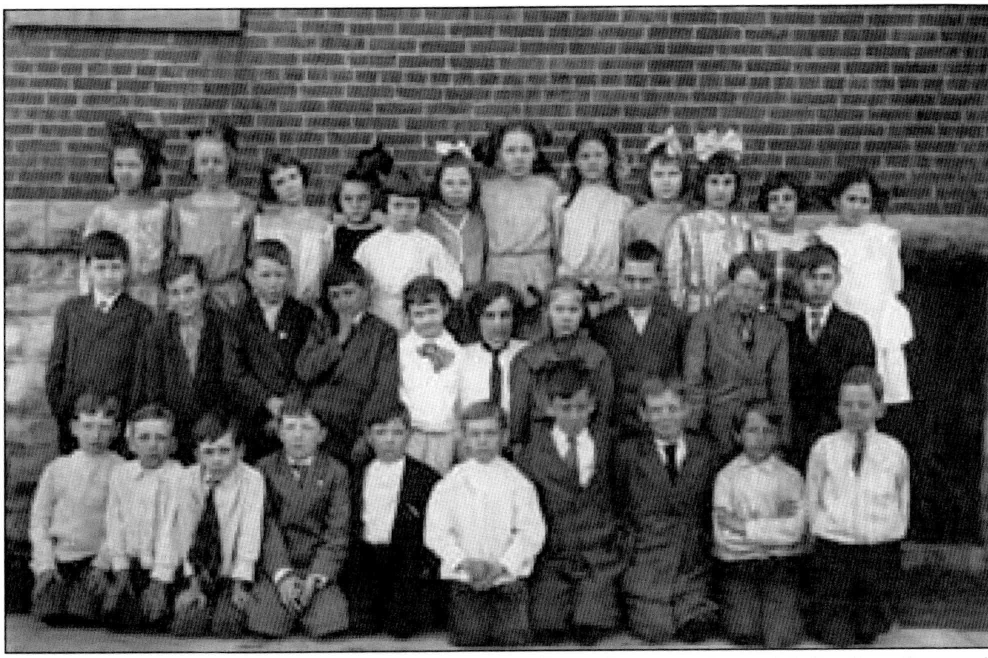

There were two elementary schools in Louisiana in the early 1900s: Central School on the north end of town and Eugene Field School on the south end of town. The children seldom socialized with each other, partly due to the lack of in-town transportation. The third grade at Eugene Field School is seen here in 1911. The child in the front row, sixth from the left is John J. Zook, father of coauthor Martha Sue (Zook) Smith. (Courtesy Betty Jane Allen.)

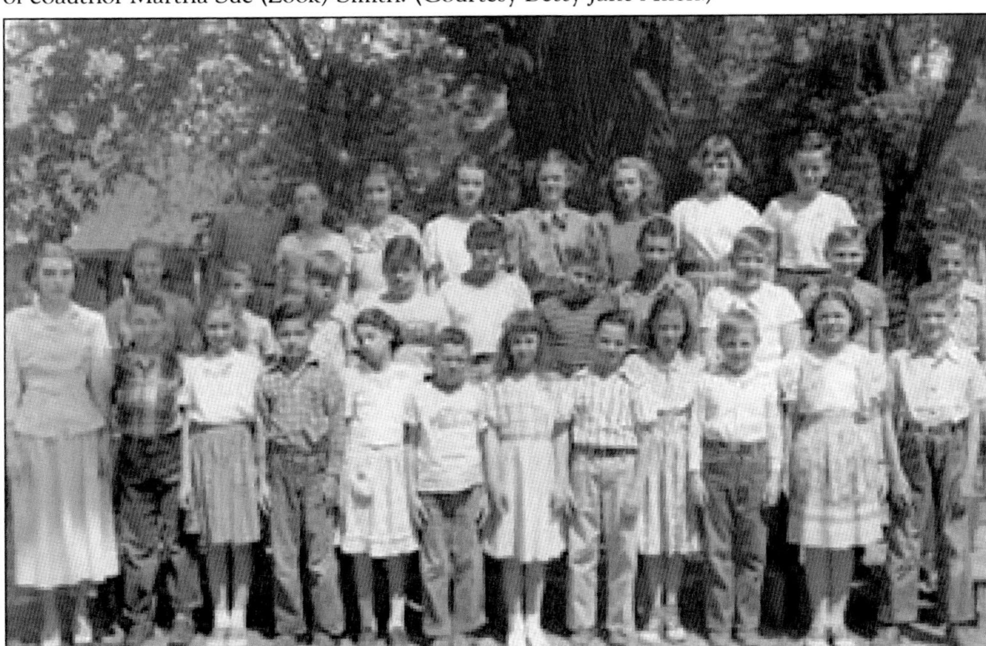

This sixth-grade class at Eugene Field School poses with its teacher, Jean Rice. This class graduated from high school in 1955. (Courtesy Betty Jane Allen.)

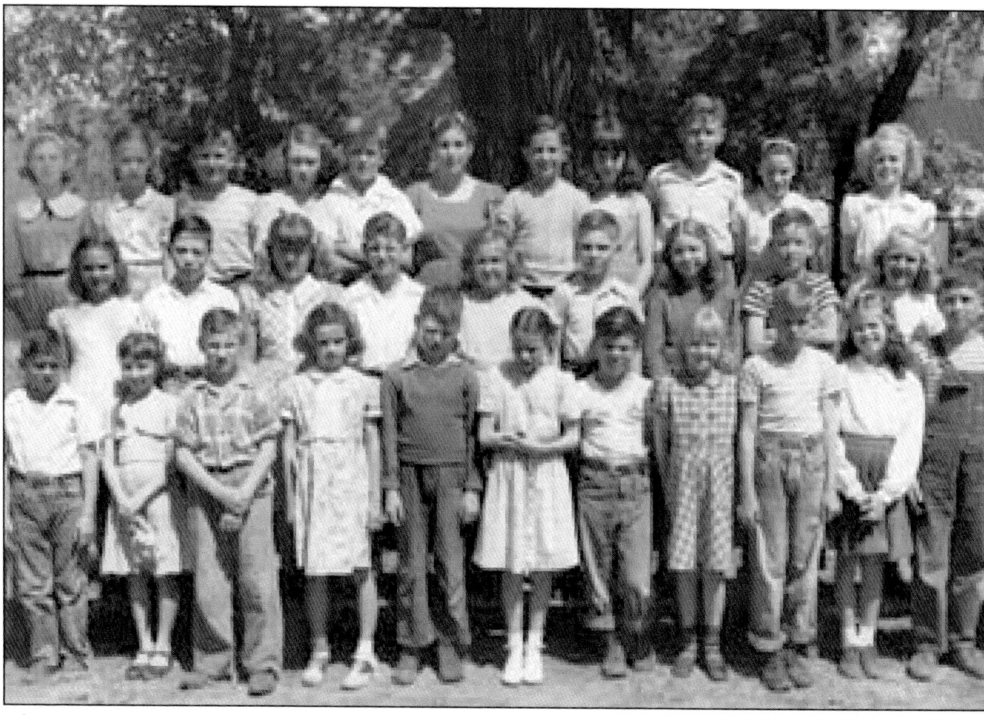

The 1956 high school graduating class members gathers for their photograph when they were in elementary school at Eugene Field School. (Courtesy Louisiana Area Historical Museum.)

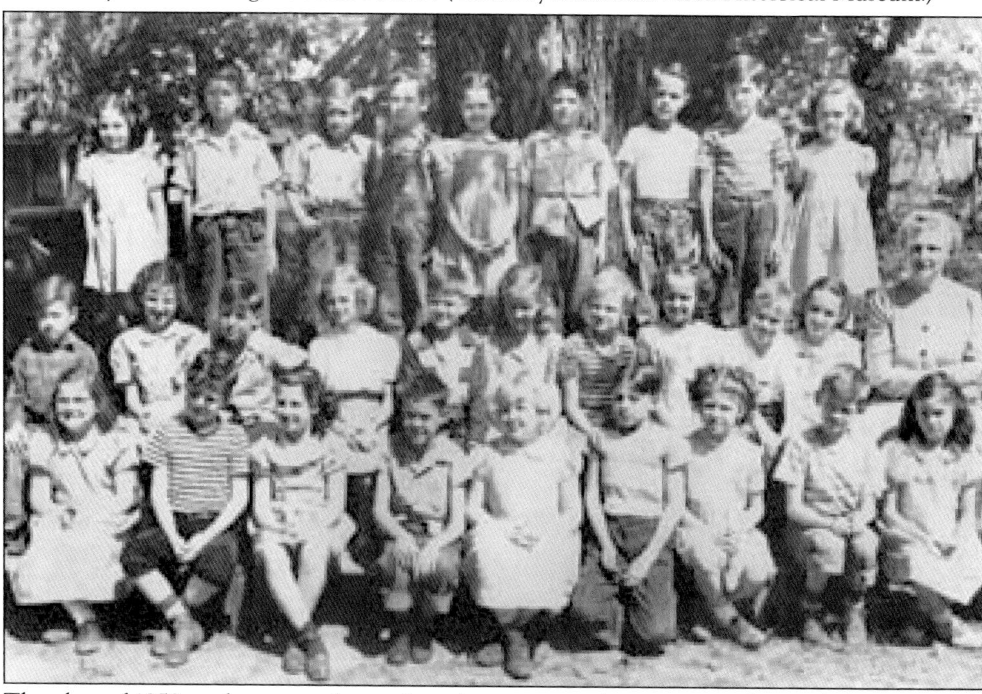

The class of 1958 students pose here when they were much younger and attended Eugene Field School. First row, third from the left is coauthor Martha Sue (Zook) Smith. (Courtesy Louisiana Area Historical Museum.)

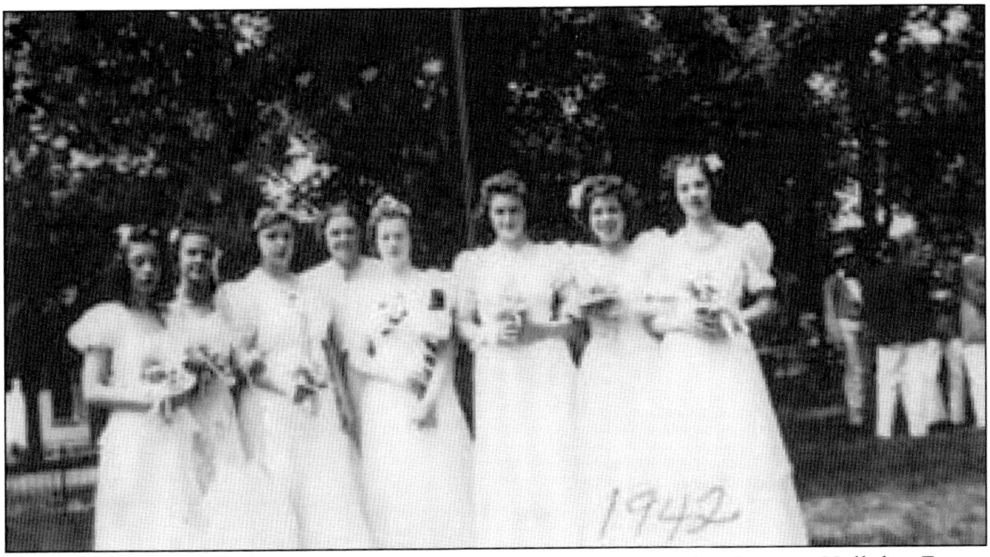

From left to right, Naomi (Rubemeyer) Gottman; Bea (Henry) Goodin; Daynice Holliday; Emma Naxera, principal and eighth-grade teacher; Juanita (Walker) Beddies, 1942 Maypole Queen; Bonnie (Hudson) Morton; Suzanne (Goodman) Smith; and Peggy (Boyd) Readey comprise the 1942 Eugene Field School May Day Court. (Courtesy Bea Goodin.)

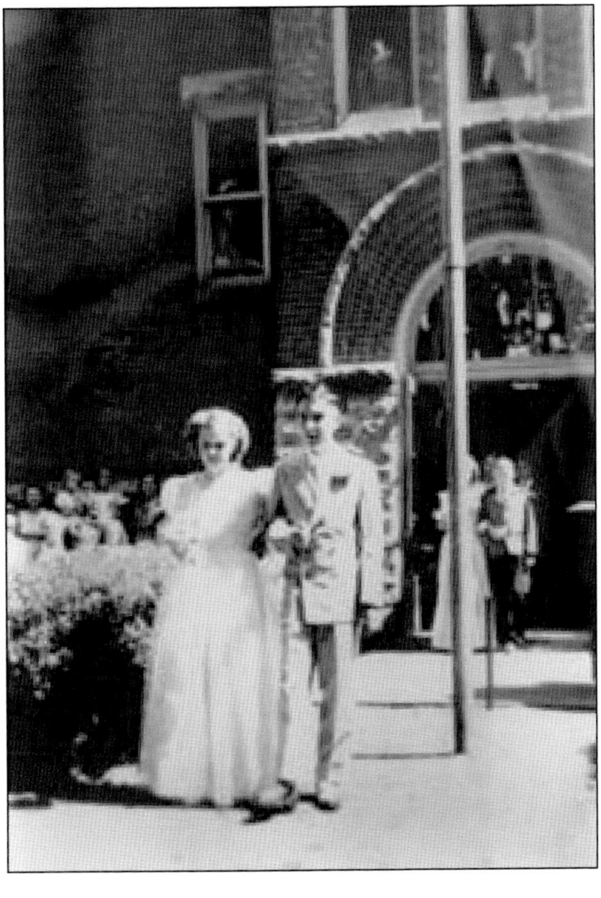

Robert Ray Gast Jr. escorts Betty Jane Akers through the arched doorway of Eugene Field School in the spring of 1947. Gast and Akers were king and queen of the annual May Day celebration. They were graduating eighth-graders heading for high school in the fall. They took their seats in the honored spot to watch other students dance around the May pole, weaving colorful ribbons in and out and then reversing direction to unweave them. (Courtesy Gail Gast Sidwell.)

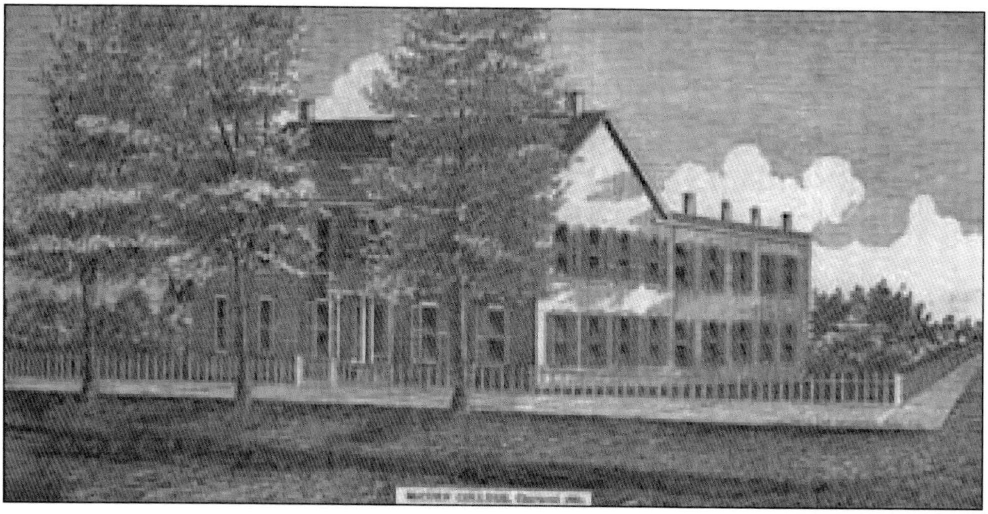

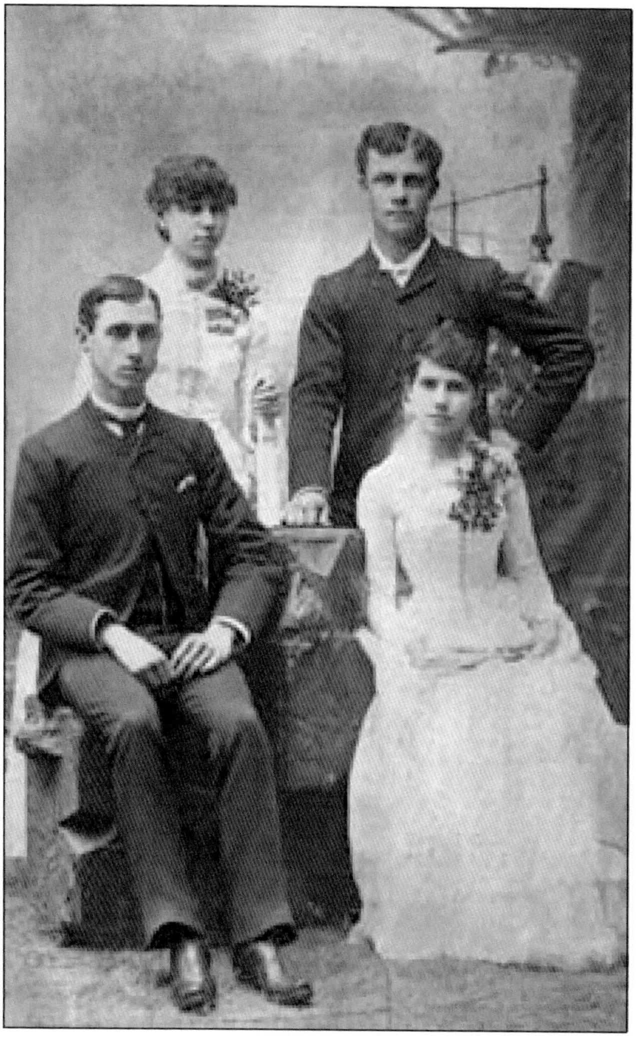

Pardee College (above) was established through the Old School Presbyterian Church in Louisiana in 1868. In 1871, it was sold to the Baptists, who had incorporated the Louisiana Baptist College in 1869. A. Judson McCune, the president of the Mercantile Bank of Louisiana, and later the mayor, financially supported the college for its entire existence. In June 1881, the Louisiana Baptist College was reorganized as McCune College and incorporated under the laws of Missouri. The college closed in 1895. (Courtesy Betty Jane Allen.)

Roxa West and Joe McCune (seated) and Eva Keith and Malcolm Campbell (standing) attended McCune College in 1883. West and McCune married on May 17, 1887. Their only child, Tinsley West, was born on September 29, 1889. He married and raised a family and lived to be 97 years old. He had the first filling station and the first hearse in Louisiana. (Courtesy Dorothy McCune Sansing.)

Four

FUN AND FESTIVALS

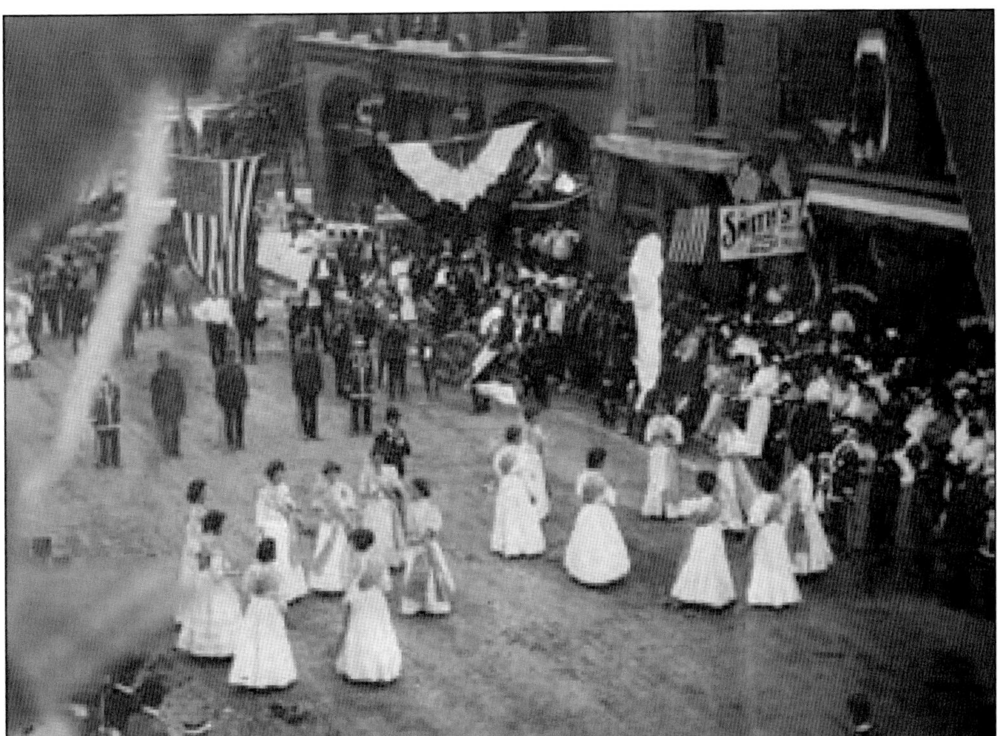

The Fourth of July parade gathers at the corner of Third and South Carolina Streets in front of the Grand Hotel in 1890. The Citizen's Band, with the drummer in the center right, was assembling, and attractive young ladies were receiving instructions. Decorations were in place, the streets were crowded, and the patriotism was visible. (Courtesy John Wood.)

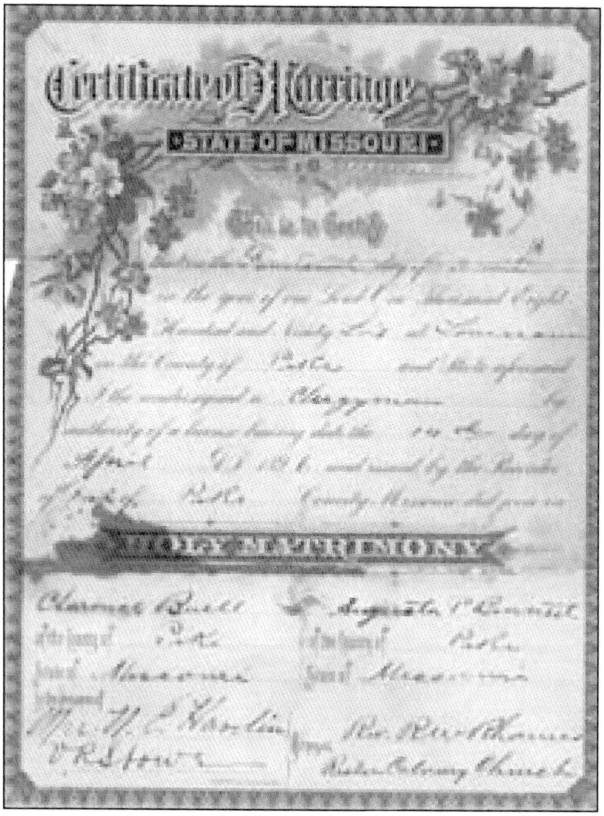
Certificate of Marriage
STATE OF MISSOURI
This is to Certify
HOLY MATRIMONY

Clarence Buell and Augusta P. "Gussie" Burnett were married on April 14, 1896, by Rev. R.W. Rharnes, the rector at Calvary Episcopal Church. Gussie's father, Frank Burnett, was issued a ferryboat license in 1843, owned numerous properties, and had the Burnett Theater built. The family is buried in Riverview Cemetery. (Courtesy Trent Meyers.)

After the theater was built, Clarence Buell became a partner and manager of the theater. And the name was changed to the Burnett-Buell Theater. The theater, which survived two fires, was a popular cultural center for plays, graduations, civic events, and area festivities. (Courtesy Trent Meyers.)

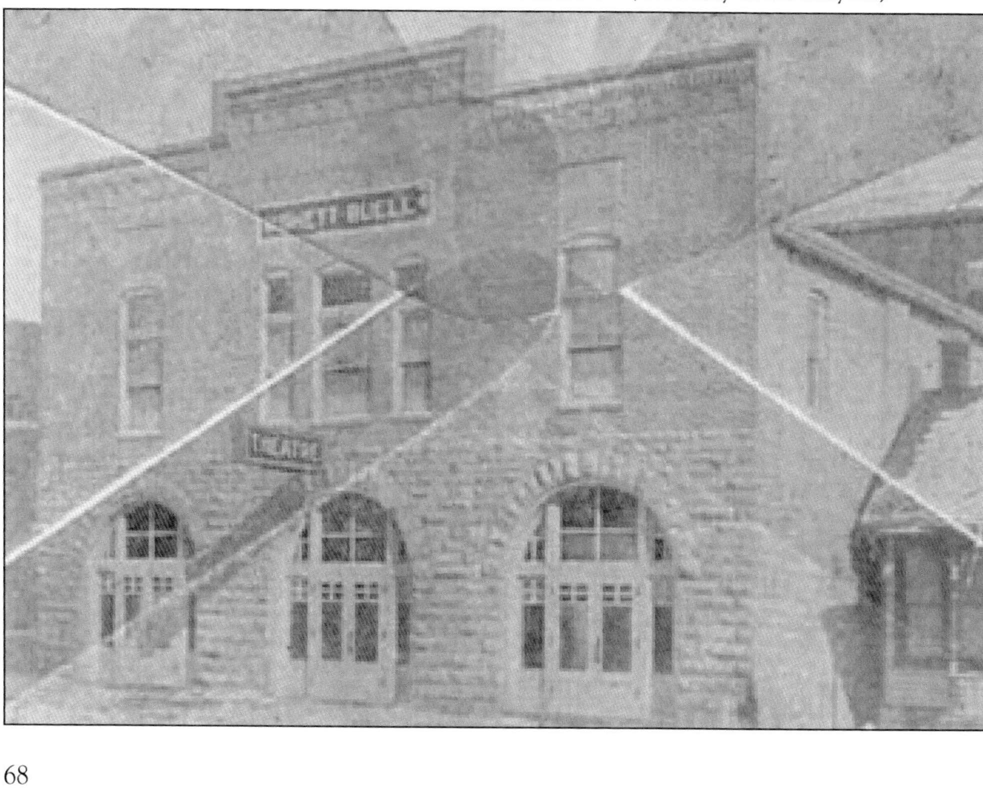

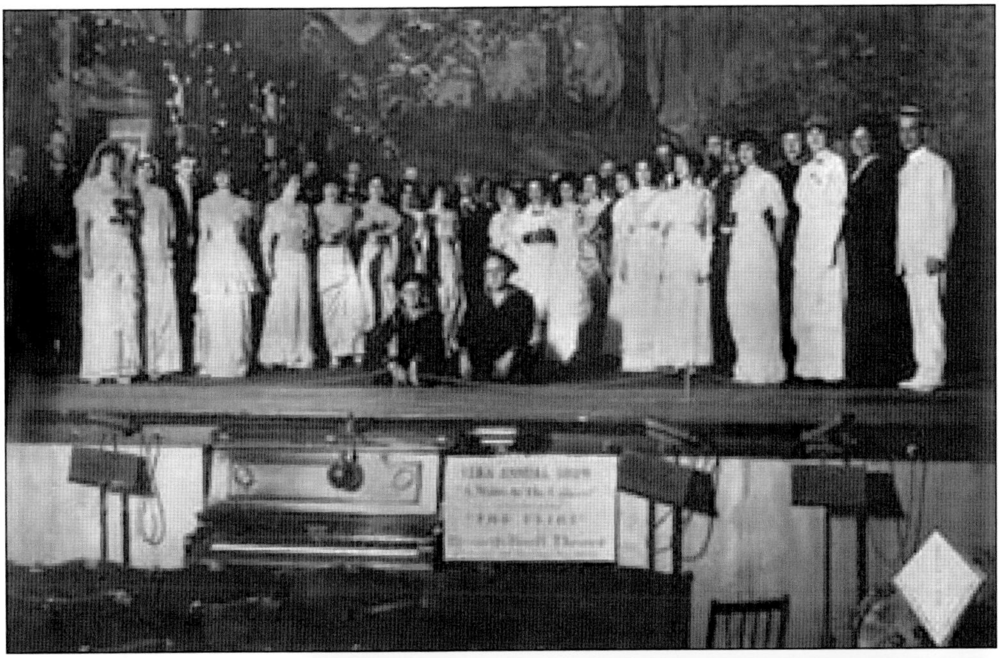

The annual Elks Show, "A Night At The Cabaret," billed as "The Flirt," ran on Wednesday and Thursday nights, November 26 and 27, in the early 1920s at the popular Burnett-Buell Theater. Talented young people and enthusiastic audiences enjoyed evenings of delightful shows together. (Courtesy Betty Jane Allen.)

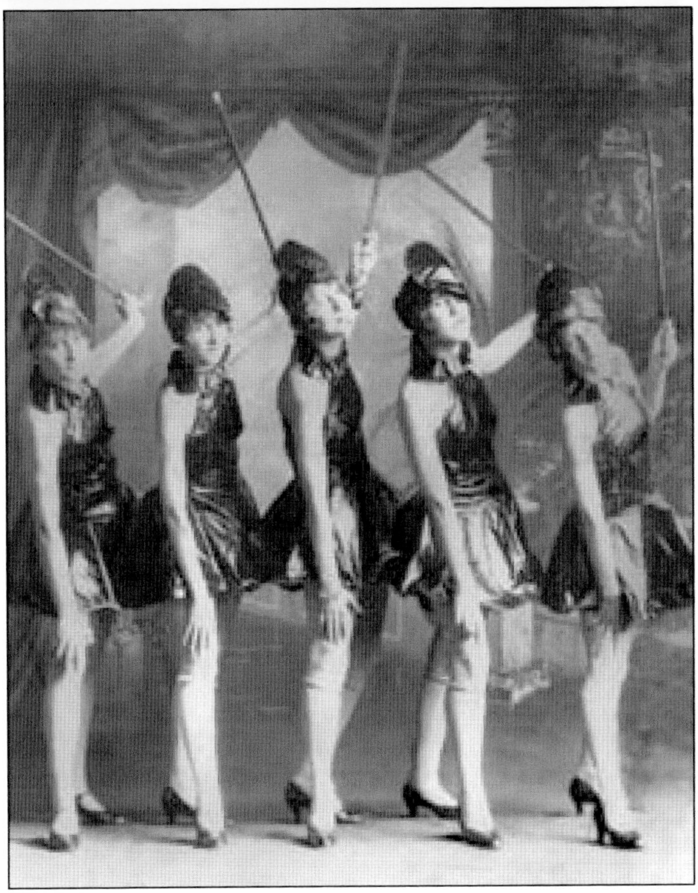

These fine ladies perform at the Burnett-Buell Theater in the 1920s. (Courtesy Louisiana Area Historical Museum.)

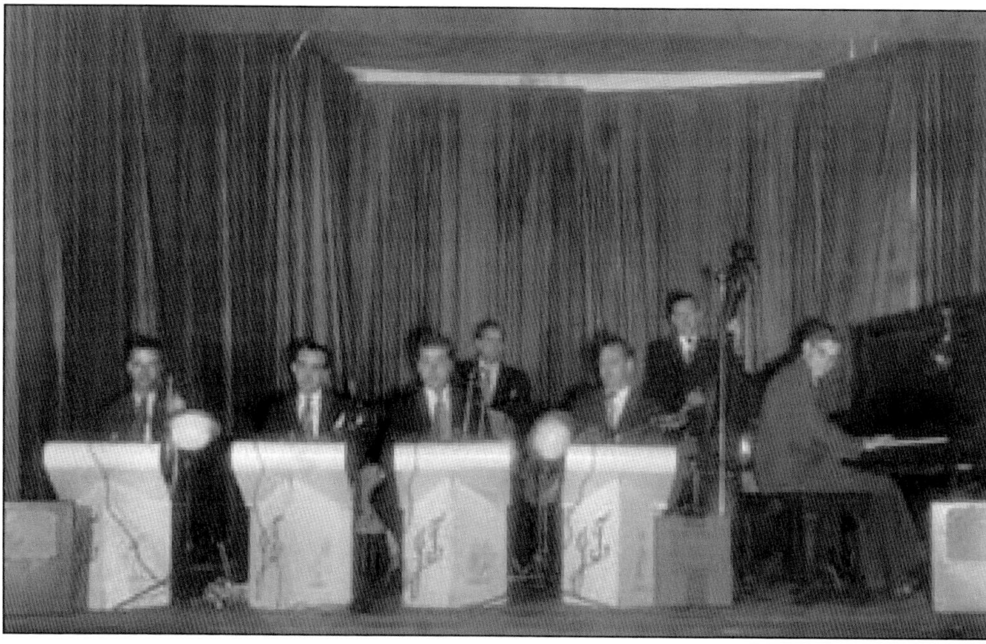

The J.T. Band takes its place for a concert at the Masonic Temple bandstand. Louisiana has been recognized for its many fine bands, large and small, that have enjoyed enthusiastic audiences. An old flyer from the Burnett-Buell Opera House featuring a band concert once proclaimed, "A town without a band is sleeping." (Courtesy Louisiana Area Historical Museum.)

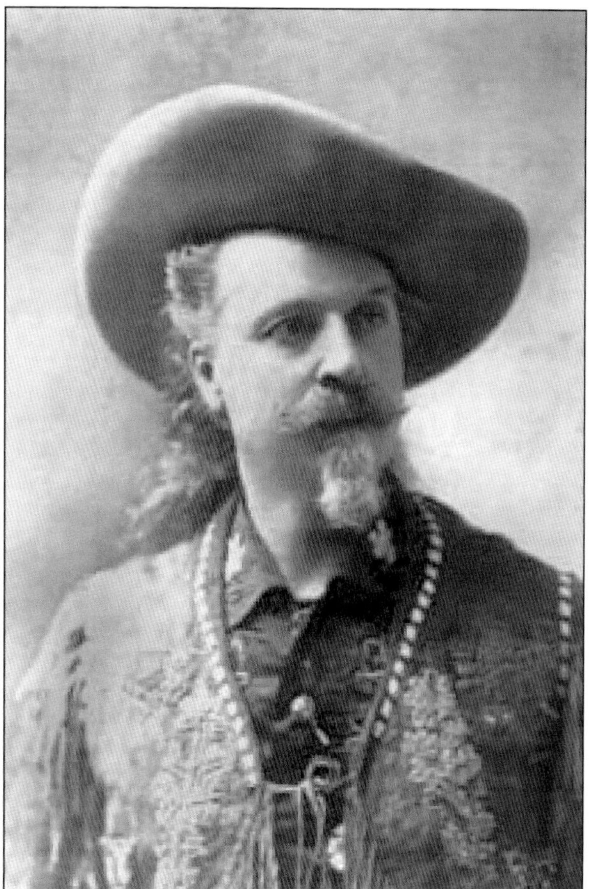

Clarence Buell (left) traveled the world over with Buffalo Bill as his advance man, booking shows. Buffalo Bill, Annie Oakley, and their troupe performed at the old fairgrounds in 1911 with local children, including Cam Hardin, in the show. (Courtesy Betty Jane Allen.)

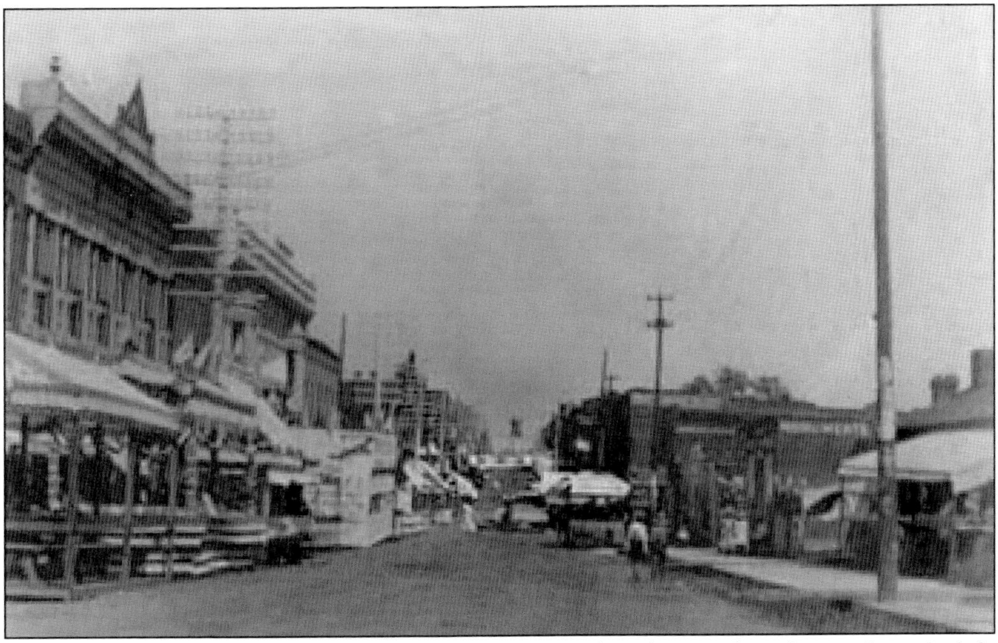

On September 5, 1900, Louisiana was preparing for a festival. A decorated vendor stands on the left. This photograph was taken looking east down Georgia Street during preparations for Louisiana's first annual street fair, which featured Buffalo Bill's Wild West Show. (Courtesy John Wood.)

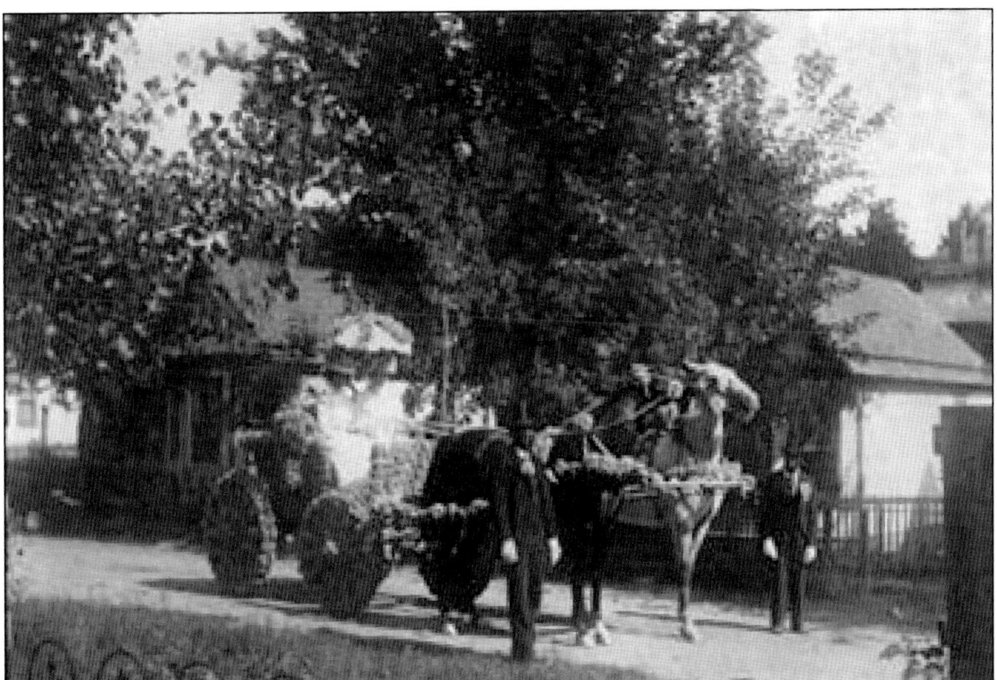

Waiting with anticipation to join in the Louisiana Street Fair—a four-day event in September 1900—are Mrs. Walter L. Tinsley and her daughter. Their elegantly decorated cart hitched to a beautiful pair of horses is being led by trainers. (Courtesy Louisiana Area Historical Museum.)

Program

OF THE THIRTY-FIRST ANNUAL GRADUATING EXERCISES OF THE

Louisiana Public School

APRIL 12, 1906 - 8 O'CLOCK P.M.

Parks Theatre

Orchestra
Chorus.....A Norse Lullaby
Prayer.....Rev. E. D. Watson
Orchestra
Address.....That Old Sweetheart of Mine.....Mr. Walter Williams, Columbia, Mo.
Orchestra
Quartette.....On Venice Waters.....Joseph Irwin, Clyde Cleveland, Victor Pitney, John Shroeder
Presentation of Class to Board of Education
Awarding of Diplomas
Chorus.....My Lady Comes to Me

SENIOR CLASS ROLL.

First Honor.........Clyde Milton Dillender
Georgia Orcth Dever
Howard Flagg
Esther Morris
Second Honor.......John Milroy Paine
Victor Max Pitney
Bessie Lorene Shepherd
John Godfrey Urban.

THE GRADUATING CLASS OF GRAMMAR SCHOOL

Egbert Taylor Adams
Louis Ayres Barnum
Cornelia Isabelle Cubberly
Mary Lucile Case
Harry Justin Dillender
Ora Erma Gilham
Bertha Mildred Harrelson
Norman Clifford Houser
Lillian Marie Howden
Clara May Ingram
Robert Hugh Ladley
Ray McCallister
Joseph Taylor Pierce
Addie Jay Reading
Gladys Lee Rose
Martha Winifred Stark
Janie Byrd Smith
Thomas Withrow Stark
Lula Mildred Wahl
Mildred Margaret Yates

Beulah Pansy Betts
William Augusta Behringer
Anna Isabel Chappell
Florence Anna DeGroodt
John Farrell
Ira Manford Howell
Laura Ellen Harrison
Vernon Judson Houser
Donald Stanley Howden
Iva Pearson Kilby
Minervia Bealle Moore
Minnie Lavenia Pool
Gertrude Ruth Rose
Trule Elsie Rose
Clara Shull
Alice Vivian Snead
Mae Deane Smith
Charles Perry Salyer
Goldie Pattie Weaver
Rhea Pearson Young

The 31st annual graduating exercises of the Louisiana Public School were held on April 12, 1906, at Parks Theatre. (Courtesy Betty Jane Allen.)

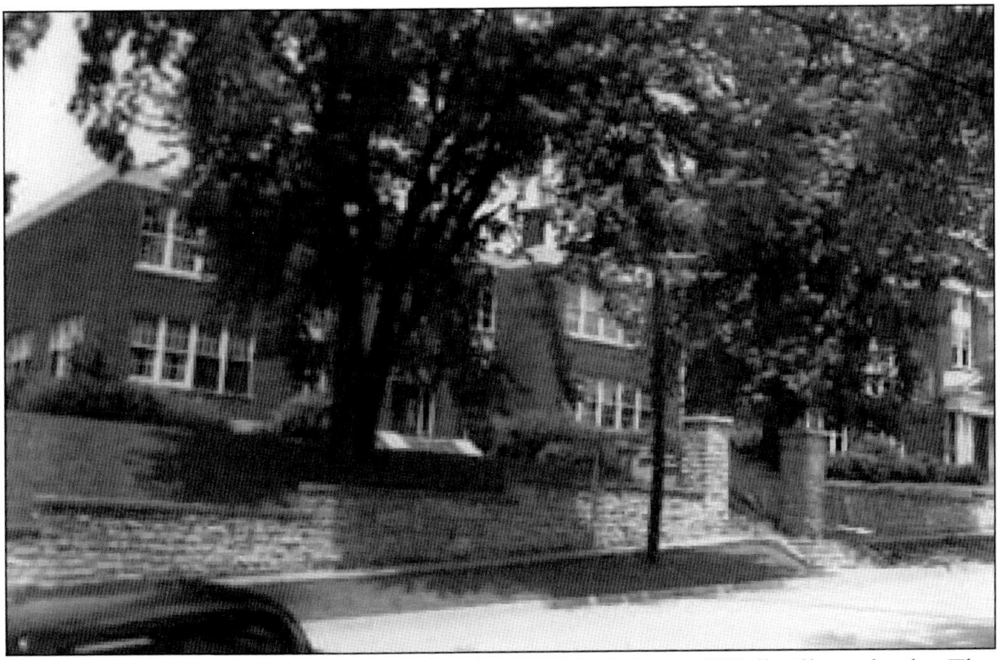

Louisiana High School and Central Grade School and the Memorial Wall still stand today. This image shows them in all their glory. The grounds are full of memories, laughter, and some tears but most of all with educated graduates exiting. (Courtesy John Wood.)

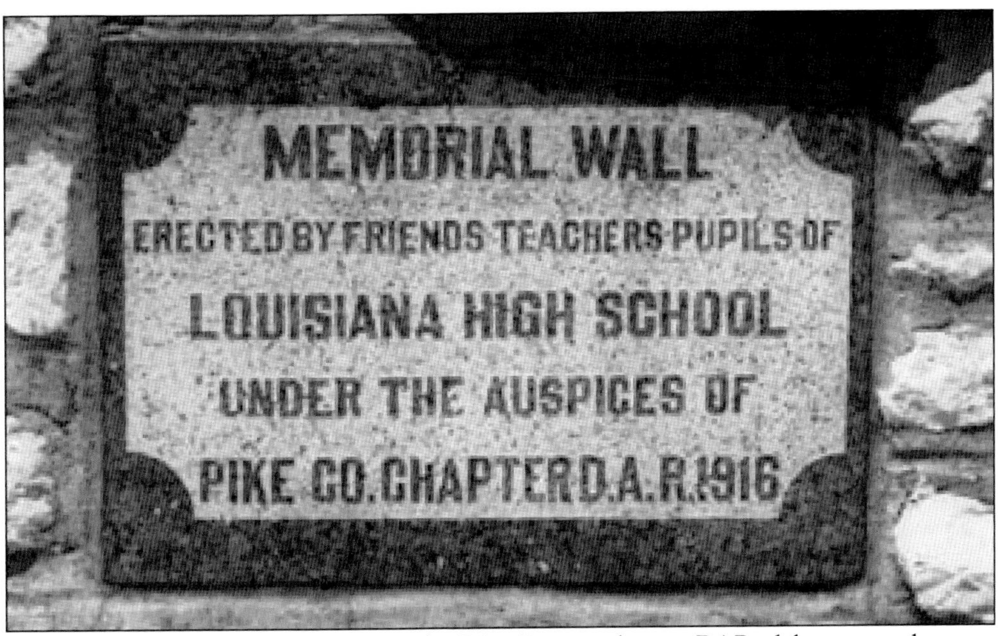

At 9:00 on Friday, October 27, 1916, the Pike County chapter DAR, delegates to the state conference of DAR, and citizens assembled for the dedication of the Memorial Wall along the entire frontage of the Central School grounds. The wall was accepted on behalf of the board of education by George E. Lynott, president. The wall is 314 feet long, 4.5 feet high, and 18 inches wide. (Courtesy Louisiana Area Historical Museum.)

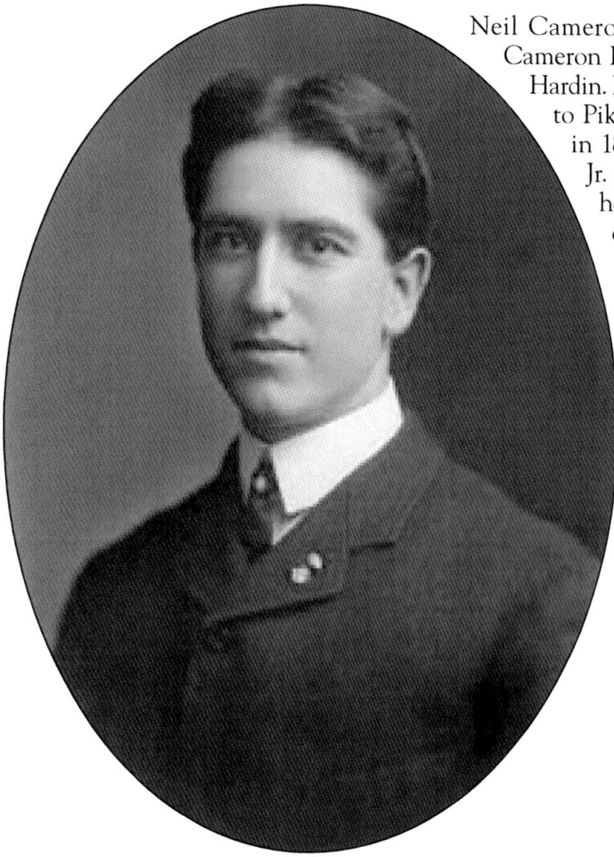

Neil Cameron Hardin Jr. was the son of Neil Cameron Hardin Sr. and Henrietta McCaskin Hardin. His grandfather Dr. W.C. Hardin came to Pike County in 1828. He built a home in 1844 at 300 North Main Street. Neil Jr. posed for this portrait in 1903, when he was in law school at the University of Michigan. Later, he was in silent movies in California for several years. Hardin Jr. died in Louisiana in 1969. (Courtesy Betty Jane Allen.)

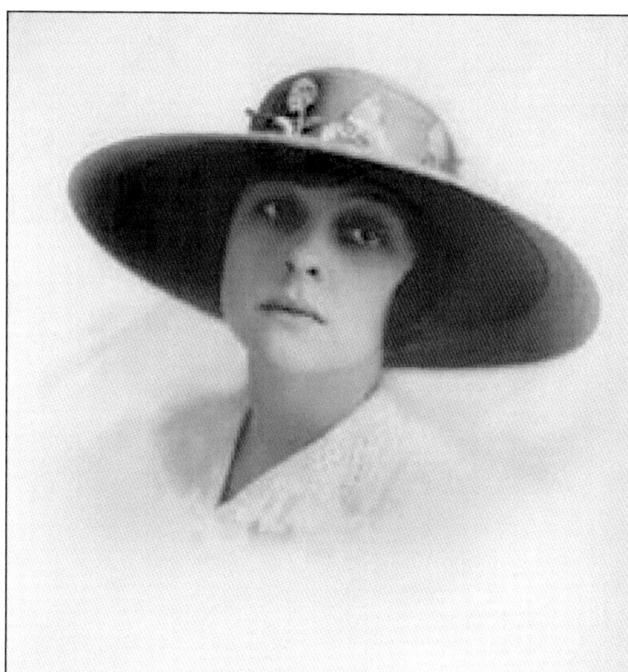

Gloria Payton Hardin left $1.7 million to Louisiana High School for scholarships when she died in 1989. Orphaned before she was seven years old, she was raised by friends of her mother's in New York and a foster aunt in California, where she met and married Neil Cameron Hardin Jr. She starred in silent movies. The Hardin Memorial Library was dedicated on November 26, 1996, at Louisiana High School. (Courtesy Betty J. Allen.)

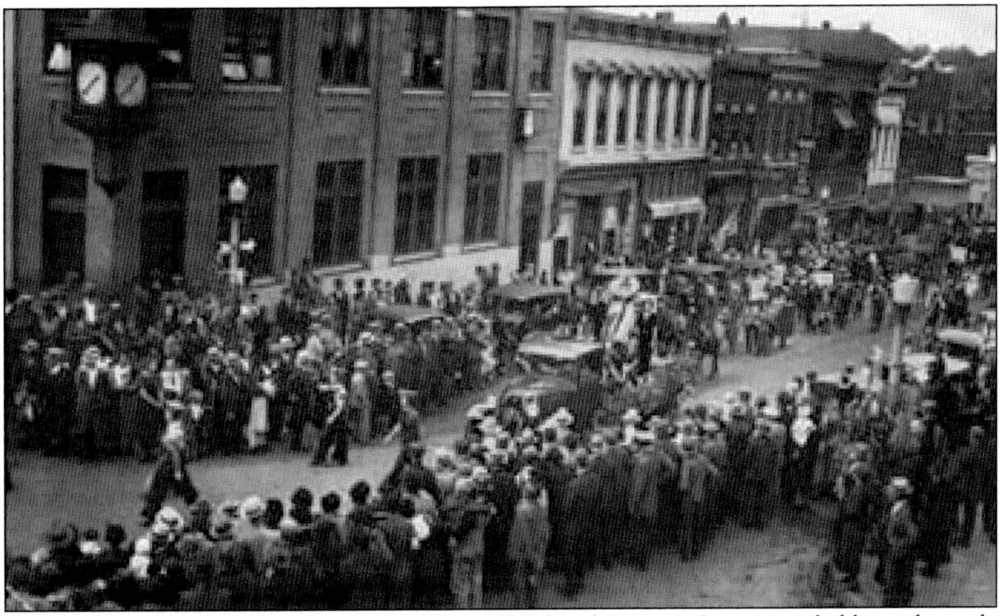

This large autumn parade turns the corner at Third and Georgia Streets, probably in the early 1930s. Parades were special, drawing many out-of-town spectators. The clock, anchored to the Bank of Louisiana building, is a town landmark, and the corner is often referred to as the Clock Corner. (Courtesy John Wood.)

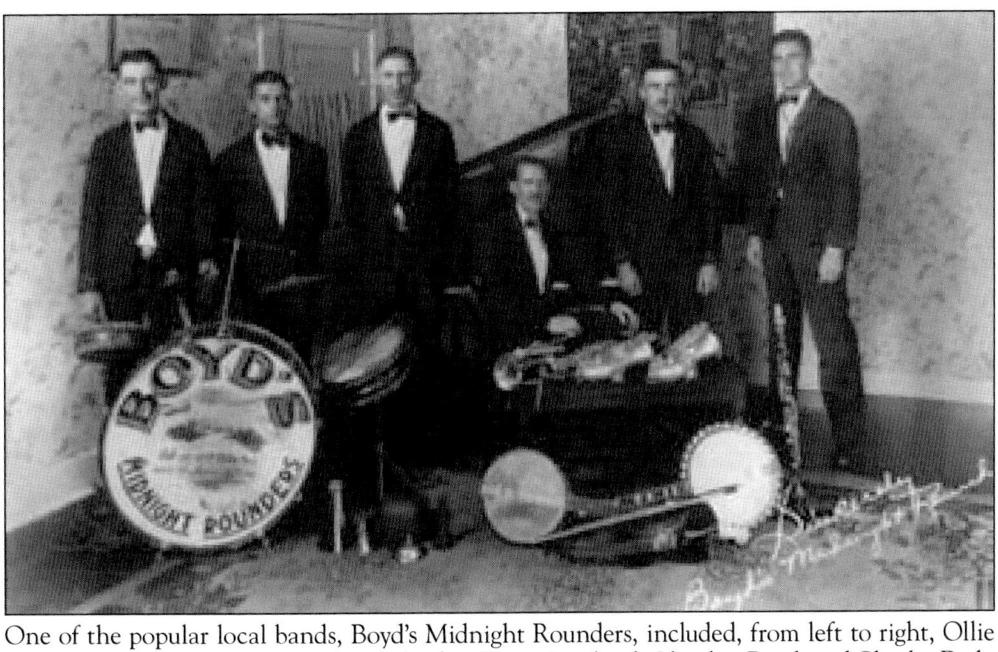

One of the popular local bands, Boyd's Midnight Rounders, included, from left to right, Ollie Bannister, Melburn Hueston, O.K. Burbridge, Fagan Rowland, Glendon Boyd, and Charles Dick. (Courtesy John Wood.)

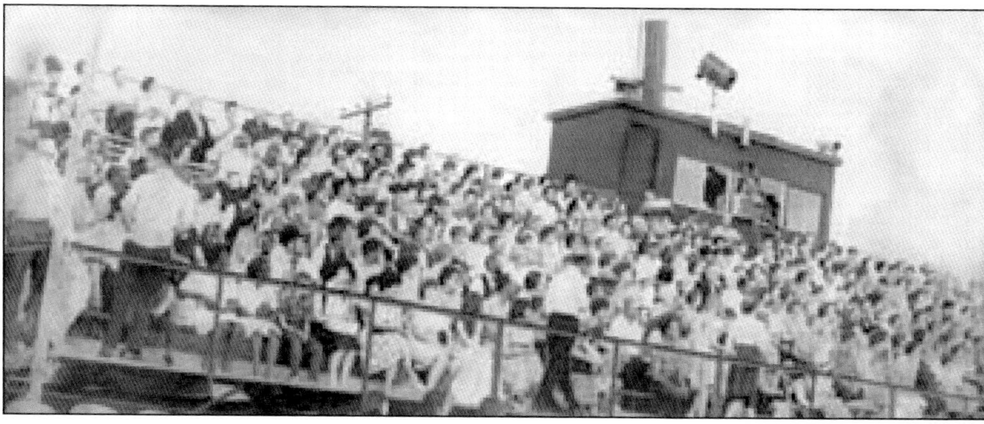

Louisiana's sesquicentennial celebration in June 1968 involved most everyone. Major events were scheduled for five days. The field bleachers at the high school stadium were packed for the queen coronation, the opening performances, and fireworks. Afterward, an Ulry's Pastries cake was served to approximately 2,000 people for two full days. The cake was 15 layers, with three tiers to a layer, and weighed 2,440 pounds. The remainder of the cake was delivered to Shriner's Hospital for Children in St. Louis. (Courtesy Irene Steers.)

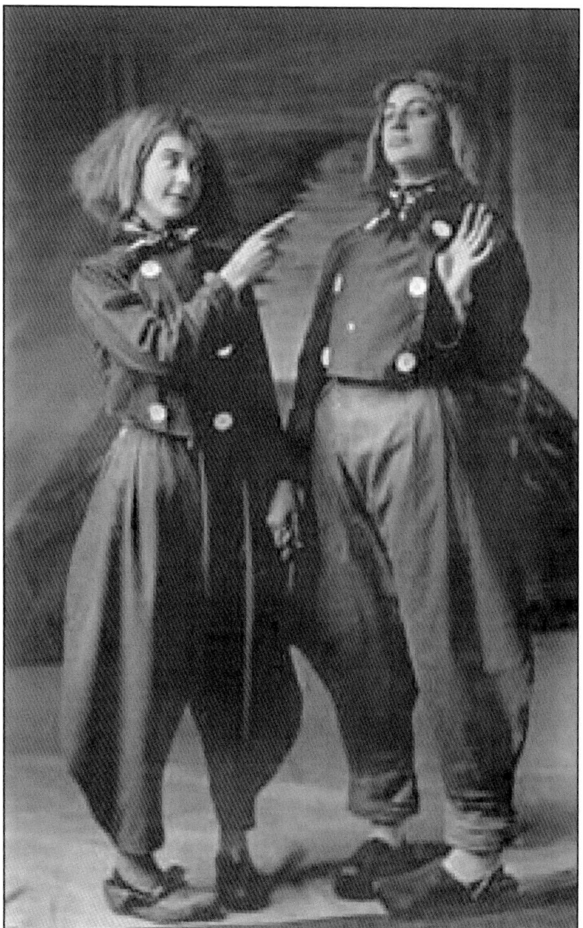

Vea Guthrie (left) and Lillian Ward ham it up cleverly, perhaps in a high school play. This postcard obviously caught the attention of a photographer who deemed it worthy of marketing, most likely in the early 1900s. (Courtesy Trent Meyers.)

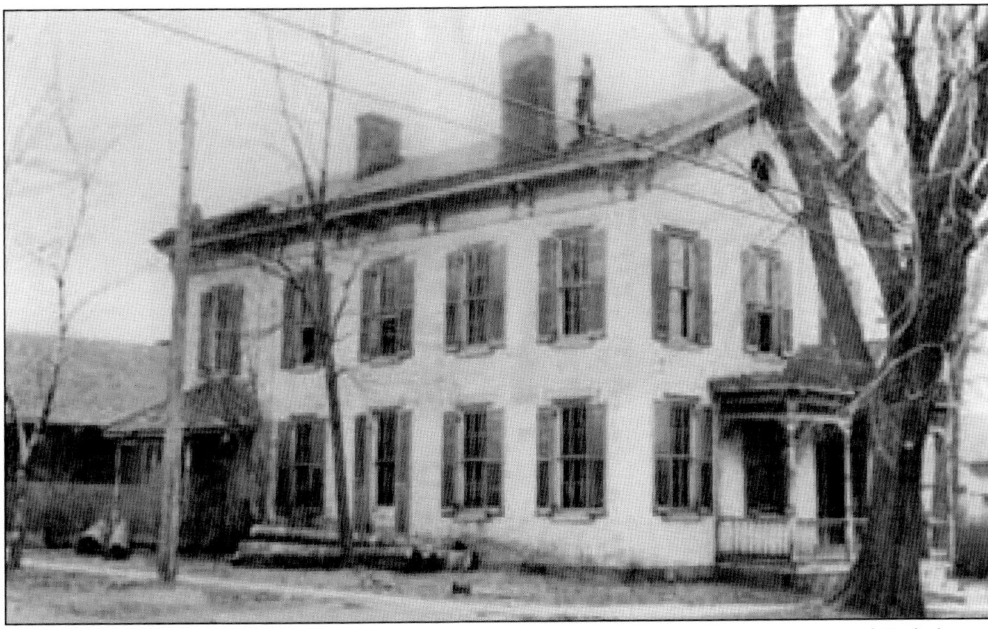

Elizabeth Whitaker, a teacher for many years, lived in this house on the corner of Eighth and Georgia Streets. The 1900 census lists her as 60 years old and living with three family members in this house. Note the man checking the chimney. Today, Dairy Queen occupies this lot. (Courtesy Betty Jane Allen.)

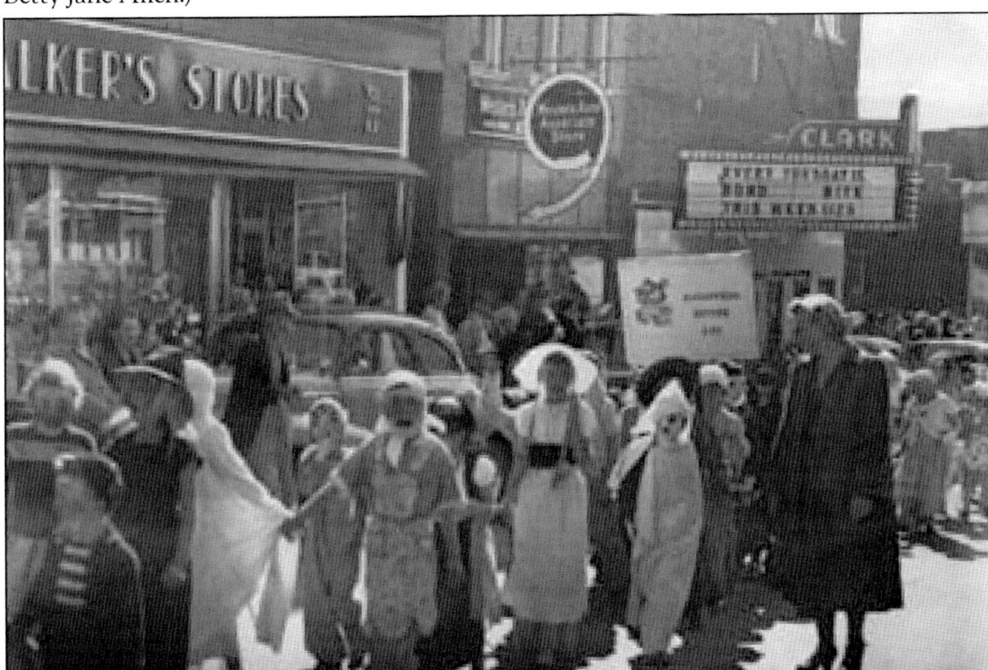

At Eugene Field School's Halloween parade, youngsters and their teacher, Mrs. Reid, drew a large crowd of parents and friends on October 31, 1949. They are between Third and Fourth Street on Georgia Street and appear to be enjoying every minute of the attention. (Courtesy Louisiana Area Historical Museum.)

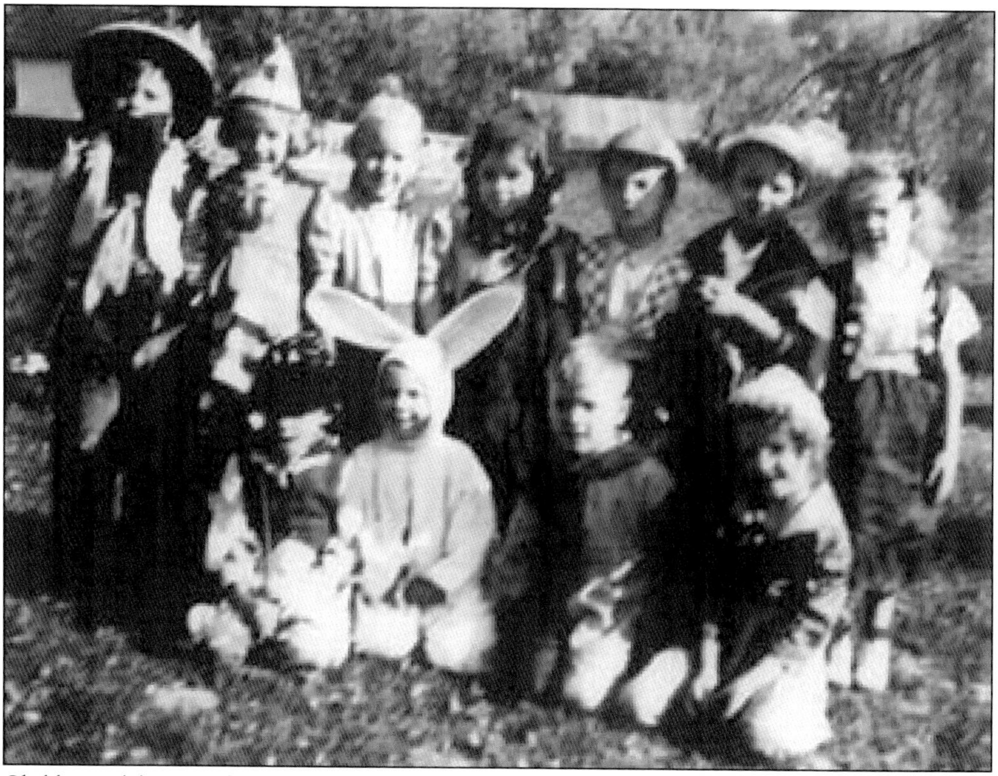

Children celebrate Halloween at the preschool operated by teacher Will Ella Gast in 1944. Neither preschool or kindergarten was a part of the public school system yet, and Gast filled an important part in many children's lives. A few faces are familiar in this picture, including Gail Gast (second row, standing, fifth from left), John Reed (sixth from left), Martha Sue Zook (first row, second from left), and Jack Dinwiddie (third from left). (Courtesy Gail Gast Sidwell.)

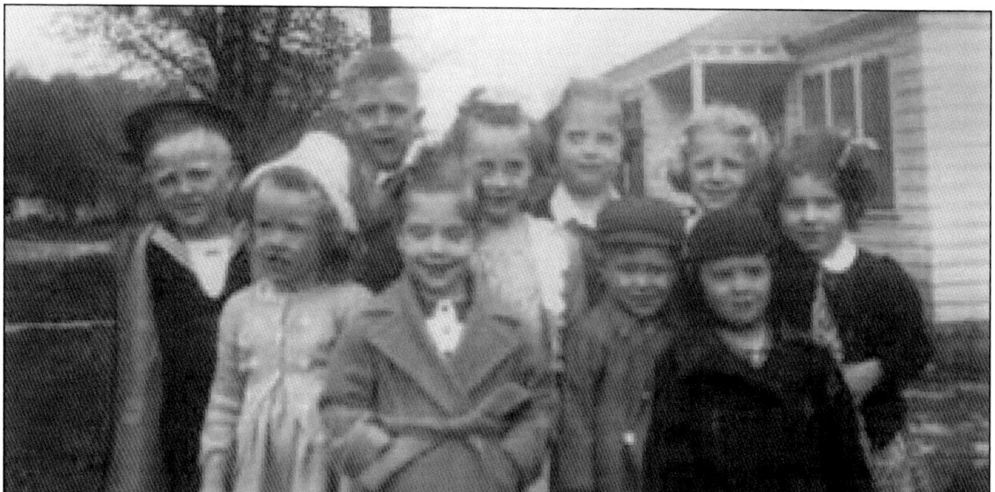

On May 6, 1944, Barbara Lee's birthday guests were, from left to right (first row) Martha Sue Zook, Jon Whiteis, and Gary Smith; (second row) Julie Anne Rogers, Phyllis Berry, and Sarah Linda Fipps; (third row) Jerry Moore, Tommy Moore, Karen Smith, and Barbara Lee. (Courtesy Barbara Lee Fay.)

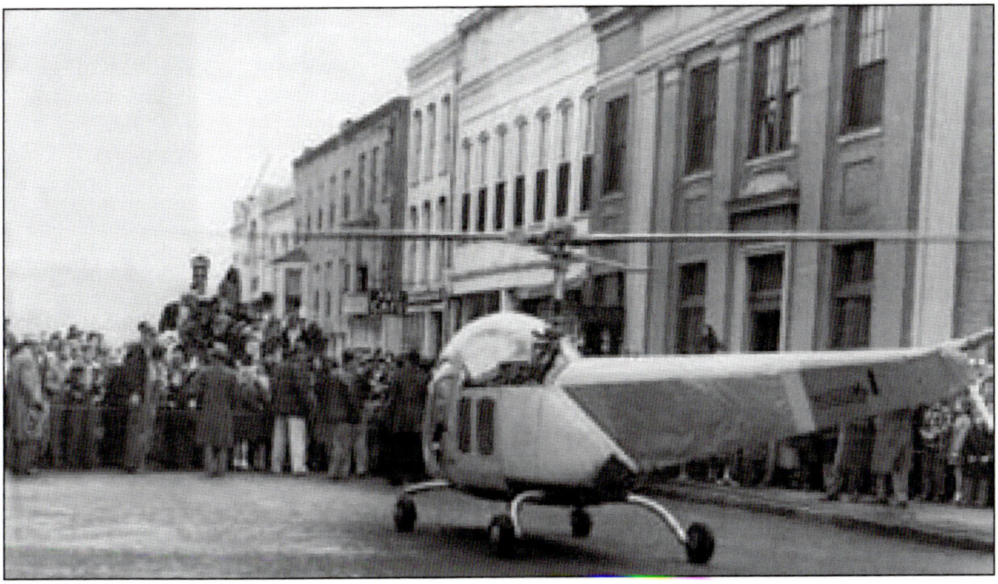

In December 1941, Santa Claus arrived at the intersection of Third and Georgia Streets in a helicopter. (Courtesy John Wood.)

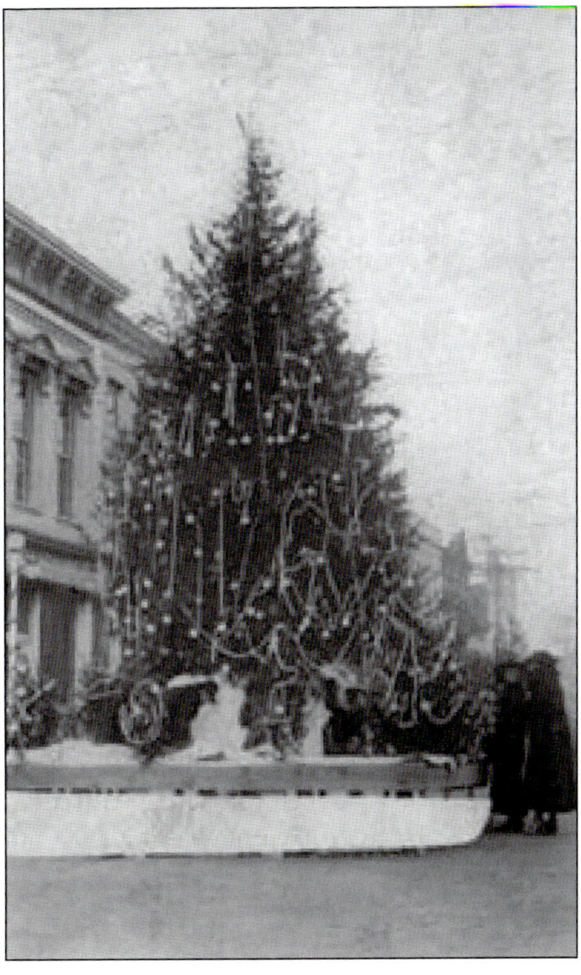

In 1916, this municipal Christmas tree was placed on display at Third and Georgia Streets. Nelson Tucker usually went out and got the tree, and in the 1950s, George Kritz piped in Christmas music to add to the season. (Courtesy Betty Jane Allen.)

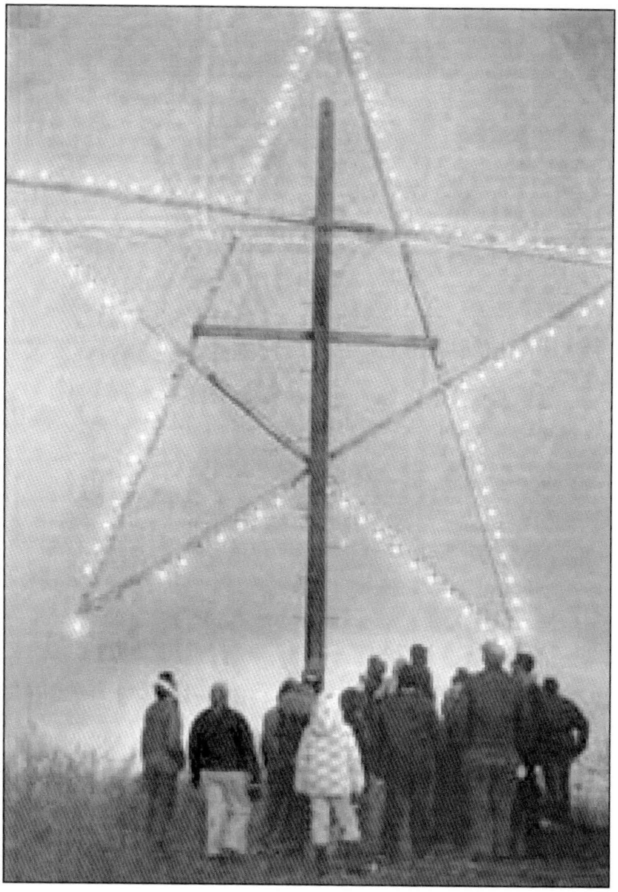

One of the greatest traditions in Louisiana is the lighting of the nearly 40-foot-tall Christmas star. Local residents look forward to the lighting with great anticipation. The Missouri Edison Company first displayed it in 1931. Originally, about 130 lights formed the outline of the star that sits atop Marzolf Hill, which now shares the name Star Hill. The position of the star can be seen from almost anywhere in town and for miles around. (Courtesy Linda Ince Beer.)

The eight Boy Scouts below, posing in the mid-1930s, included, from left to right, Leon Cochran, Ralph Ince, Clarence Blessing, Ben Lee Henderson, Buddy Andrews, Wilson Mitchell, Chad Sims, and Carl Barr. There is a proud Scouting tradition in Louisiana. (Courtesy Linda Ince Beer.)

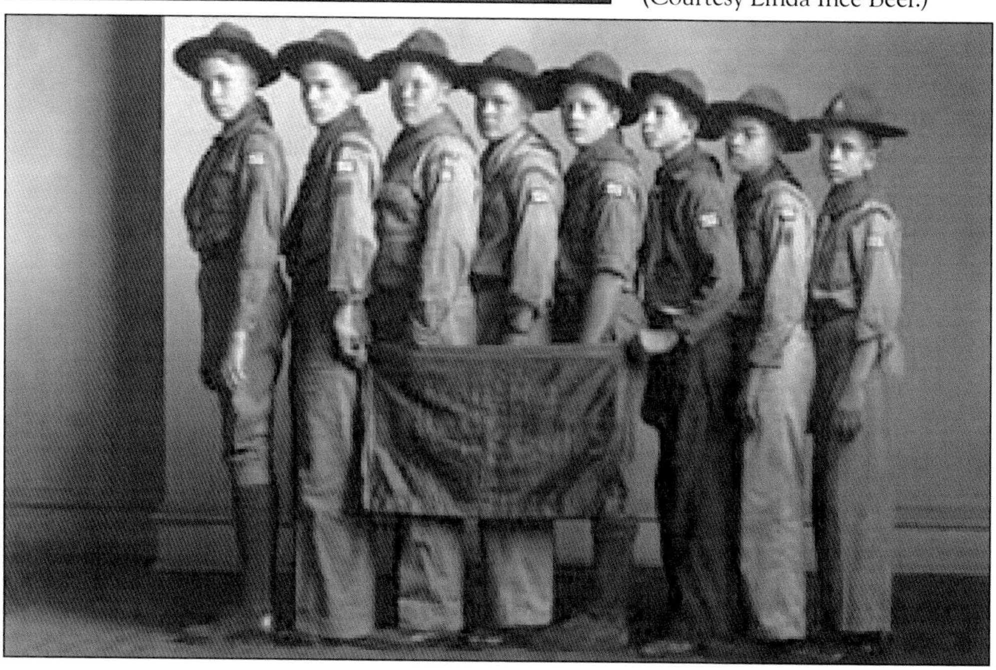

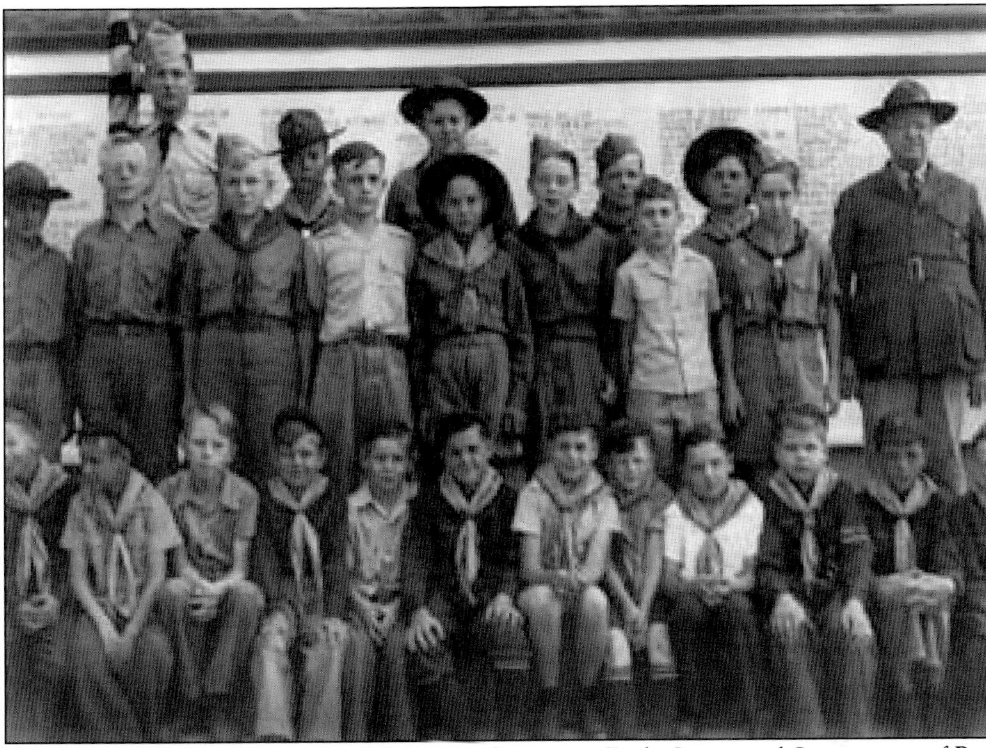

Dr. James Ligon (second row, far right) was a dentist, an Eagle Scout, and Scoutmaster of Boy Scout Troop 155 in the 1940s. Scout Troop 1 of Louisiana was organized in 1916. In 1955, the Hercules Company, Inc., sold an office building to the Louisiana Rotary Club for $1 to become a new Scout house. (Courtesy Linda Ince Beer.)

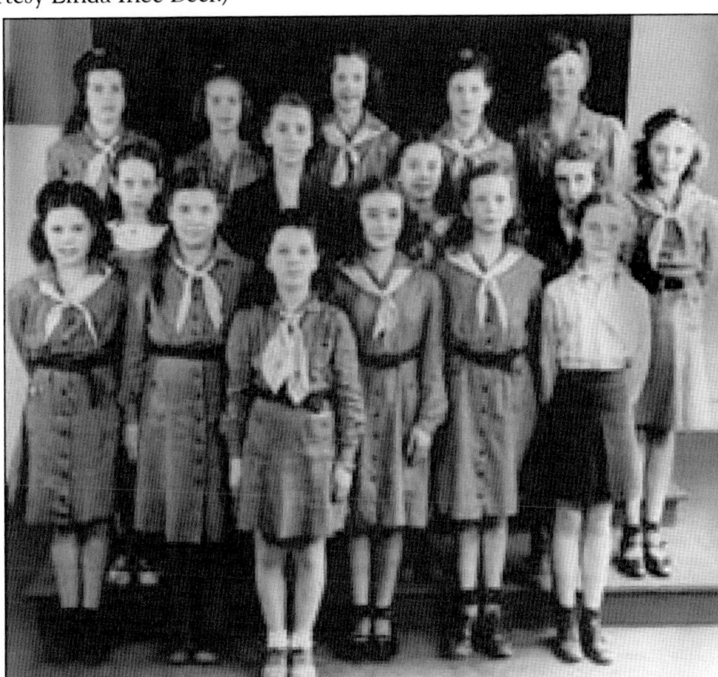

A troop of Louisiana Girl Scouts stands at attention and poses for the camera. (Courtesy Louisiana Area Historical Museum.)

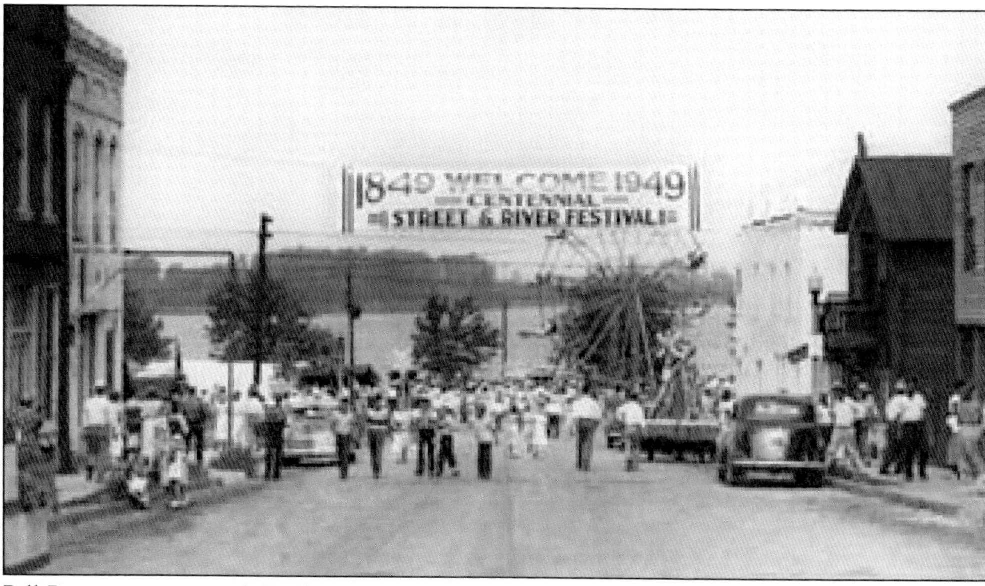

Bill Rottman organized the first Street and River Festival in 1946, which attracted thousands of people. The festival continued every summer until 1985, when the Fall Louisiana Country Colorfest replaced it. (Courtesy Betty Jane Allen.)

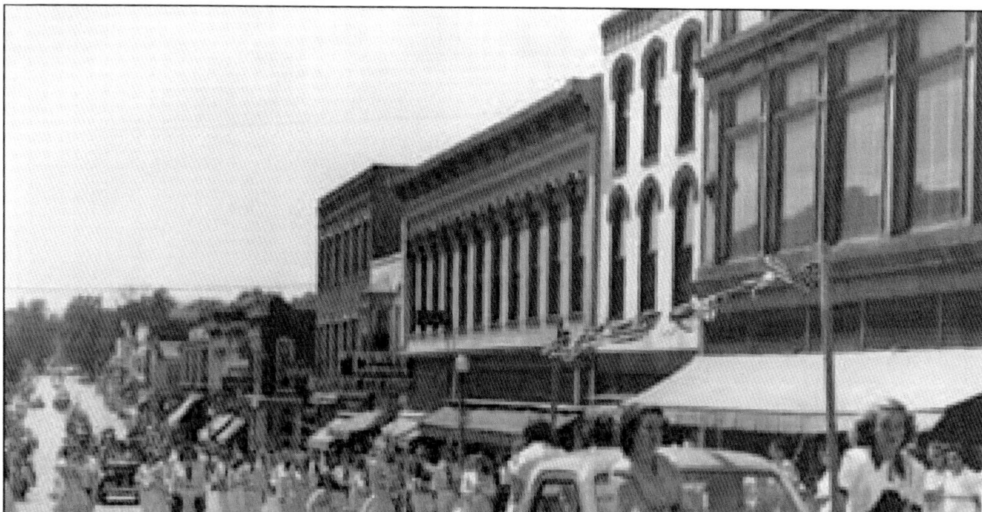

The annual Street and River Festival weekends were well attended, with queen candidates, the Louisiana High School marching band, convertibles, floats, fire trucks, and horseback riders. This 1948 parade, with queen candidates Jean Verdier (left) and Imogene Shields on the car bumper, is three blocks from the Mississippi River. (Courtesy Irene Steers.)

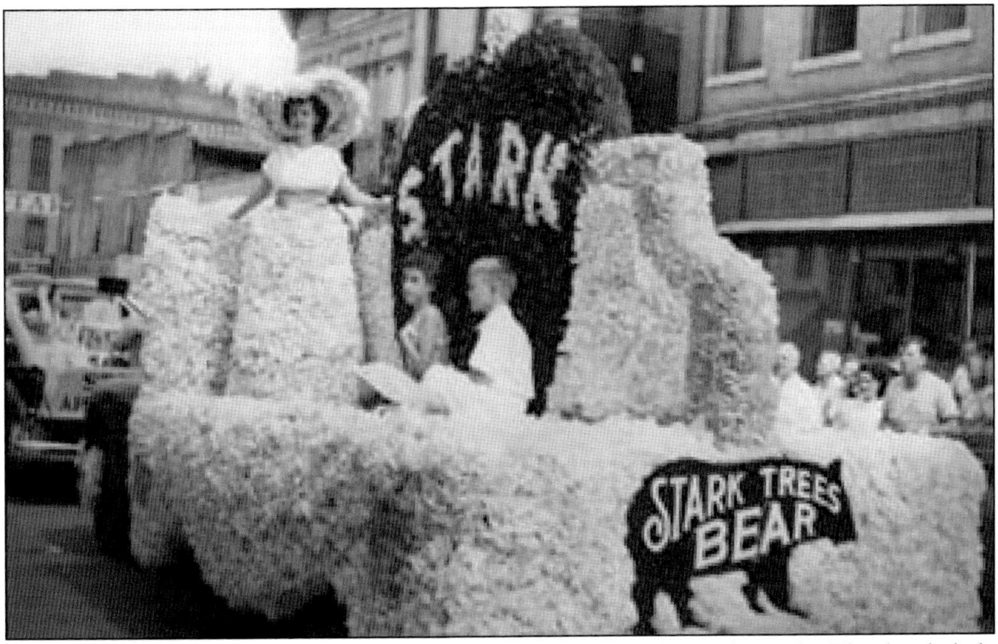

This beautiful float participated in an early Street and River Festival parade. This lovely lady and these children waved to the crowd on the parade route. The bear symbol is the trademark of Stark Bro's Nurseries & Orchards Co. and is recognized throughout the world. (Courtesy Louisiana Area Historical Museum.)

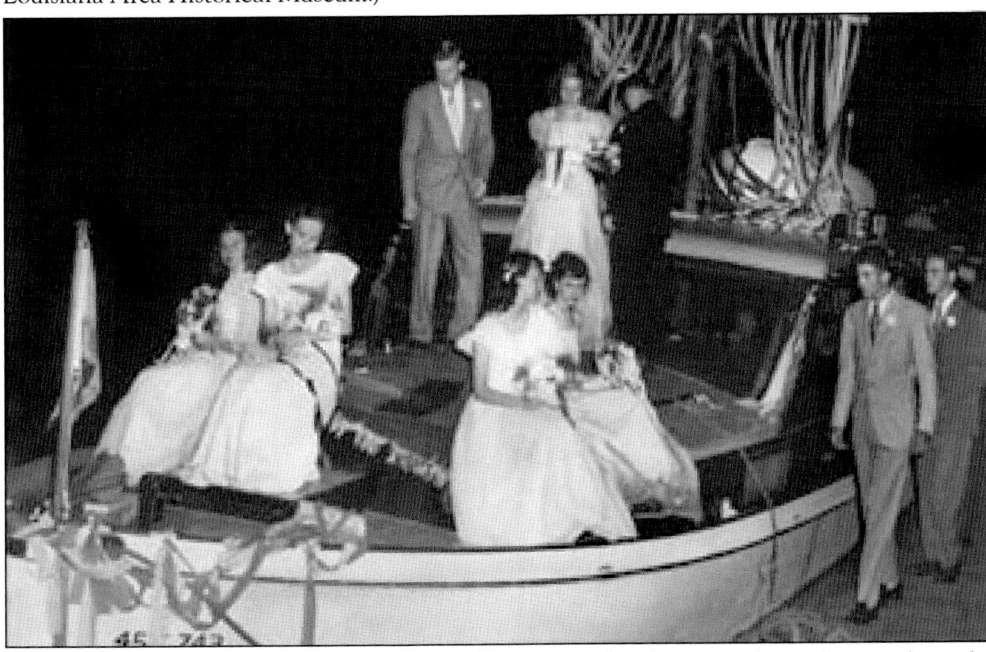

The Street and River Festival used to begin with Dr. Druey Goodman on a barge floating down the Mississippi River singing and playing the part of "Old Man River" until docking at the Louisiana riverfront. The queen and her court followed. The festival then continued with a parade, carnival rides, entertainment, music, cotton candy, and more. It helped local businesses, and it was fun. (Courtesy Louisiana Area Historical Museum.)

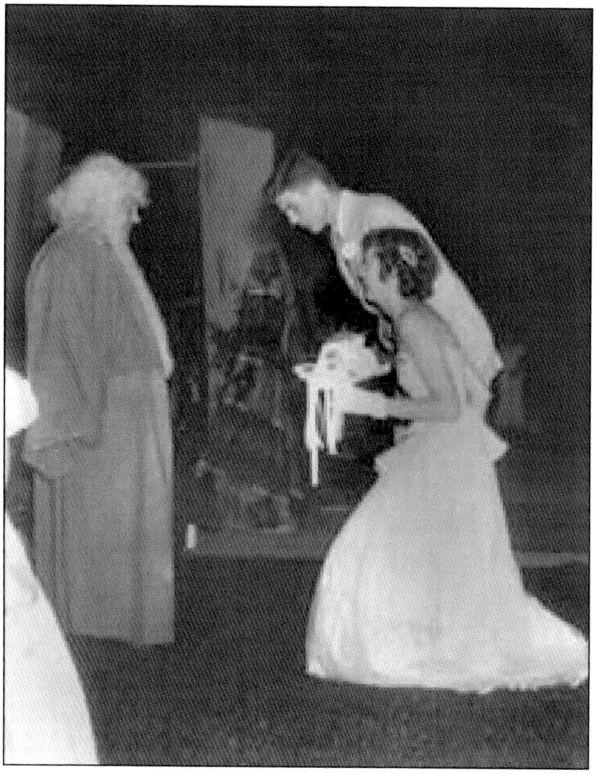

Dr. Druey Goodman's "Old Man River" smiles his approval as 1949 Street and River Festival queen Peggy Reneau curtsies gracefully and her escort, Bob Conrad, bows respectfully. Goodman and the royal court came by barge to the Louisiana riverfront, where a crowd awaited their arrival. (Courtesy Louisiana Area Historical Museum.)

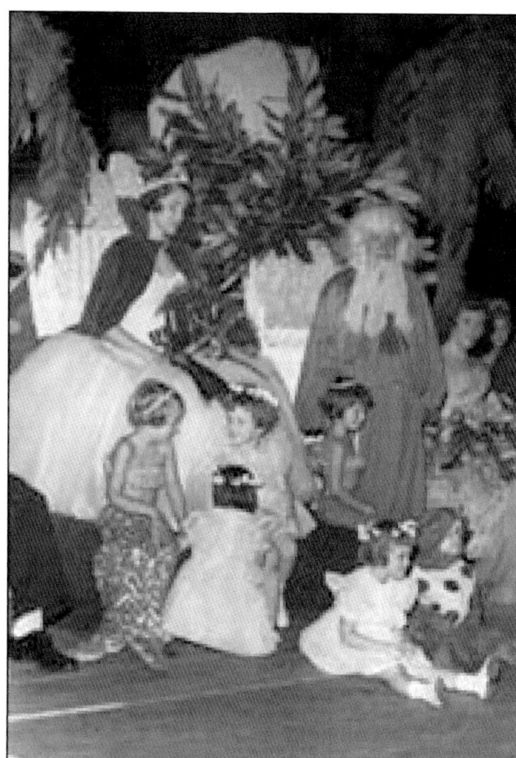

Dr. Druey Goodman is seen again as the 1955 Street and River Festival queen arrives. Joyce Powell held the honor that year and Dolores Skelton is to the right of Dr. Goodman. Precious mermaids, creatures, and children are in the forefront. (Courtesy Louisiana Area Historical Museum.)

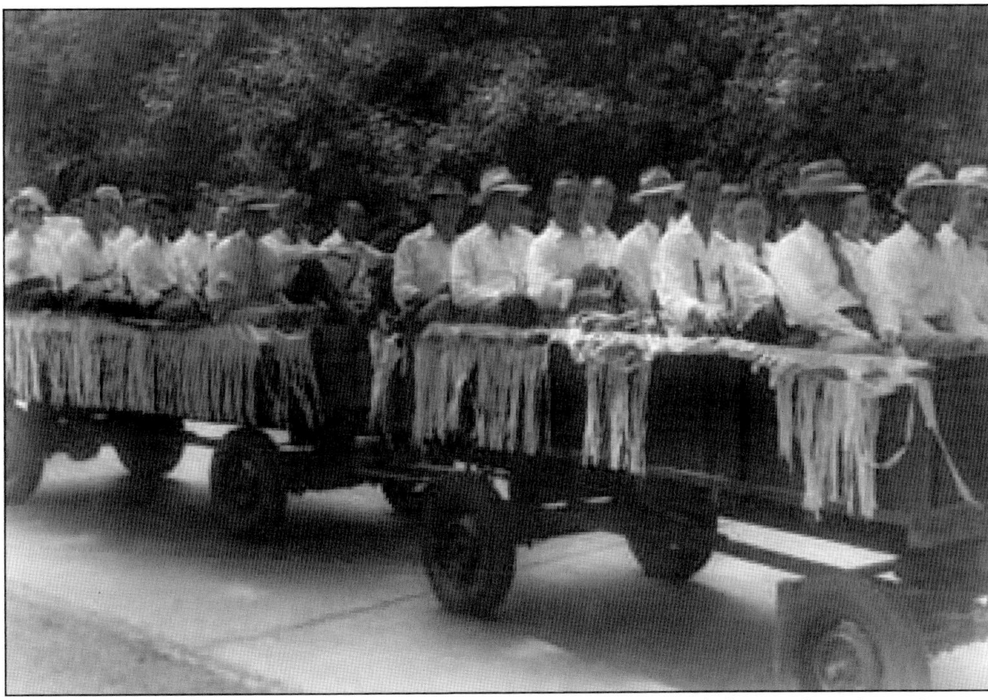

This group of men was part of a parade singing "Old Man River" while traveling down Georgia Street to the river. Griff Rule, a local farmer, loaned seven wagons to carry the group, which delighted the crowd. They were led in song by Dr. Druey Goodman and John Mayfield. (Courtesy John Wood.)

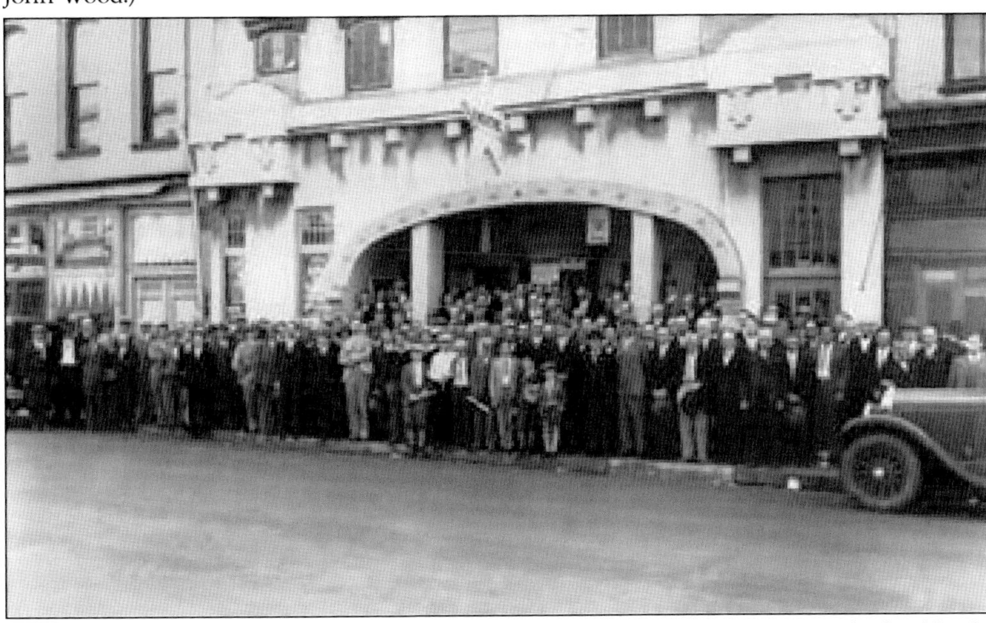

The Star Theatre, run by proprietor W.A. Boyd, had a center advertisement in the booklet for the Louisiana Fall Festival Association, October 2–4, 1924. These men and boys gathered before entering the theater for a concert by the Citizen's Band, which always played during the festival. At the time, Louisiana was an enterprising city of 6,500 people. (Courtesy John Wood.)

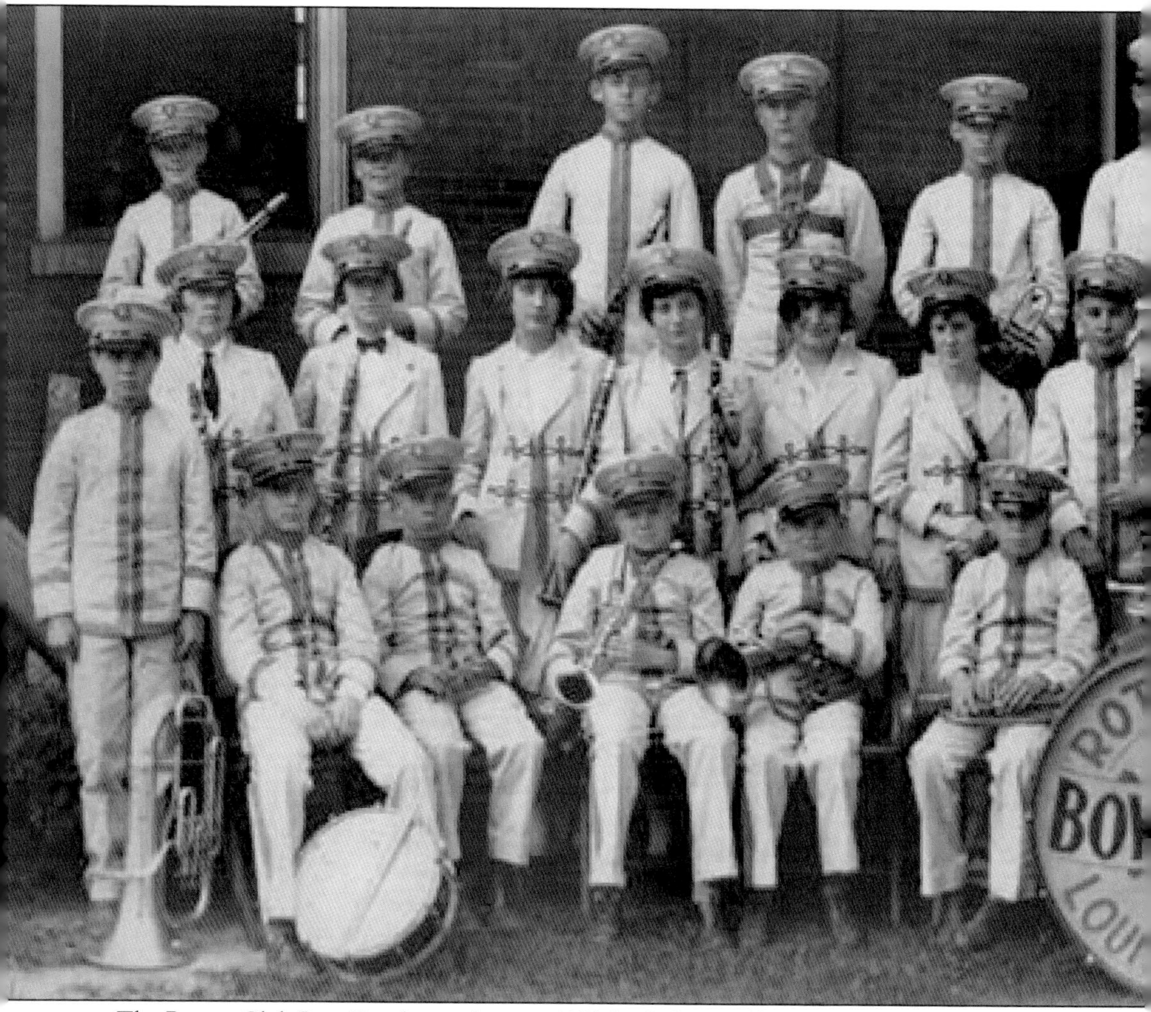

The Rotary Club Boys Band, seen here in 1930, had plenty of boys—and even a few girls—who participated in school and community functions. Their snappy uniforms were courtesy of the Louisiana Rotary Club. The Louisiana Rotary Club was admitted on February 1, 1924, as Charter No. 1618, into Rotary International, sponsored by the Mexico, Missouri, Rotary Club. Active

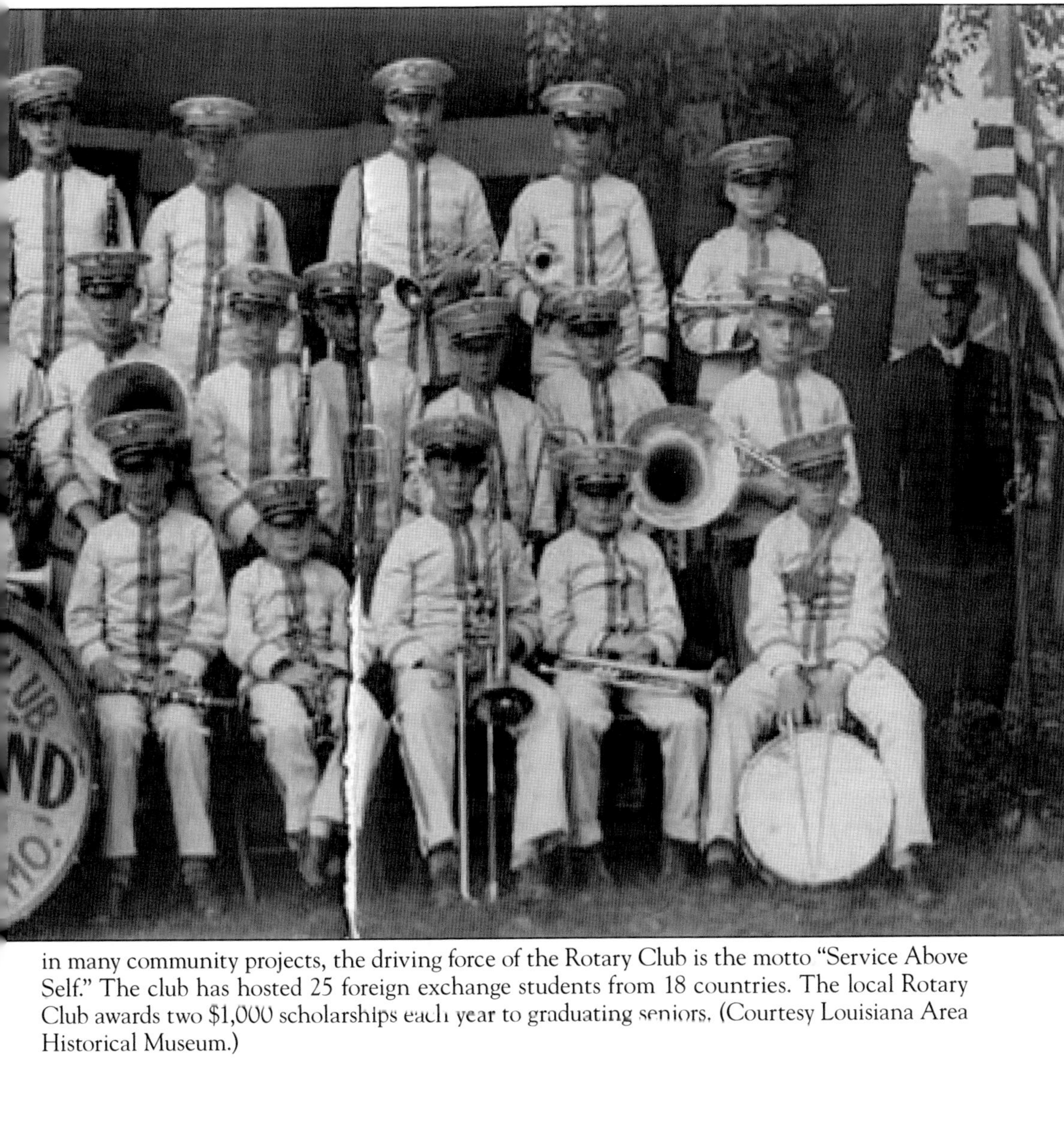

in many community projects, the driving force of the Rotary Club is the motto "Service Above Self." The club has hosted 25 foreign exchange students from 18 countries. The local Rotary Club awards two $1,000 scholarships each year to graduating seniors. (Courtesy Louisiana Area Historical Museum.)

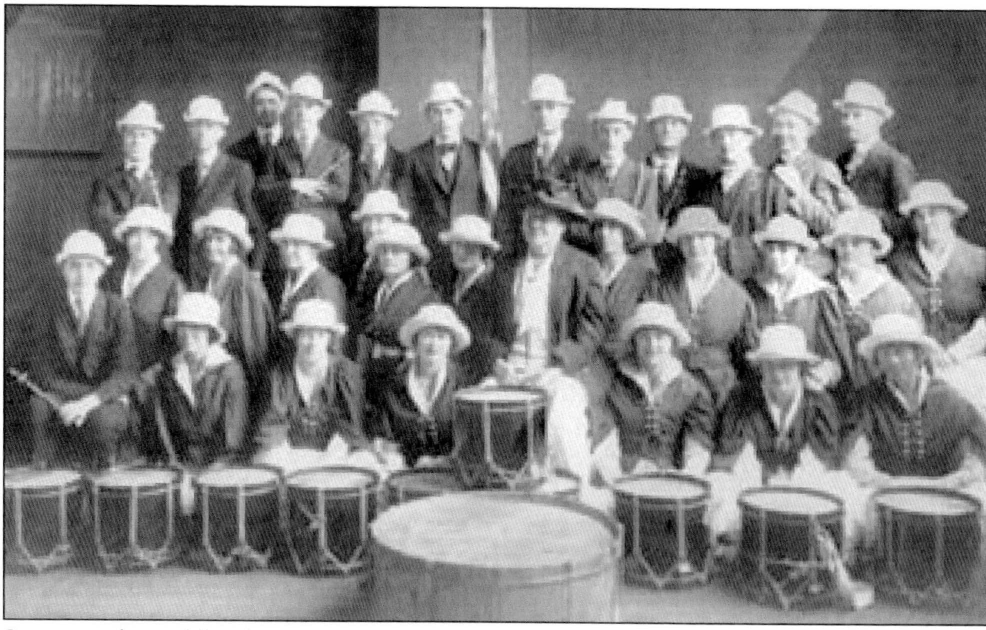

Sitting in the middle of Louisiana's first drum corps is Nell Dunphy (fifth from left, front row). Her older sister Maggie Dunphy was a milliner in Louisiana for more than 65 years and was like a mother to Nell. Eventually, Nell came to live with her sister and became a part of the Drum Corp. She is likely wearing one of her sister's creations here. (Courtesy John Wood.)

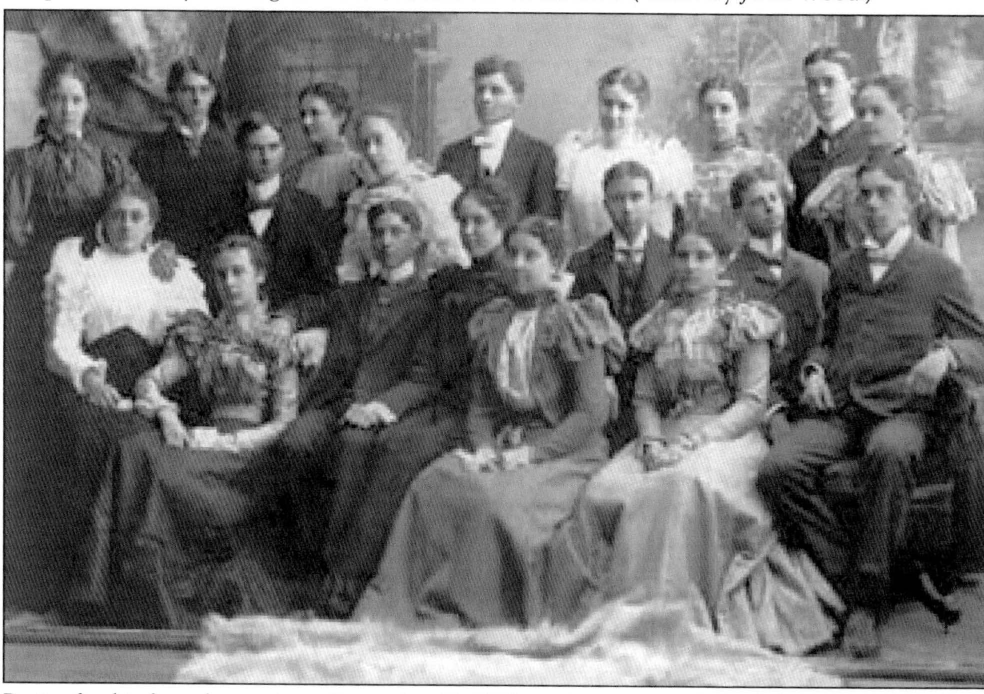

Posing for this formal portrait on September 19, 1897, are (in no particular order) Ora Long, Margaret Rupert, Oscar Lynott, Maud Lake, Emma Bowen, Marie Naxera, Freeman Culver, Ray Pearson, Ira Miller, Bob Robinson, Erma Estes, Emma Culver, Will Naxera, Suella Pribe, Frank Bowen, Sadie Campbell, Jake Pettibone, Berry Hannah, and Alice Payne. (Courtesy Betty Jane Allen)

Five
NOBLE CAUSES

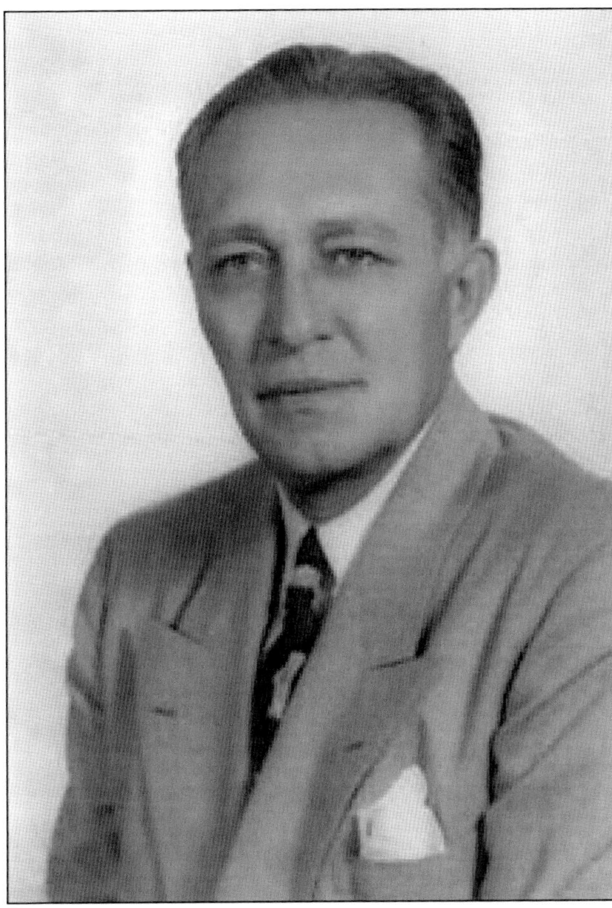

Eric A. Cunningham, born in Centralia, Missouri, on October 21, 1898, was a physician and surgeon in Louisiana for 31 years. He came to Louisiana in 1928, the year Pike County Hospital opened. Often, he was known to tell a patient, "If you aren't able to pay me and the hospital, pay the hospital." He was instrumental in organizing the hospital medical and surgical staff and was active in civic organizations. He died on May 6, 1969, and is buried in Riverview Cemetery. (Courtesy Louisiana Area Historical Museum.)

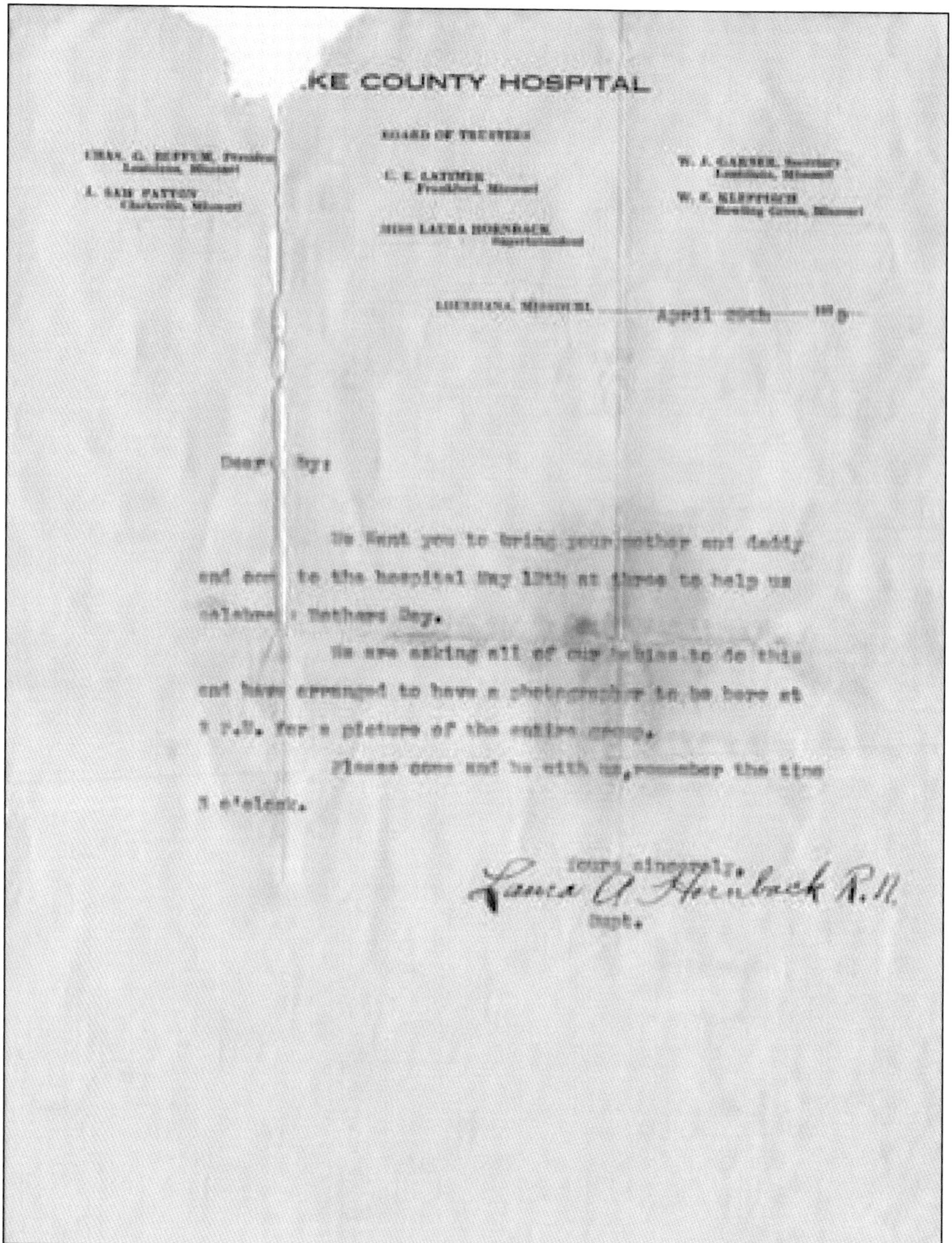

.KE COUNTY HOSPITAL

BOARD OF TRUSTEES

MISS LAURA HORNBACK
Superintendent

LOUISIANA, MISSOURI April 29th 19

Dear Boy:

We want you to bring your mother and daddy and come to the hospital May 12th at three to help us celebrate Mothers Day.

We are asking all of our babies to do this and have arranged to have a photographer to be here at 3 P.M. for a picture of the entire group.

Please come and be with us, remember the time 3 o'clock.

Yours sincerely,
Laura A Hornback R.N.
Supt.

This letter was sent by nurse Laura A. Hornback to the parents of the babies delivered at Pike County Hospital in the first year it was open. (Courtesy Irene Griffith.)

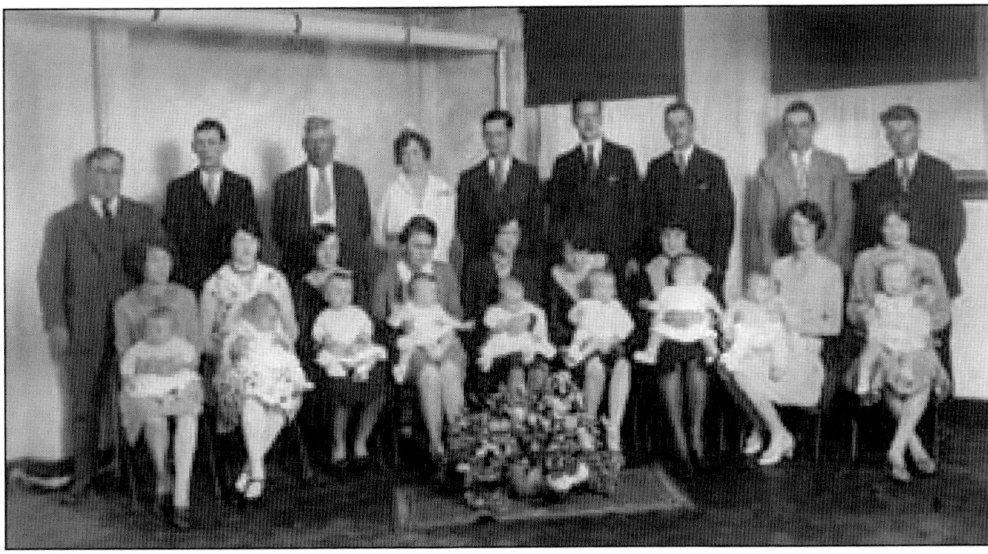

The letter of invitation on the previous page was sent to these families: (from left to right) Mr. and Mrs. R.C. Carroll and son, Robert Calvin, Clarksville; Mr. and Mrs. Lynn Bryson and son Isaac Newton, Louisiana; Mrs. Robert Benton Mackey of Clarksville, her father, Dr. J.E. Bankhead, and son Joseph Benton; Mrs. Richard Middleton and daughter Sue Pledge, Clarksville; Laura Hornback, hospital superintendent; Mr. and Mrs. C.E. Hord and son Charles Edmund, Louisiana; Mr. and Mrs. Clay Agee and daughter, Anne Adams, Louisiana; Mr. and Mrs. Clinton Johnson and son Langdon Goodlove, Louisiana; Mr. and Mrs. Roy Sanderson and son Robert Albert, Bowling Green; and Mr. and Mrs. Ira Griffith and son Ira Jr., Clarksville. (Courtesy Irene Griffith.)

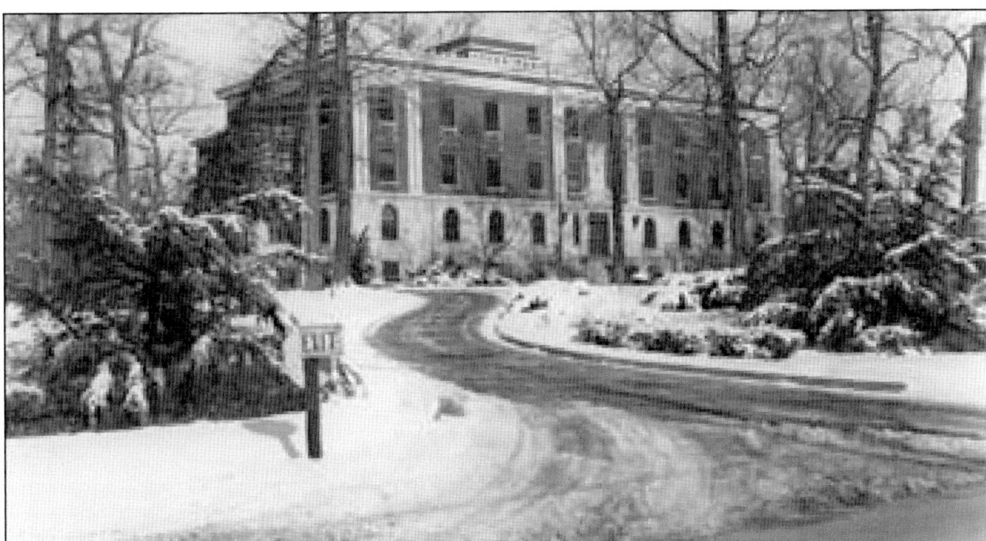

Pike County Hospital opened on June 30, 1928, and six people were treated that first week. The Century Club had purchased the location for $3,031.88. Susanah Barr, a milliner, left her estate for the building of a hospital, and J. Otis Smith, an 1883 Louisiana High School graduate who became a wealthy New York City businessman, left $100,000 for the same purpose. Donations covered the small remainder. Later, the name was changed to Smith-Barr in honor of the hospital's benefactors. (Courtesy Betty Jane Allen.)

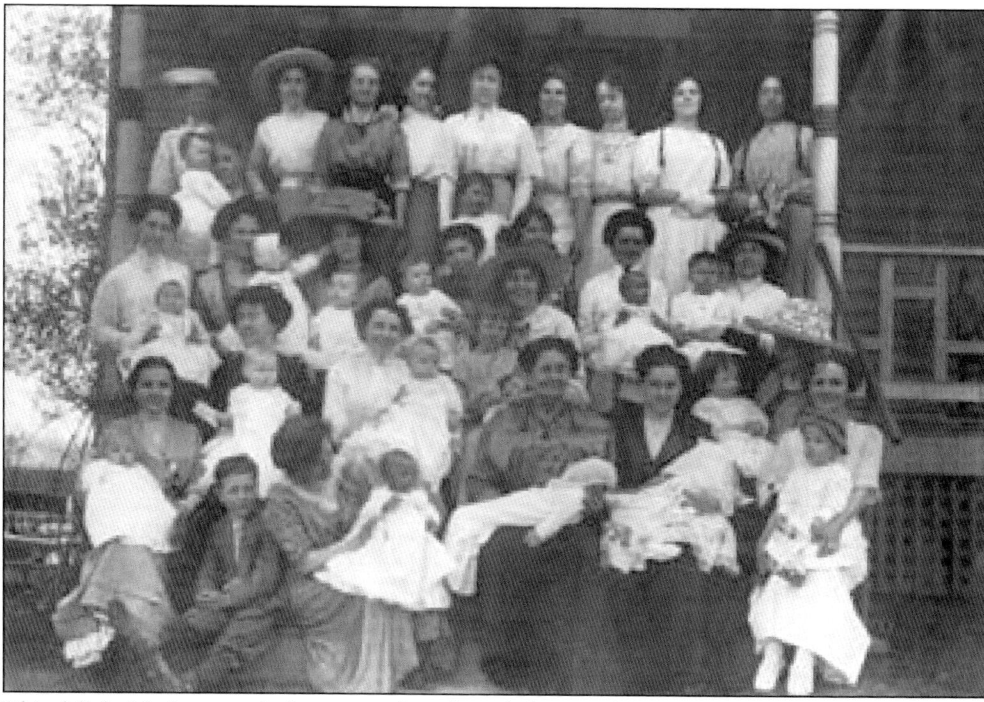

This delightful photograph shows proud mothers, babies, and friends posing on a porch. (Courtesy Betty Jane Allen.)

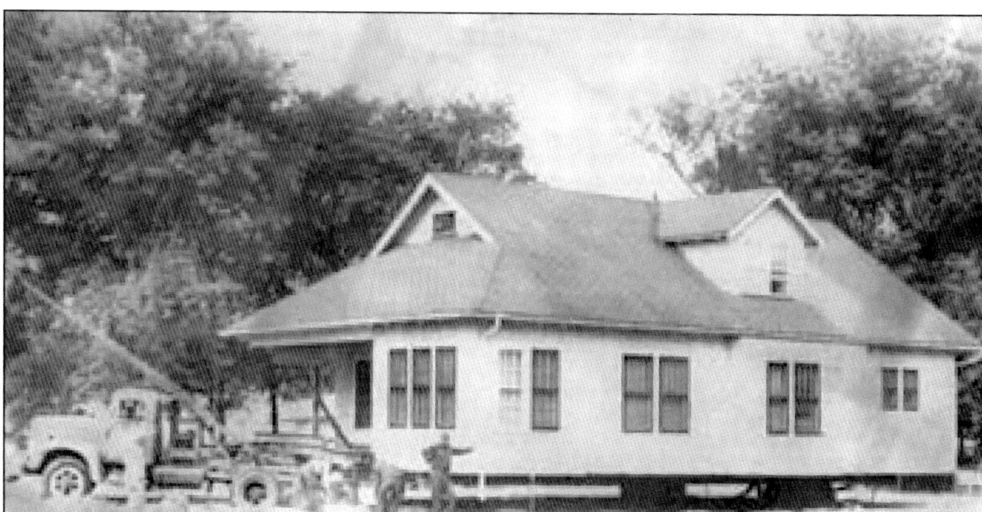

This house was on West Georgia Street near Smith-Barr Hospital and was used for nurses' quarters. When it was no longer needed, it was moved nearby to 2314 Kentucky Street and sold for a residence. (Courtesy Louisiana Area Historical Museum.)

Andrew Murphy Sr. (pictured) noticed a newspaper story about industrialist Andrew Carnegie funding libraries across the nation and wrote to Carnegie in 1902, when he was 32. Carnegie replied that if a site was obtained, a board of directors named, and a city maintenance tax approved, he would fund $10,000 for a free library. Murphy put the administration in place, and the library was built. (Courtesy Louisiana Public Library.)

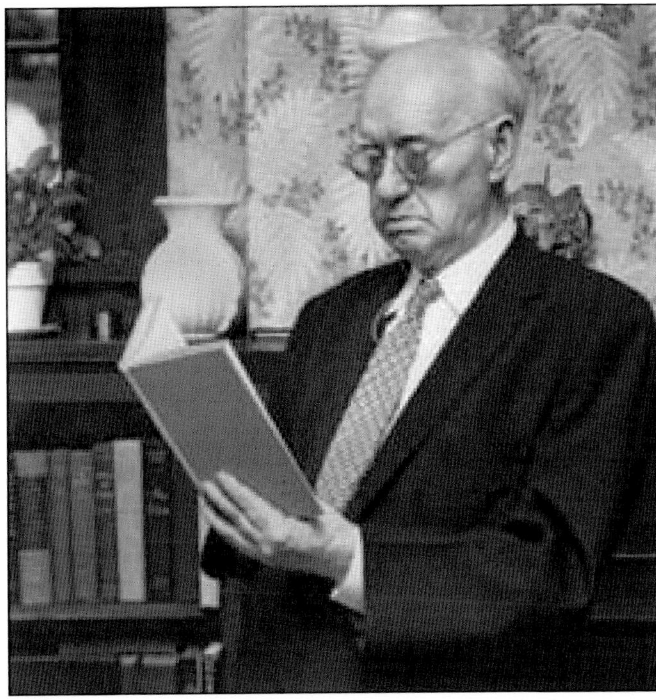

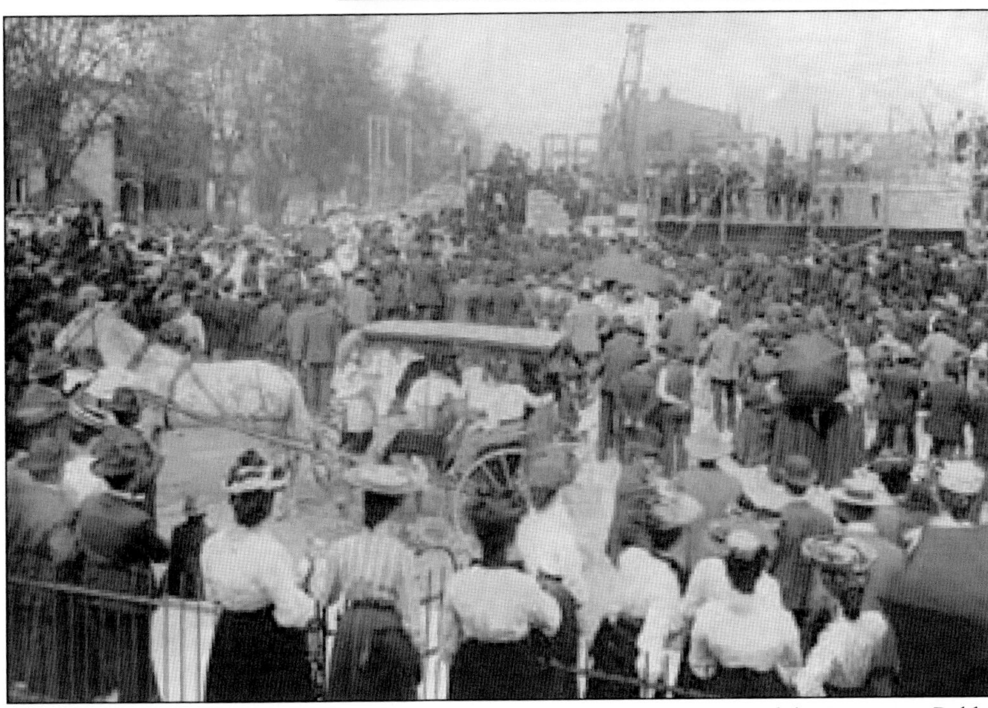

On May 4, 1904, this crowd gathered for the placing of the cornerstone of the Louisiana Public Library. The doors opened to the public on January 15, 1905. It was one of the first 10 Carnegie libraries in Missouri and it has always been supported by a property tax. Having recently undergone an addition to enlarge the building, the Louisiana Public Library remains an integral part of the town. (Courtesy Louisiana Public Library.)

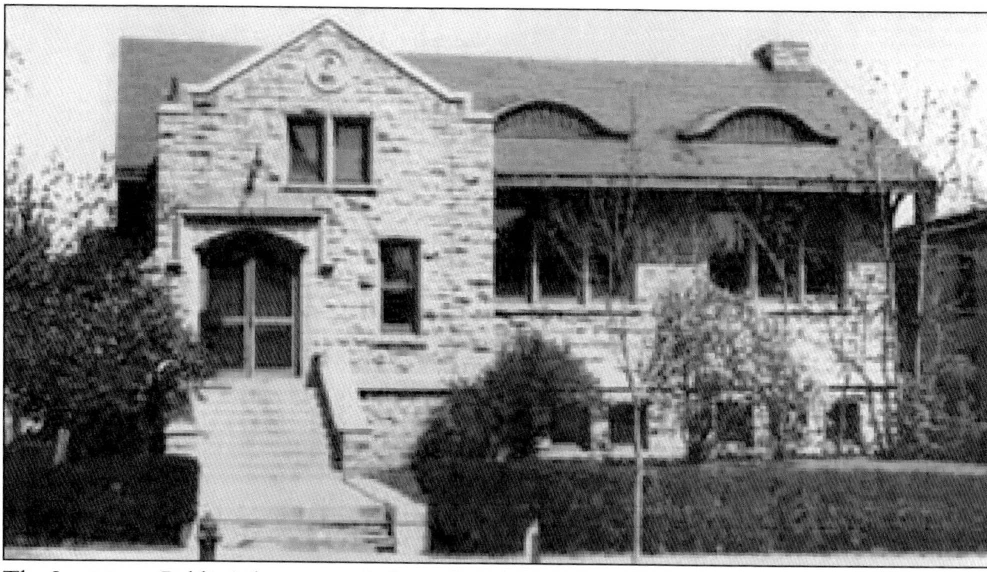

The Louisiana Public Library was dedicated on May 4, 1904. Six sites were considered, but the Glenn livery stable site won. Citizens could vote many times for a site, but had to pay $1 each time. The corner of Third and Tennessee Streets won, and $3,100 was raised. (Courtesy Louisiana Public Library.)

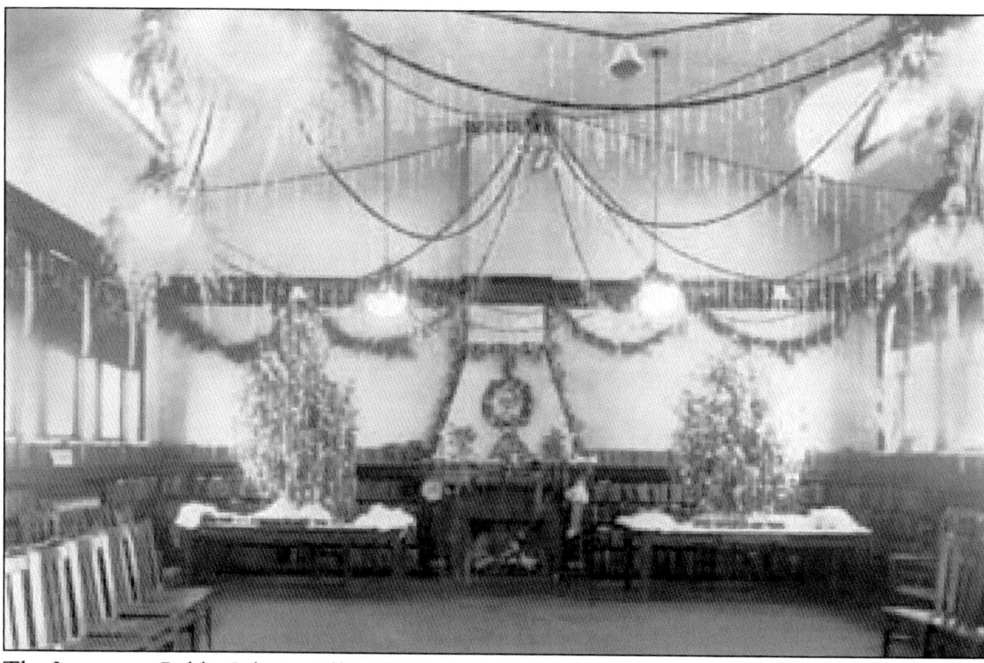

The Louisiana Public Library officially opened on January 15, 1905. In July, 2,268 visitors were recorded and 1,067 books were checked out. Anna Draper was the first librarian, and she was assisted by Elizabeth Irvin, who served 45 years, and Elizabeth Anderson. The library was added to the National Register of Historic Places in 1997. The library reading room has original electric fixtures, backup gas fixtures, and tables and chairs. A grandfather clock, which still graces the entrance, was given to the library in December 1905 by Molly Templeton of Salt Lake City, Utah, who taught in Louisiana in the 1860s. (Courtesy the Louisiana Public Library.)

The Masonic Temple was dedicated on April 28, 1910. Excavation had begun on April 15, 1908, and the cornerstone was laid on June 26, 1909. It is a replica of the Tuscan Lodge building in St. Louis, in the Ionic architectural style. When it was built, each member furnished his own chair, which had his name with a brass plaque on it. A Parks piano made in Louisiana is in the ballroom. That ballroom has been the scene of many social events in the past 100 years. The Masons are still very active in Louisiana. Today, the Order of the Eastern Star ladies are an integral part of the Masons organization as well. (Courtesy Marilyn Johnson and Louisiana Area Historical Museum.)

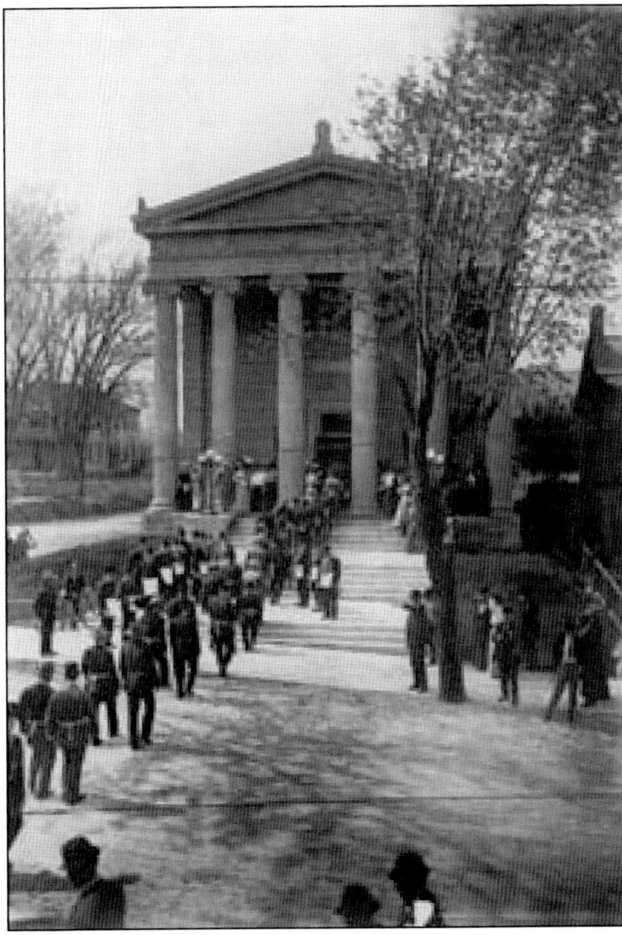

The Masonic Temple is on the left in this image, taken from Seventh Street looking down Georgia Street toward the Mississippi River. (Courtesy Betty Jane Allen.)

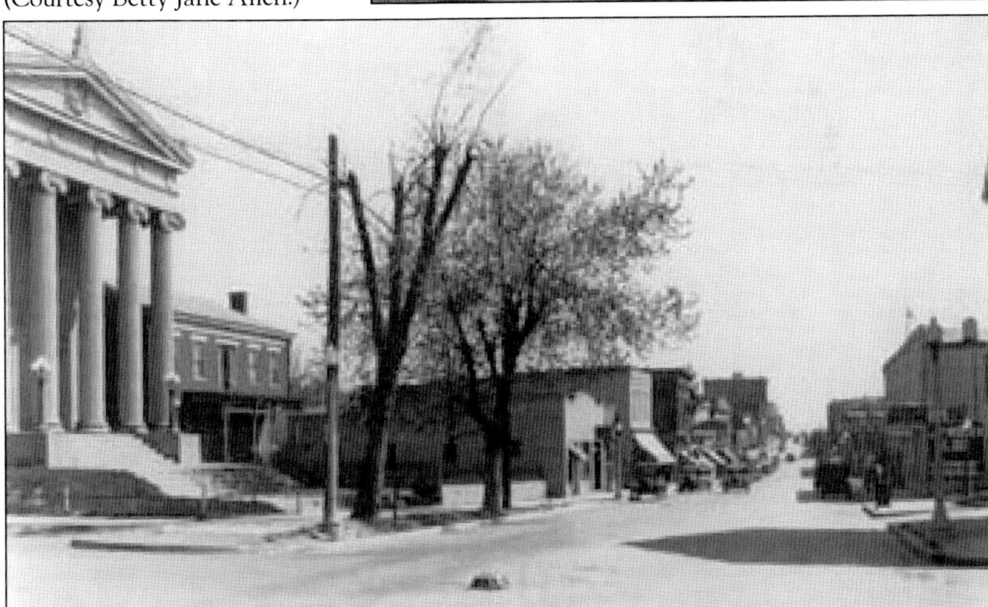

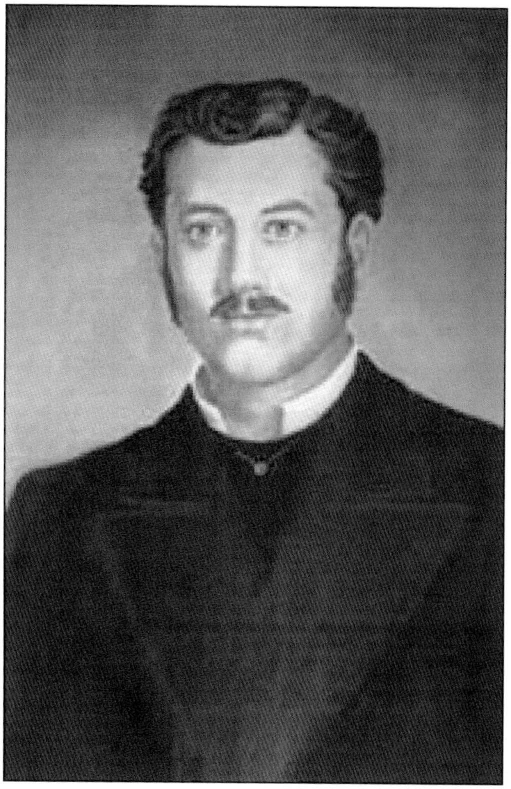

George William Trimble, a retired Seattle banker with roots in Louisiana, died in 1929 and left a trust fund of $900,000, some of which benefits the Smith-Barr Memorial Hospital and the local Elks lodge. A percentage of the earnings is still distributed annually. Another project supported by the Trimble fund is the Trimble House, a center for senior citizens. Trimble, his wife, Martha, and sister Bue Shaw are buried in Riverview Cemetery. (Courtesy Nathan Lilley and Louisiana Area Historical Museum.)

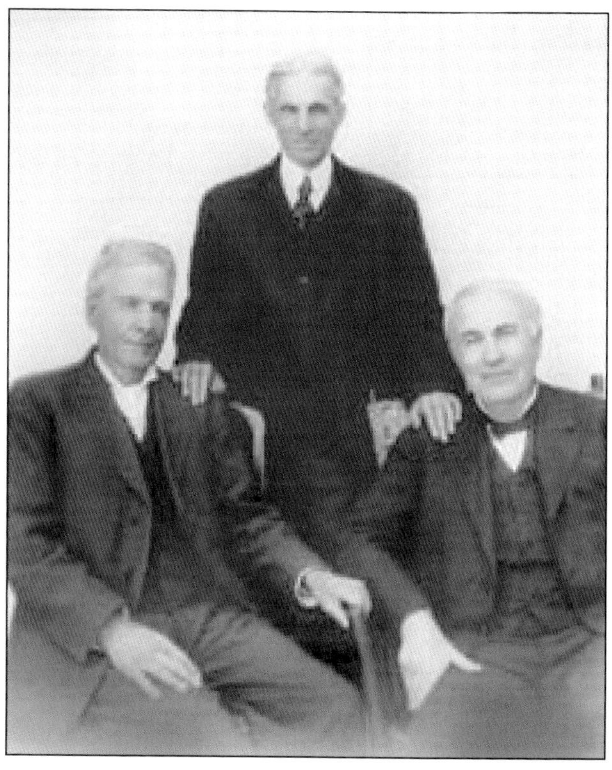

These three men, Luther Burbank (left), Henry Ford (standing), and Thomas Edison all made huge impacts on Americans' lives. The three were friends and constituents and each made significant discoveries in their individual fields. Burbank's name is synonymous with horticulture, Ford's with automobiles, and Edison's with electricity. Before his death in 1926, Burbank instructed his wife to pass on his horticultural legacy to the Stark Bro's Nurseries & Orchards Co. (Courtesy *The Stark Story* and Louisiana Area Historical Museum.)

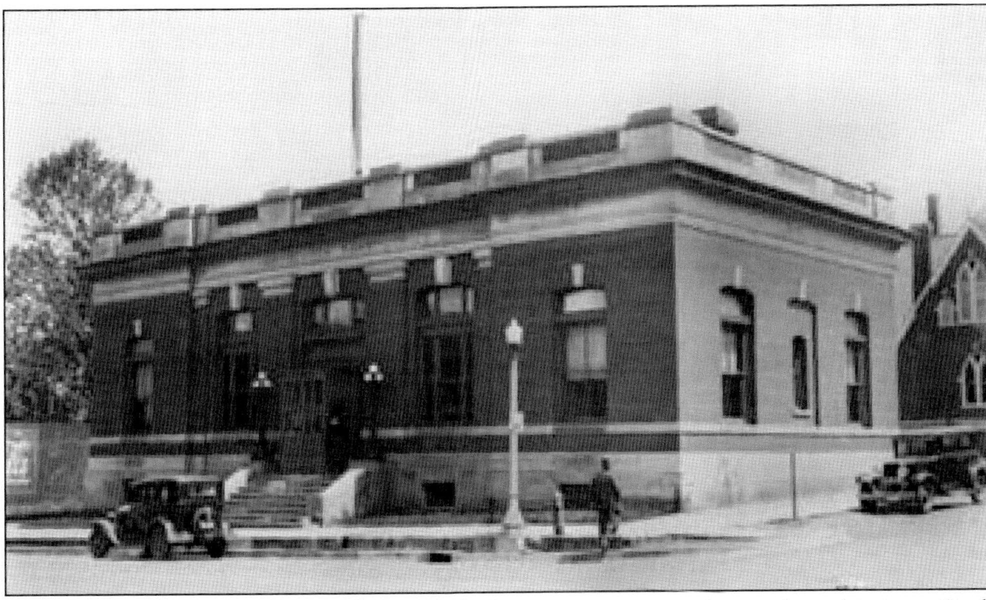

In February 1903, at the request of Champ Clark, the government agreed to purchase this site on Sixth and Georgia Streets, which had been selected and approved by the town council for the Louisiana post office, for the sum of $4,900. The post office entrance was remodeled in 1978, becoming accessible by federal law. At one time, brass railings graced the steps. (Courtesy John Wood.)

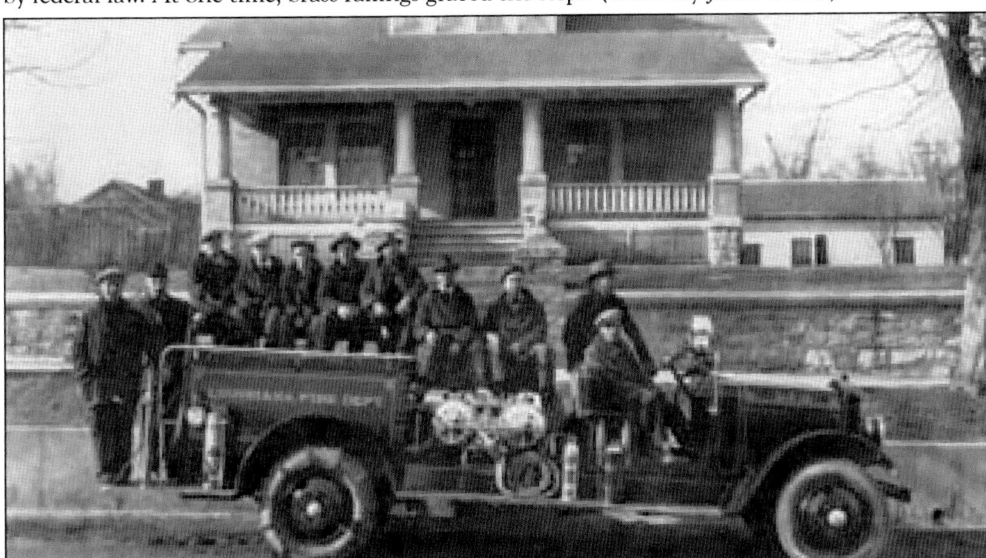

In December 1871, the Louisiana Volunteer Fire Department moved to its first firehouse in the 600 block of Georgia Street. The department was officially organized on April 6, 1870, with Ordinance No. 572, and was housed in the Suda Market House on Fourth Street, and later on Tenth Street. Members of the department in 1935 included, from left to right, Naldy Bell, Henry Pribe, W.A. Jordan Sr., W.H. Smith, John Clay, Charles Osterhold, Note Mitchell Sr., George Browning, Earl Frederick, Ben Houchins, and Charles "Chick" Reed. Champ Clark was a member of the volunteer fire department in the early 1870s and, along with J.W. Watson and James Lewis, he wrote the by-laws and constitution for the department. (Courtesy J. Note Mitchell and Louisiana Fire Department History.)

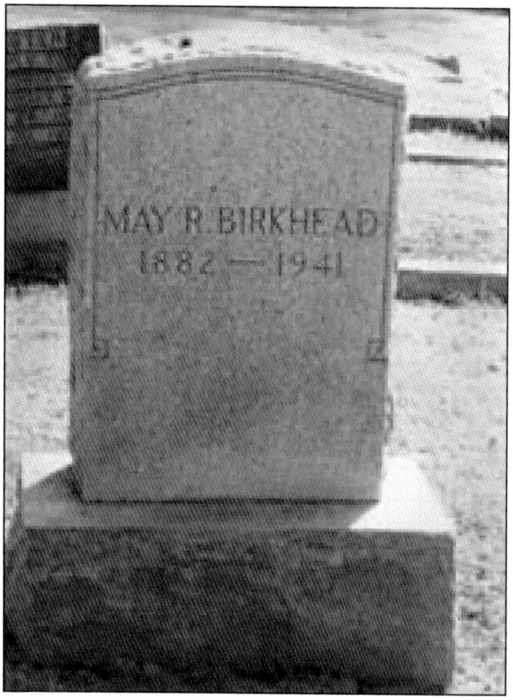

May Rule Birkhead (1882–1941) was a 30-year-old, accomplished seamstress in Louisiana. She traveled on the *Carpathia* with her aunt Eva Sue Rule and was an eyewitness to the tragedy of the *Titanic*. A reporter with the *New York Herald* had recently interviewed Birkhead's mother regarding her father's friendship with Champ Clark. The reporter knew Birkhead was going to be on the *Carpathia* from the interview. He wired her after hearing of the tragedy. His wire was the last to go through. She immediately began writing an article for the *Herald*. The *New York Herald* realized her writing abilities and hired her and moved her to Paris to cover society there. She later wrote for the *Chicago Tribune* in the same capacity. Birkhead is buried in Louisiana's Riverview Cemetery with her parents. (Courtesy Carolyn E. Allen.)

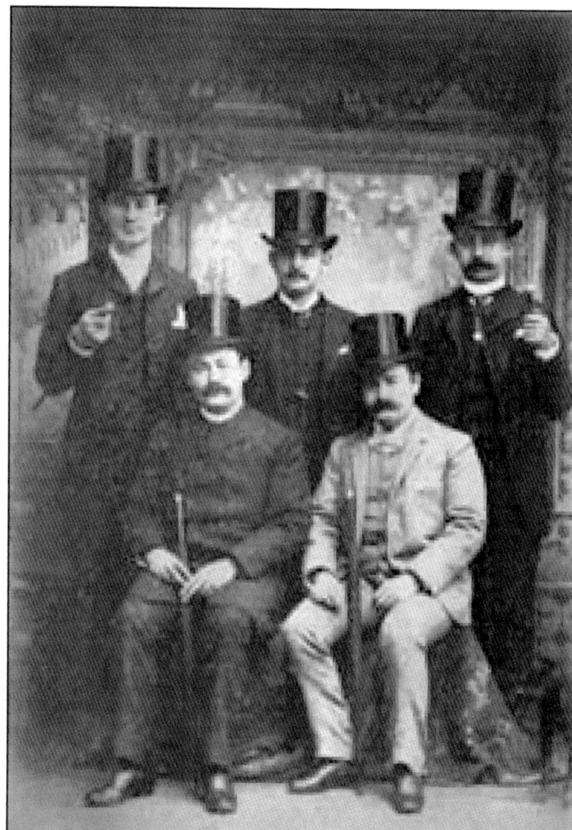

This group cut a fine swatch in men's fashion. They include, from left to right, (first row) Marvin Ford and Ed Jamison; (second row) brothers Isadore, Mike, and Max Michael. The Michaels had a dry goods store at 211 Georgia Street. (Courtesy Betty Jane Allen.)

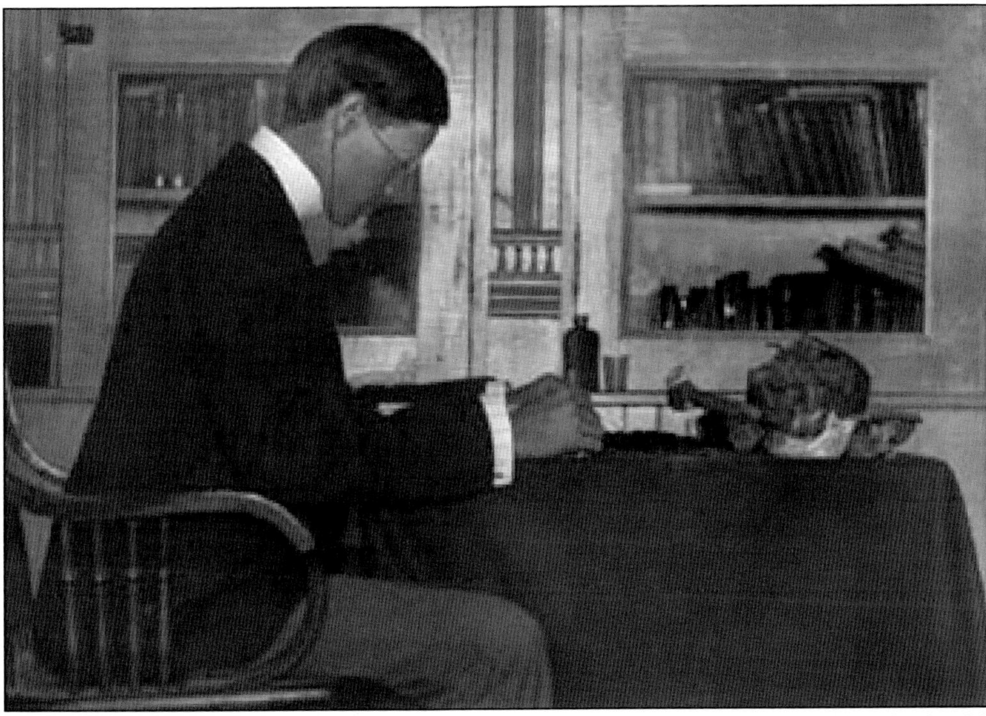

Charles Louis Meriwether, seen here at his desk, was a dentist for 18 years before his health failed. He and his wife, Marie Naxera Meriwether, had a son, Charles L. Meriwether Jr. (Courtesy Charlotte Griffith.)

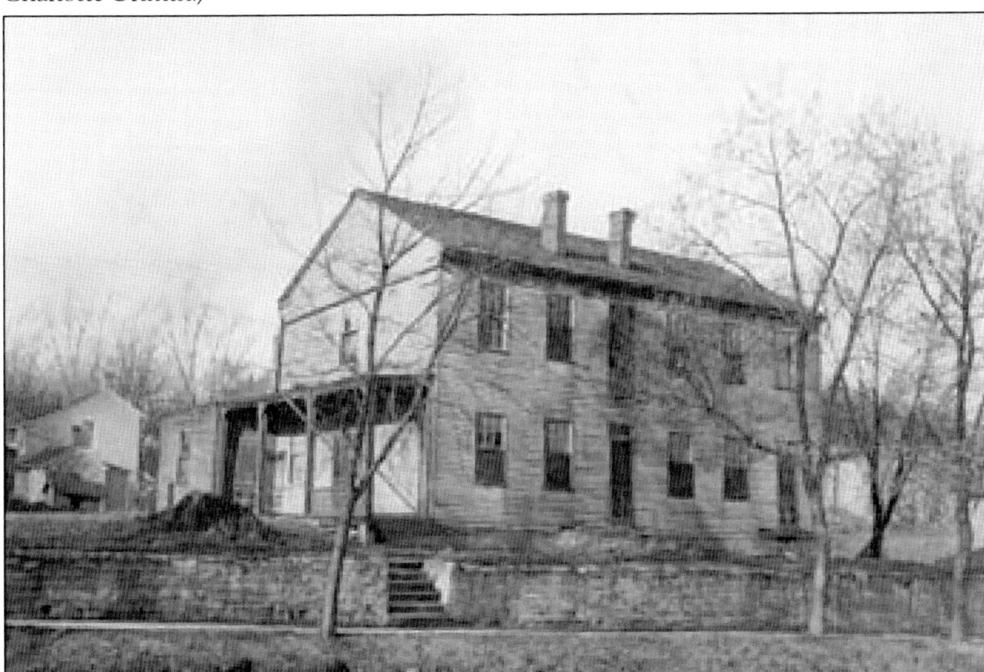

This building, across the street from the N.E. Methodist Church on the corner of Tennessee and Seventh Streets, was a school for several years in the 1800s. (Courtesy John Wood.)

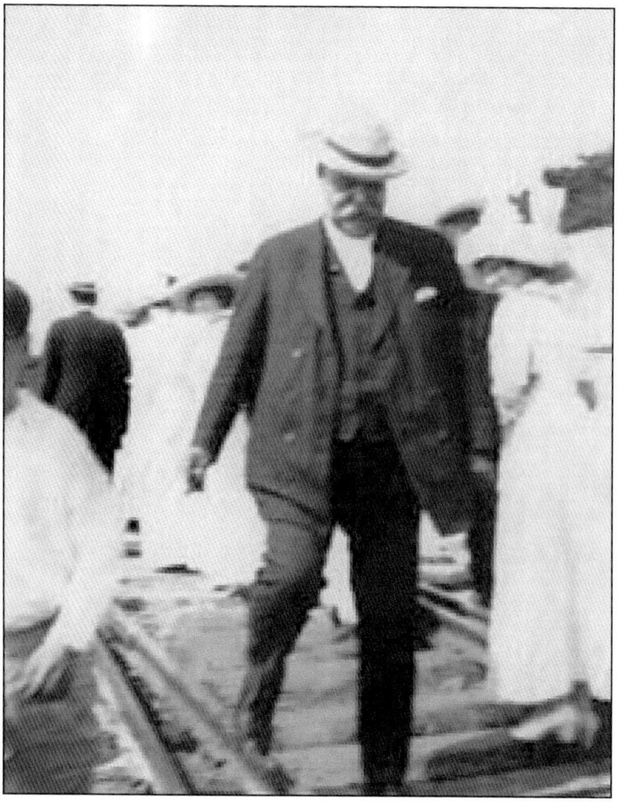

Pres. William Howard Taft (left) visited Louisiana on his 1908 campaign tour. Pres. Theodore Roosevelt stopped by three times, once drawing a crowd of between 7,000 and 10,000 people at the Burlington Railroad station. (Courtesy Betty Jane Allen.)

The gigantic white oak tree stood in the family cemetery of Christopher Jackson (January 8, 1768–July 12, 1831) and Catherine Jackson (July 19, 1768–October 30, 1857) until the early 1990s. A landmark, the tree was about 20 feet in circumference and is estimated to have sprouted in 1492. Many people studied and admired it. In the 1980s, it was declared the largest white oak tree in Missouri, and a state certificate was issued. (Courtesy Betty Jane Allen.)

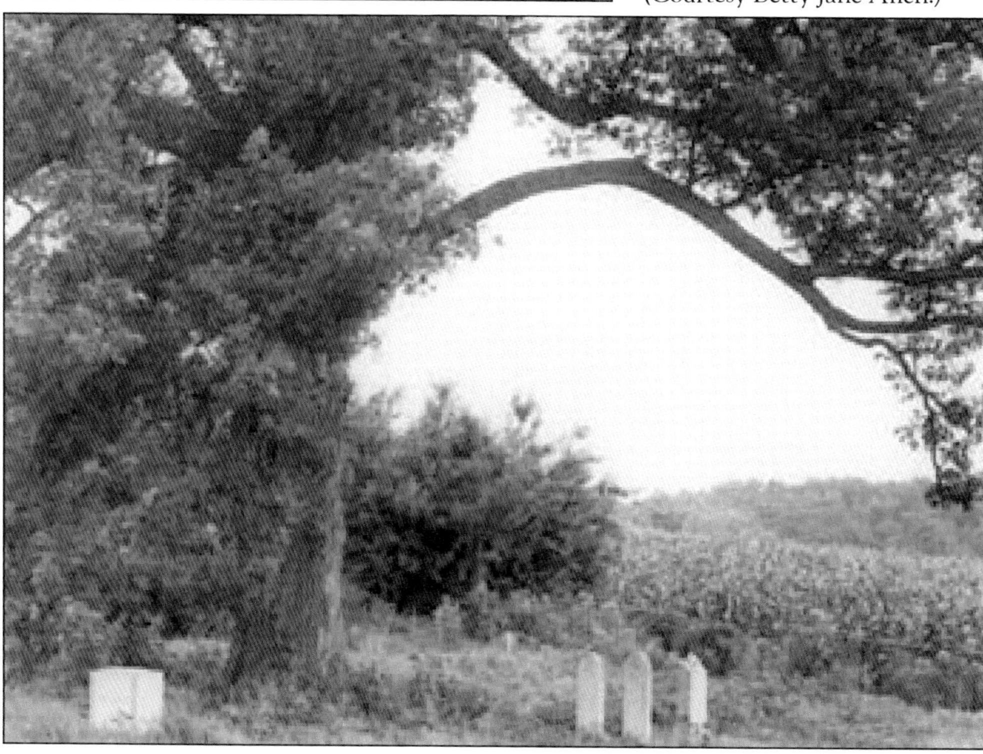

Brothers Charles G. Buffum and Frank W. Buffum, sons of the founder of the LaCrosse Lumber Company, Gustavus Adolphus Buffum, built these similar houses next to each other on West Georgia Street. The family came to Louisiana in 1873. Frank's home, on the left, was finished in 1895, and Charles's was finished in 1896. Millwork, stained glass, and various woods including curly maple, birdseye maple, red oak, cypress, and quartered white oak were used extensively throughout. The original carriage structures, now garages, still have horse stalls, tack rooms, and upstairs hay-storage areas. Additional acreage behind the homes was used for horses, a cow, and chickens. Known locally as the Buffum Houses, they are indeed still grand dames. (Courtesy Betty Jane Allen.)

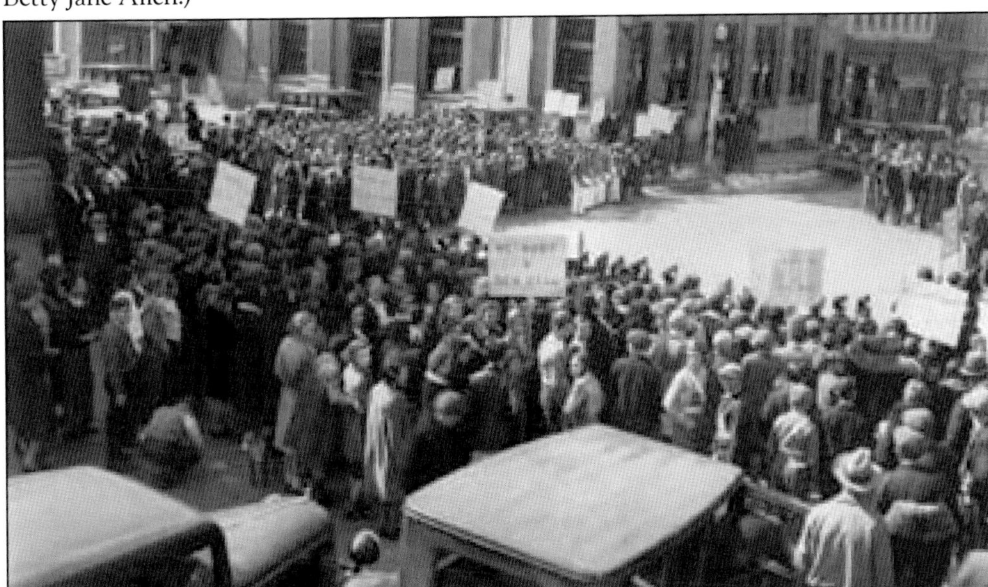

This group of folks proclaiming "We want a New Deal" assembled at Third and Georgia Streets around 1931, after the Great Depression hit Louisiana. (Courtesy John Wood.)

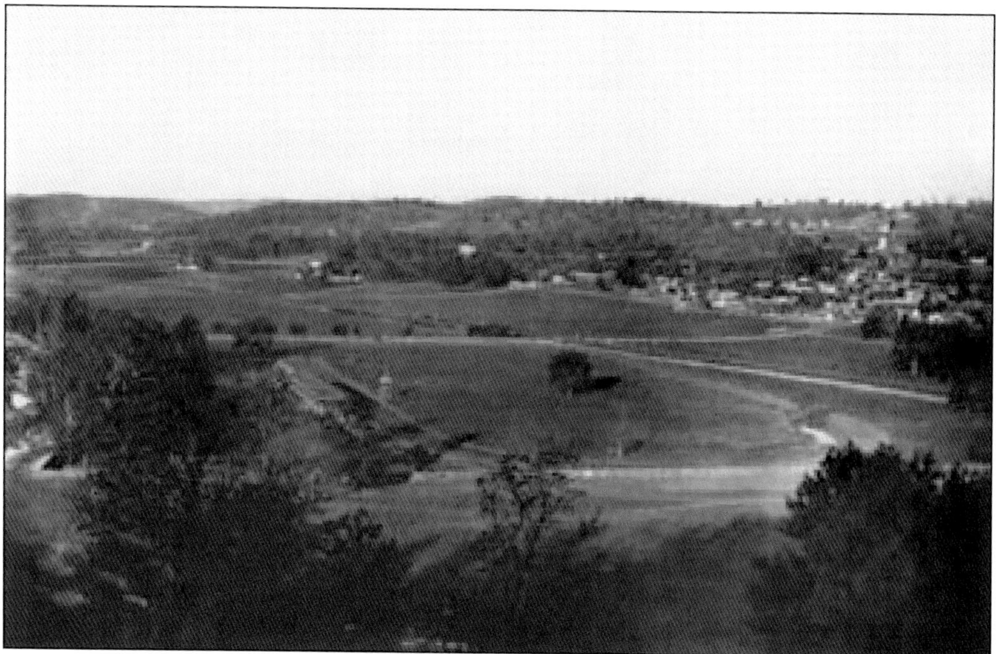

This aerial view of the old fairgrounds was taken from Clinton Hill. The fairgrounds were south of Louisiana, and in early years, the track was used for horse races. It was used for football in the 1930s and for Little League softball teams. In 1982, Wallace Park was opened for these activities. (Courtesy John Wood.)

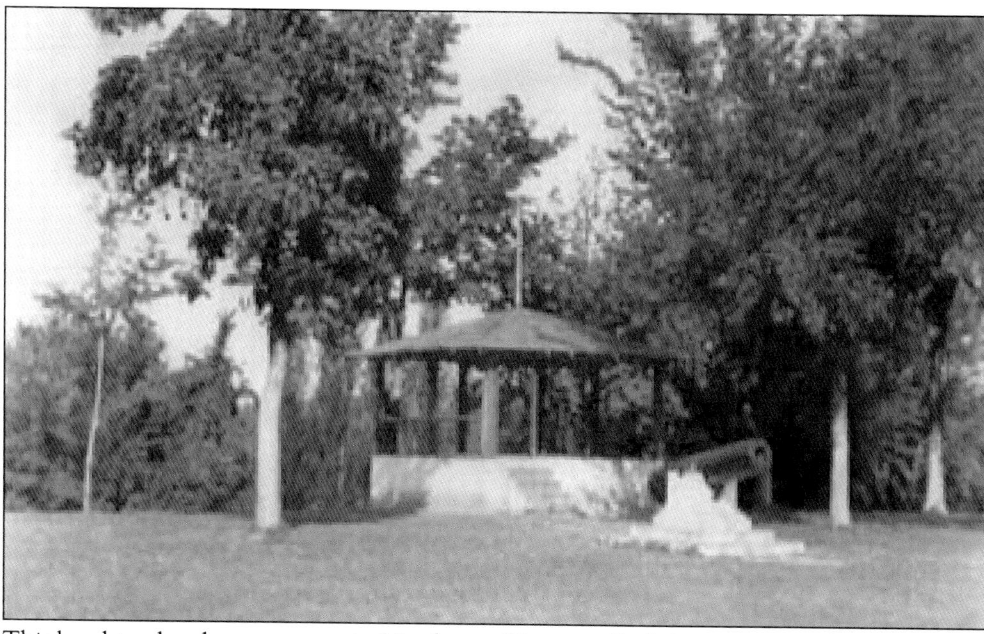

This bandstand and cannon were in Henderson Riverview Park for many years, but the cannon was dismantled and sold for scrap iron during World War II. Children went door to door in 1942 collecting scrap for defense weapons. Sliding on the cannon was fun for the youngsters. Sen. John B. Henderson and his wife deeded the land to the city for a park on May 2, 1903. (Courtesy John Wood.)

J.R. Morrison joined the *Press Journal* on May 21, 1923. With only a grade-school education, he became a respected and trusted editor-reporter for 36 years, locally and statewide. He was born in Kentucky on February 5, 1867, and died on January 2, 1960, at age 93. (Courtesy Betty Jane Allen.)

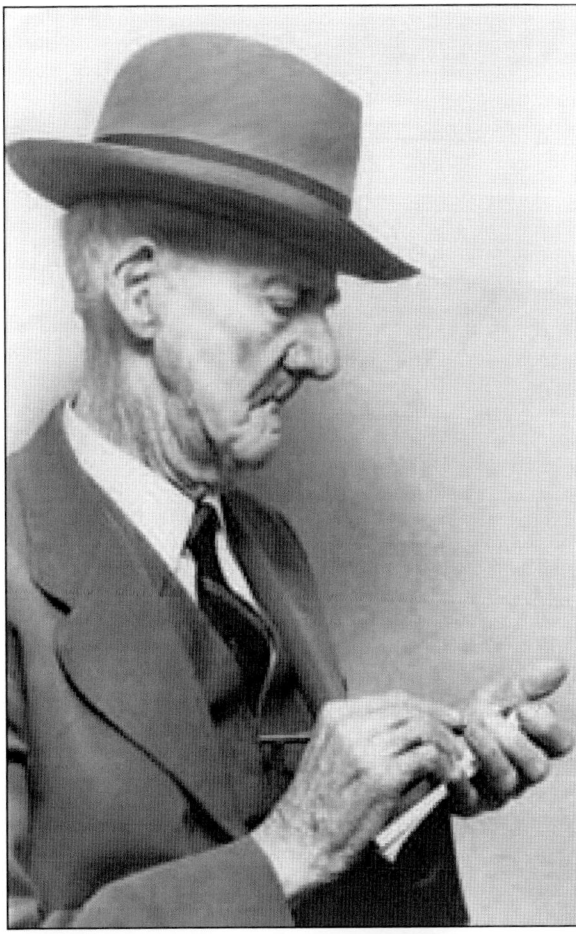

J.R. Morrison's office at the *Press Journal* was complete with all he needed to record the life of the community he so loved and the people who knew their "Mr. Morrison" not only for his reporting but also for his quiet, numerous "random acts of kindness." Louisiana photographs were added to his wall periodically but never discarded. He was a bachelor and is still remembered most fondly. (Courtesy Betty Jane Allen.)

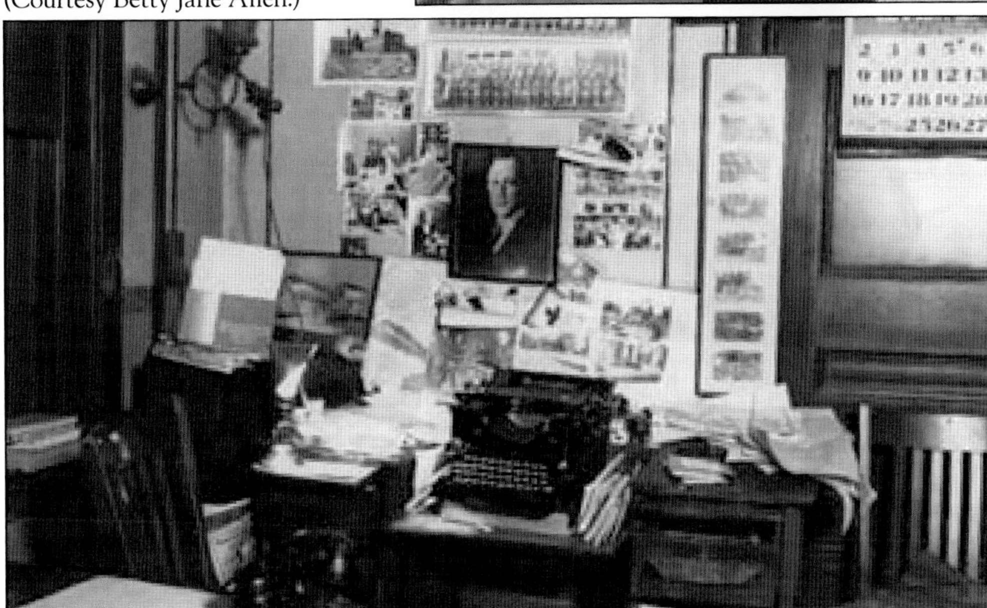

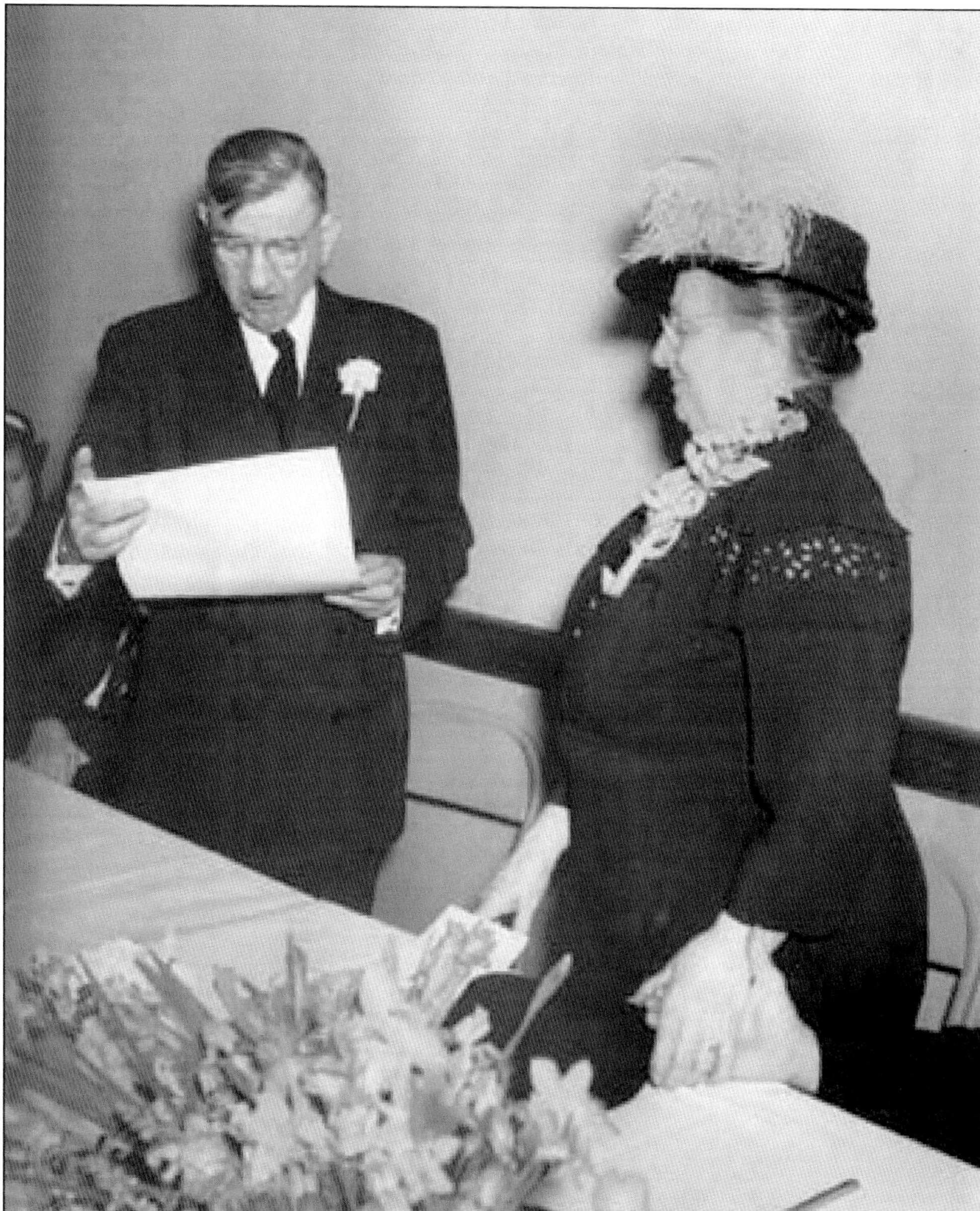

Marie Meriwether listens to Congressman Clarence Cannon read a certificate of merit and appreciation at a banquet honoring her. The civic-minded Meriwether was a well-organized lady and a supporter of many organizations, especially school-related ones. She served on the school board and on the library board, encouraged the organization of Girl Scouts, and was active in the Pike County Historical Society and the Democratic Committee. Meriwether Elementary School was named for her in 1954. Cannon was from nearby Elsberry, Missouri. He represented the Ninth Congressional District of the state for many years. Meriwether died on February 4, 1965. When Cannon died, the president at the time, Lyndon B. Johnson, and three ex-presidents attended his funeral in Elsberry on May 12, 1964. (Courtesy Louisiana Area Historical Museum.)

Six

Odds and Ends

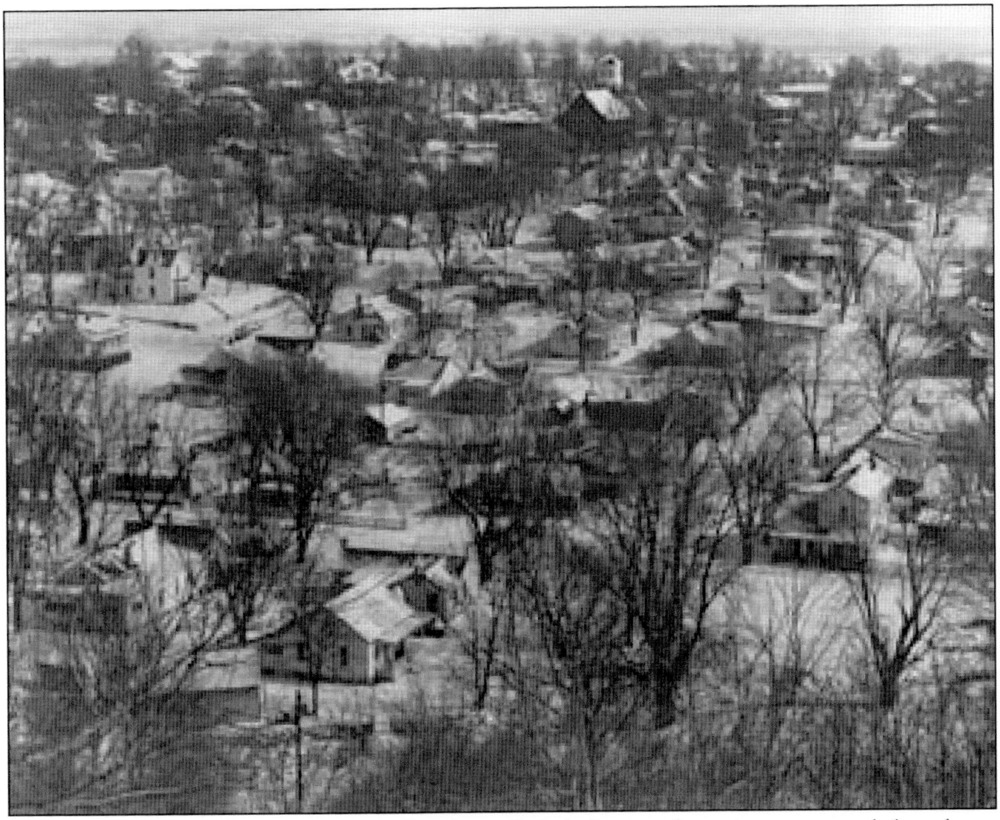

Taken from Marzolf Hill, or "Star Hill," above Eighth Street, this winter-carpeted shot shows the town in the early 1930s. St. Joseph's Catholic Church is in the distance in the center. Many streets running east and west were named for southern states and those running north and south were numerals. (Photograph courtesy Irene Steers.)

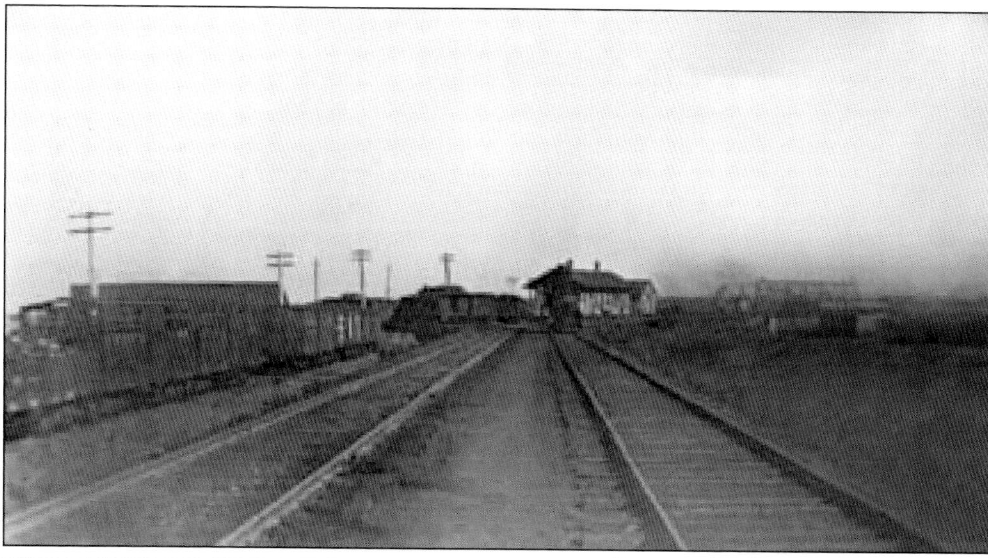

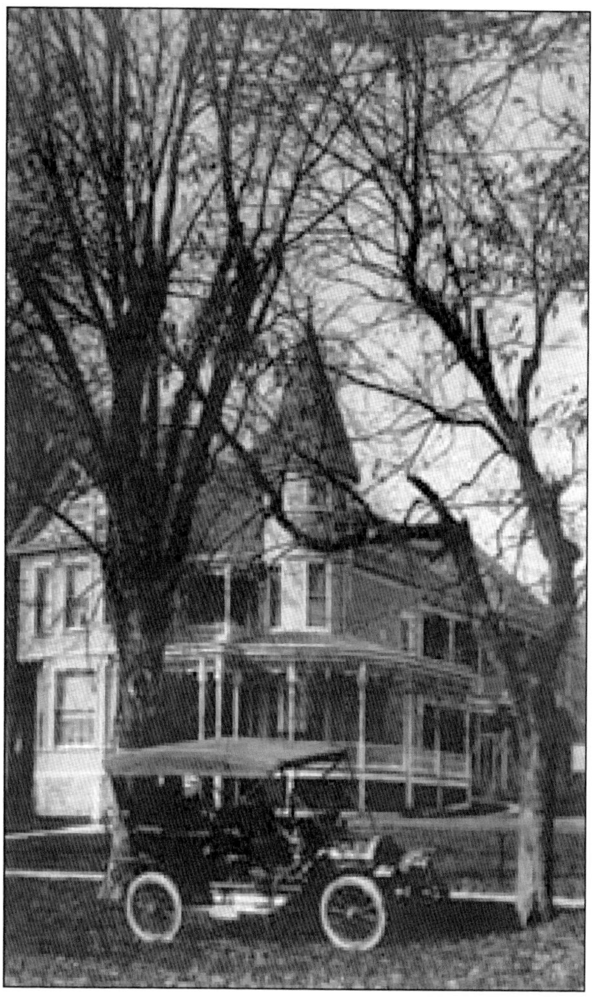

River and rail access impacted Louisiana's industrial boom. At one time, records indicate that 23 trains were coming into and through Louisiana, plus the trains that originated here. Noix Creek Bridge was to the right of the depot for vehicle use. On April 29, 1903, Pres. Theodore Roosevelt arrived by rail with six Pullman Coaches, secret service men, and his presidential party to give a campaign speech. Speaker Champ Clark introduced him at the grand, gala affair that drew several thousand spectators. (Courtesy John Wood.)

This elegant home was at the northwest corner of Fourth and Tennessee Streets. Although the original owner is unknown, it later belonged to Alexander and his wife, Mollie Wernert. Alexander, driving his high-spirited horse in his polished sulky, was a classy figure around town. The first automobile in town, parked in front, was an E.F. Studebaker with brass lamps and fittings and was owned by Joe McCune. (Courtesy Betty Jane Allen.)

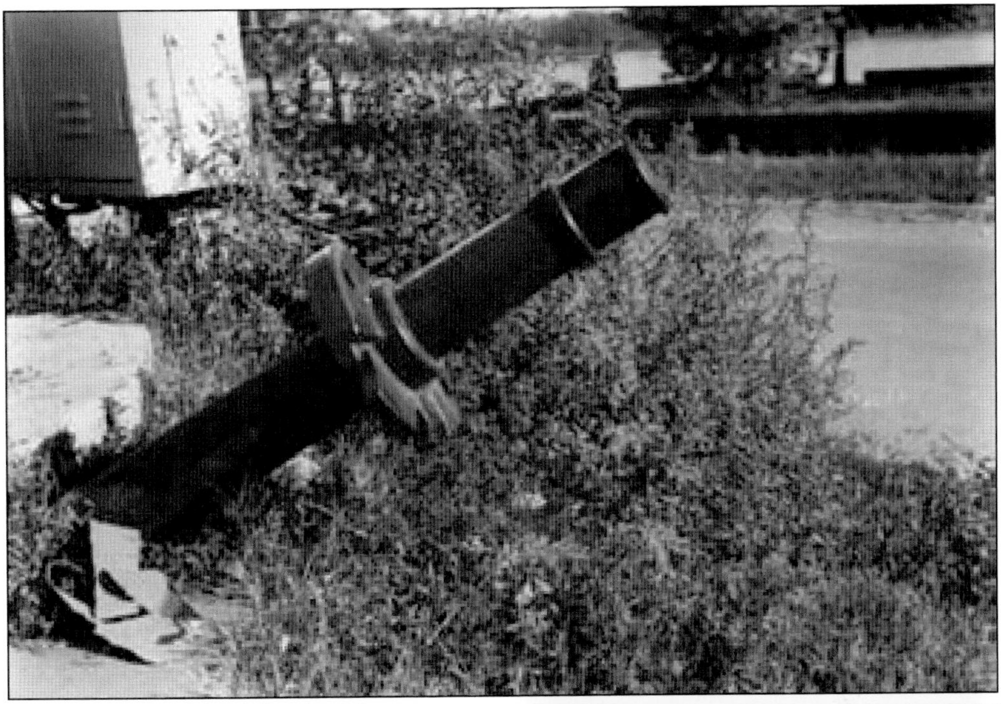

The shaft of an old paddle wheel from a steamboat sits at the foot of Georgia Street near the Mississippi River. It was used to tie up boats when they stopped in Louisiana. (Courtesy Betty Jane Allen.)

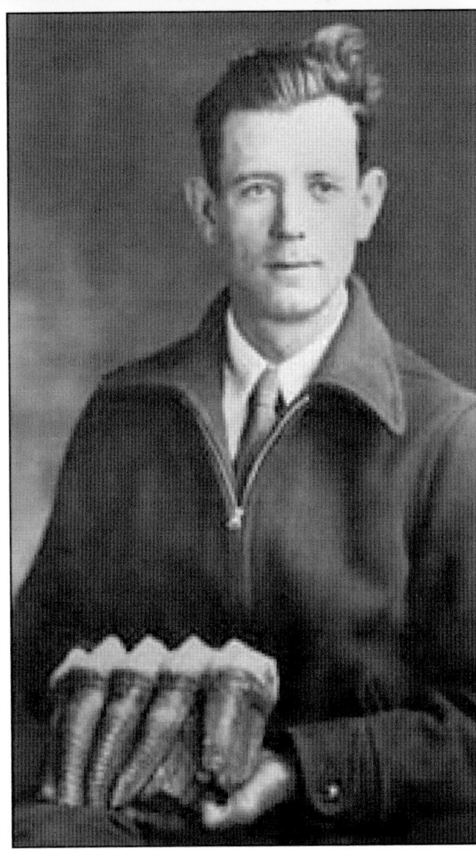

This mastodon tooth was found in the spring of 1936 when crews were excavating for Highway 79 near Louisiana. Dow Morton noticed a lump in the dirt but was told he would have to come back after hours to check it out. Morton kept it for his children, though the Smithsonian Institute wanted it. His daughter Katherine Todd often displays it and tells the story to school classes today. (Courtesy Linda Ince Beer.)

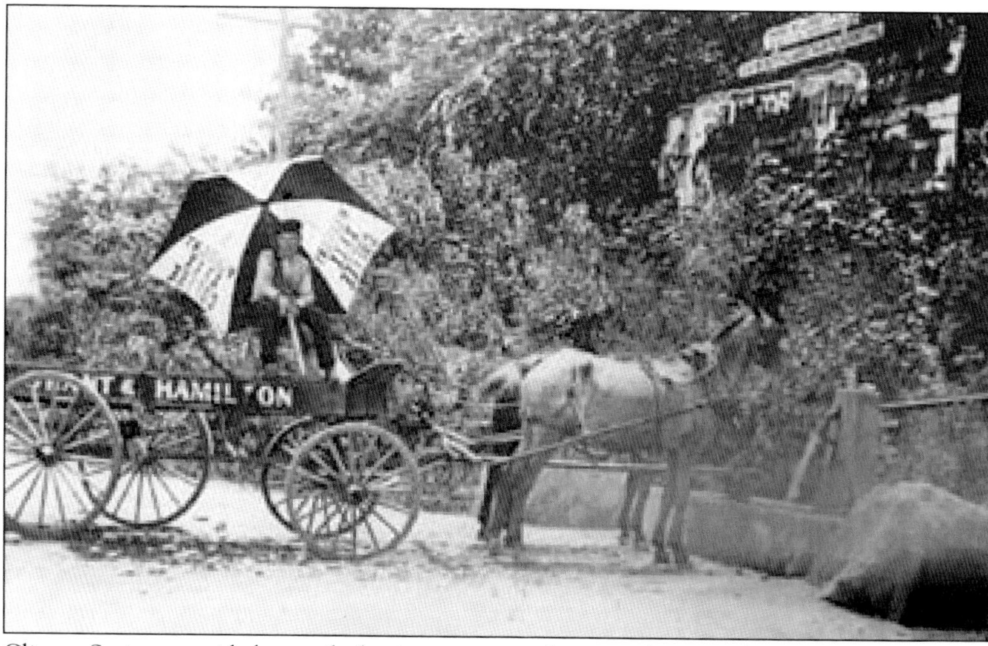

Clinton Springs provided water for business teams and carriage horses. This Grant and Hamilton delivery wagon, seen here around 1905, was for a grocery store on Main Street. Near the Railroad Bridge, Clinton Springs continues to serve the needs of townspeople and tourists, just as it did for early settlers of Buffalo Township. A large population of buffalo once roamed Pike County, giving the township its name. The county was named for Zebulon Pike. (Courtesy John Wood.)

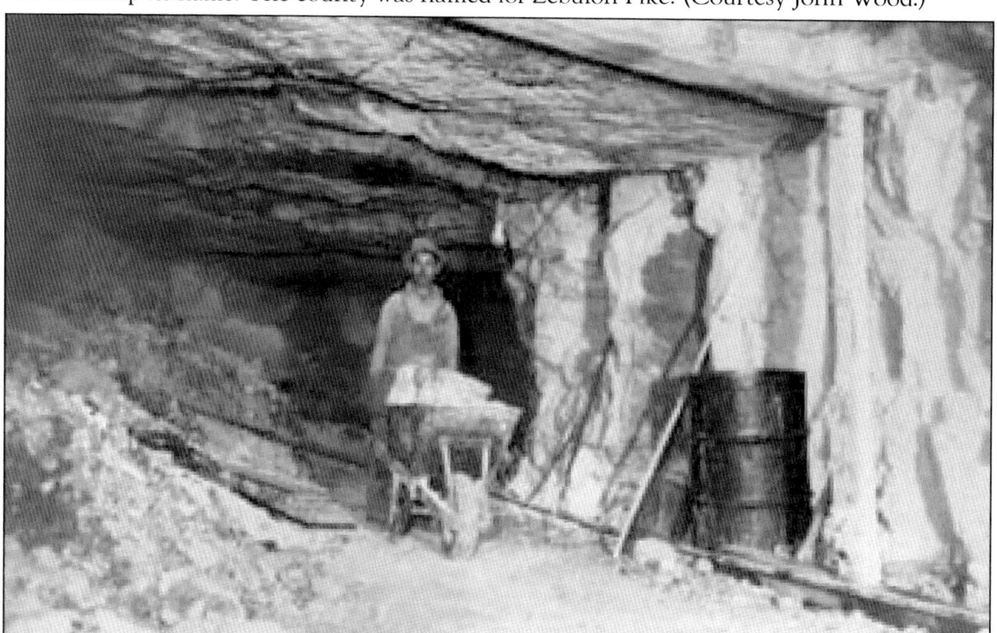

Putty rock mined from Clinton Hill near Clinton Springs was used to make cement at a nearby cement company. Hart Quarry ran trolleys up Vandeventer Hill for loads of limestone rock used for the foundations of many Louisiana homes as well as the library. The original limestone Hart Quarry office still remains. (Courtesy John Wood.)

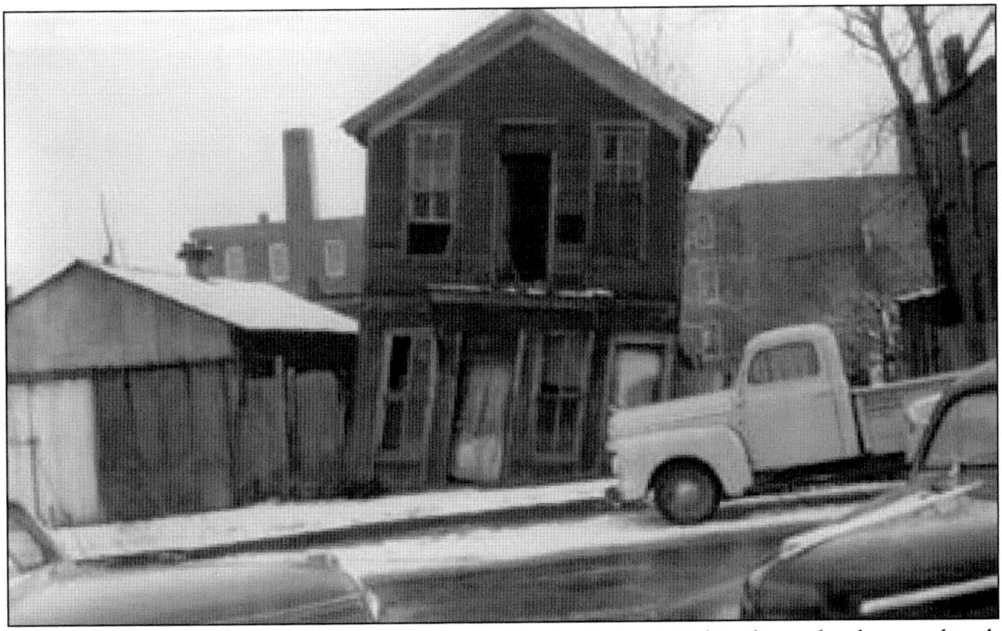

This "Leaning Tower" house was owned by Guy Rudd, who operated a salvage, hauling, and junk business. His office was upstairs. The house lacked a foundation, and weakened and rotted over time, causing it to lean uphill to the right. It was on the south side of Georgia Street between Water and Main Streets and was occupied until the late 1940s. The Leaning Tower house has appeared in LIFE magazine. (Courtesy Betty Jane Allen.)

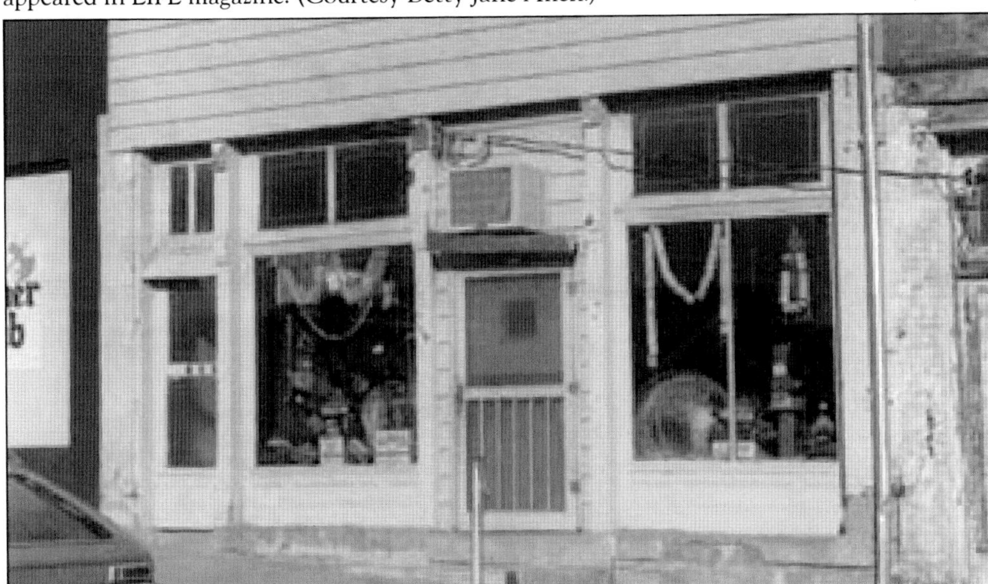

Sam Morris was a shipper of hides in the early 1900s, purchasing locally and shipping to dealers. He also furnished fishing gear and supplies here and by mail order catalogue. His son Mark assisted him and continued after his father's death. An attorney, Mark was in the military and was sent to the Nuremberg trials to observe them. This unpretentious store was important to fishermen, trappers, and hunters and is known statewide. The building is currently being renovated for a lunchroom. (Courtesy Betty Jane Allen.)

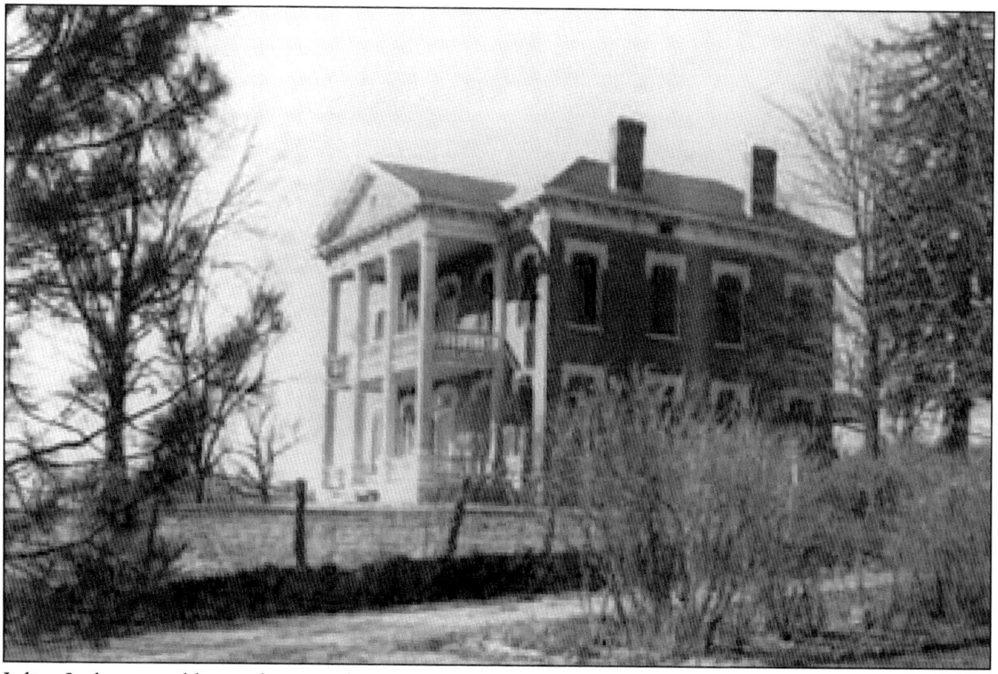

Julius Jackson and his wife came from Kentucky in 1831. He established a sawmill and built this house in the mid-1800s on land his father, Christopher Jackson, acquired through a large land grant. It was occupied by his descendants until the 1960s. The house was a copy of Pres. Andrew Jackson's Hermitage. President Jackson was Christopher Jackson's first cousin. The house is in the National Register of Historic Places. (Courtesy Betty Jane Allen.)

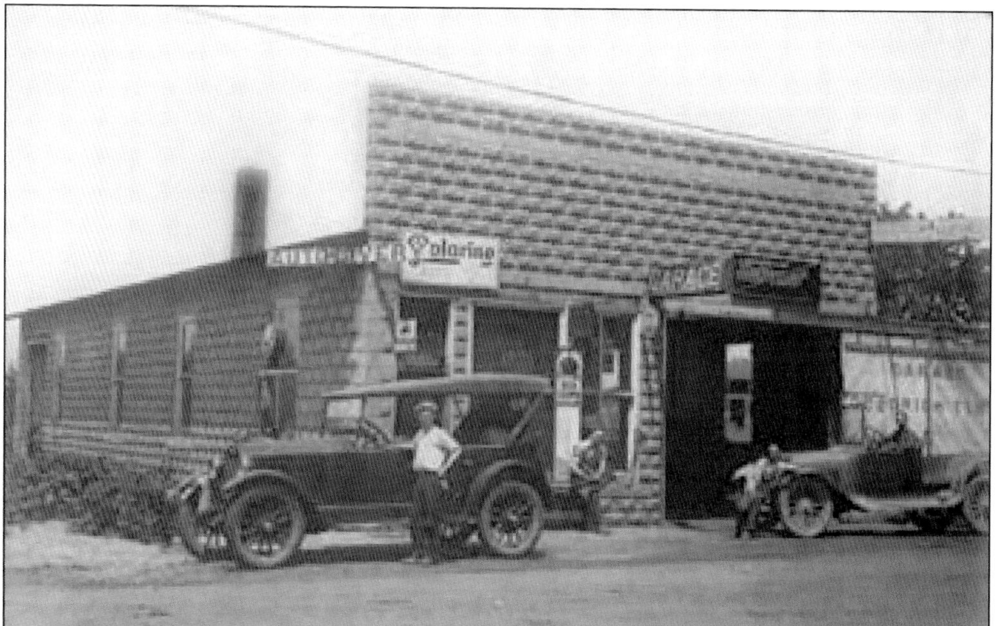

This garage was on South Carolina Street in the early 1920s. It was originally called Porter and Vaughn. After the building was destroyed by fire, the land was later purchased by Southwestern Bell Telephone Company. It is still there today. (Courtesy John Wood.)

Anna Thurman (pictured) was a fashionable 19 year old in 1904. She married Jerry Roberts, who had a saloon at 102 North Main Street. Although the couple had no children, they raised a niece, Lucille Roberts, whose mother died when she was a small child. Lucille worked for the telephone company and was well known for the beautiful flowers in the yard of her home, which she grew up in and had been left to her by her aunt and uncle. (Courtesy Trent Meyers.)

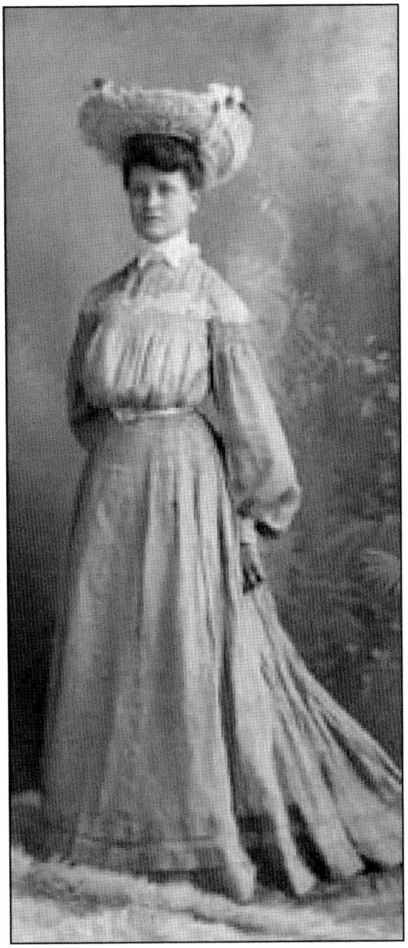

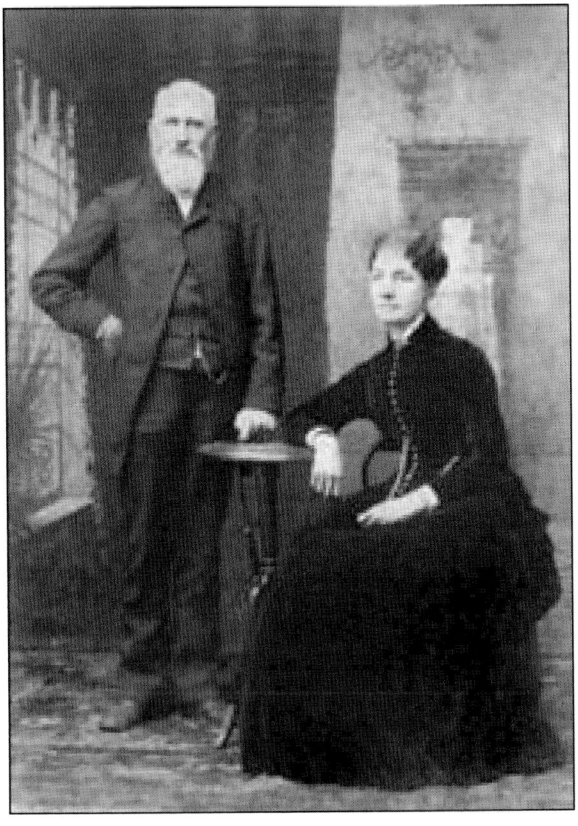

Virginia native Francis Thornton Meriwether served in the Confederate army. In 1870, he came to Missouri, surveyed a townsite, and suggested the name Aeolia, which is Latin for "windy." This neighboring town's name eventually became Eolia. In 1872, he married Elizabeth J. Dawson. Their son Charles Louis became a dentist. Francis was postmaster for four years and later the bookkeeper for the Addison Tinsley Tobacco Company. Elizabeth was one of 12 charter DAR members in 1911. (Courtesy Charlotte Griffith.)

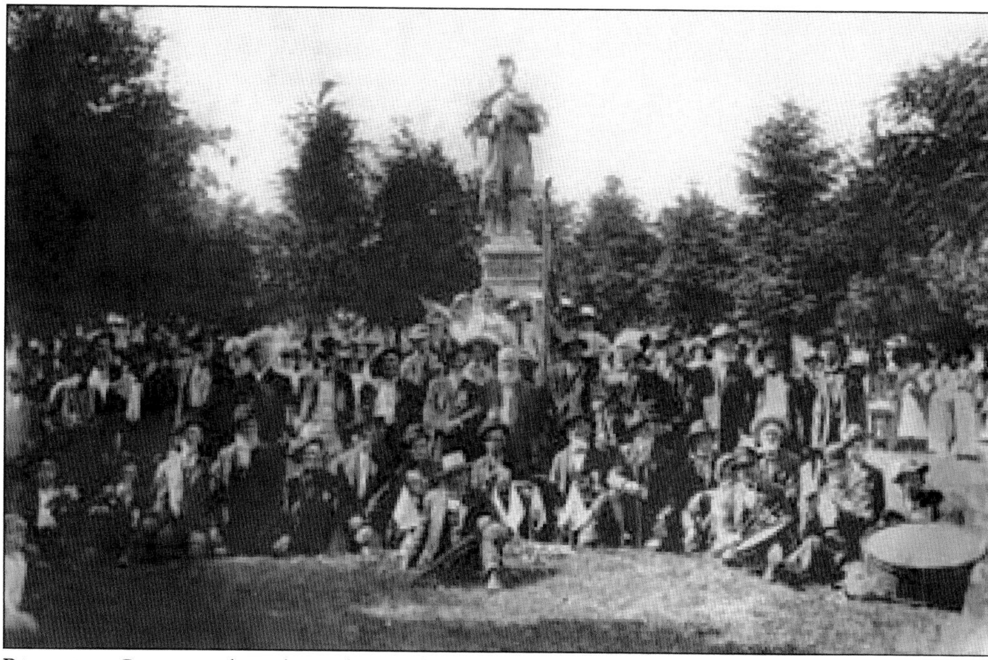

Riverview Cemetery has the only Civil War monument in Pike County. After the war, the veterans formed a Grand Army of the Republic (GAR) post in Louisiana. The GAR erected the monument in the center of a circle drive at the end of the old cemetery in 1884. In 1998, the monument was removed and rebuilt by John Wood. The American Legion funded the rebuilding of the monument, which was originally made from Detroit Bronze. The oldest record of burial is A. Fleece, who was buried on April 1, 1813. (Courtesy Louisiana Area Historical Museum.)

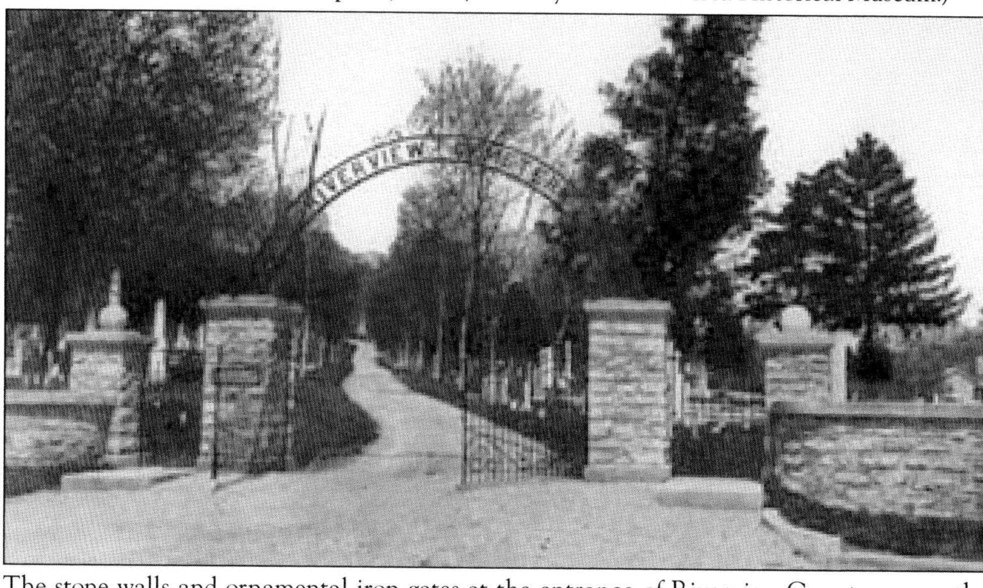

The stone walls and ornamental iron gates at the entrance of Riverview Cemetery were the first memorial projects of the DAR in 1911, the year the chapter organized. The project took five months to complete. A small stone sexton's building was also constructed. It was the largest work of any DAR chapter in the state of Missouri. At the same time, the Louisiana Cemetery Association was formed. (Courtesy Betty Jane Allen.)

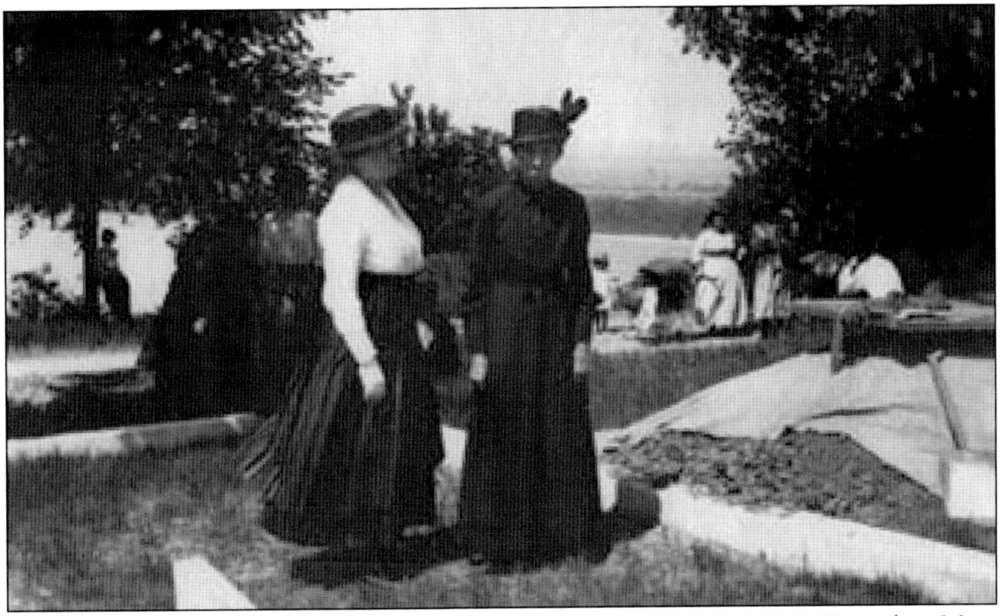

This photograph was taken after the burial of Daniel A. Kershner in 1919. His widow, Mary (right), pauses, as friends and relatives stand nearby. The burial site is at the top of Riverview Cemetery. Note the Mississippi River in the background. Daniel and Mary had one daughter who married Leonard Pounds, a longtime employee of Stark Bro's Nurseries & Orchards Co. and a 1922 Louisiana High School graduate. (Courtesy John Wood.)

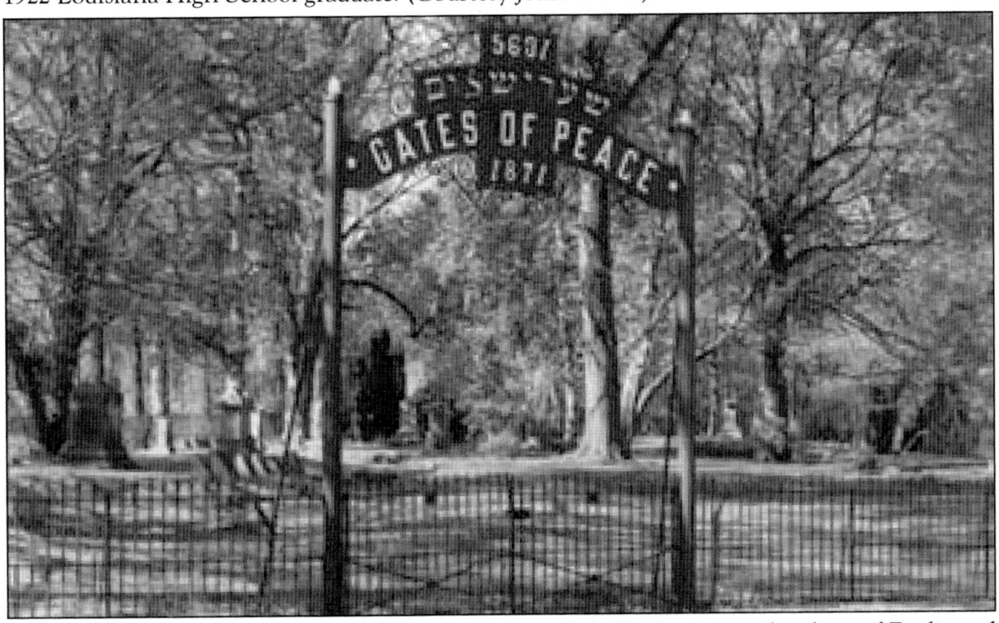

The first burial in the Hebrew Cemetery was Katie Fishell, the young daughter of Ferdinand Fishell, a local merchant. In 1871, the cemetery was one acre on the Louisiana and Bowling Green gravel road, approximately two miles west of town. The entrance gateway inscription reads, "Shaare Shalem," which means "gates of peace." Several early Jewish families made lasting and significant contributions to the town through their business enterprises and civic associations. (Courtesy Betty Jane Allen.)

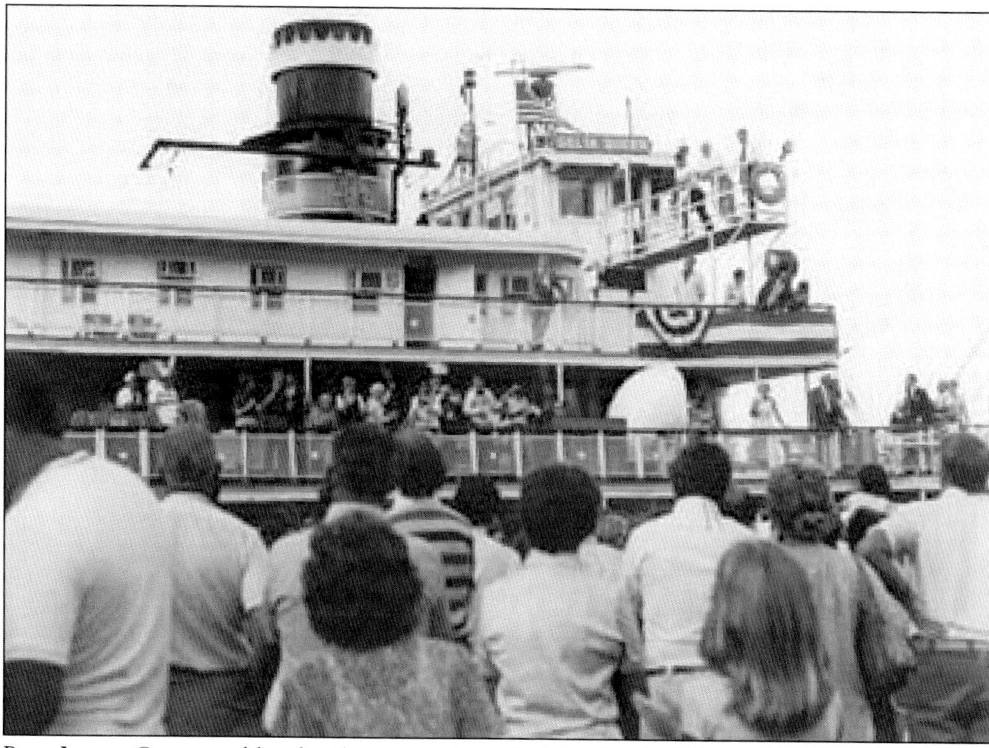

Pres. Jimmy Carter and his family appeared on deck in April 1979 as the *Delta Queen* paddle wheeler paused for him to address a crowd estimated to be more than 1,000 people. With him were his wife, Rosalynn, daughter Amy, and mother, Lillian. (Courtesy Lois Stark.)

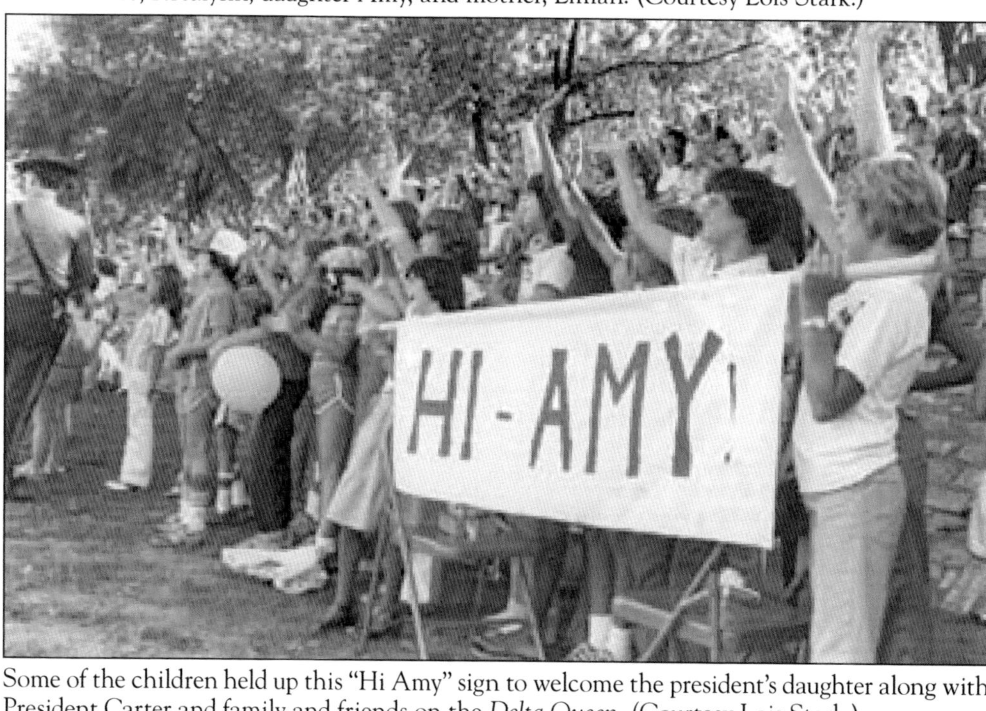

Some of the children held up this "Hi Amy" sign to welcome the president's daughter along with President Carter and family and friends on the *Delta Queen*. (Courtesy Lois Stark.)

Seven
You Might Want to Know

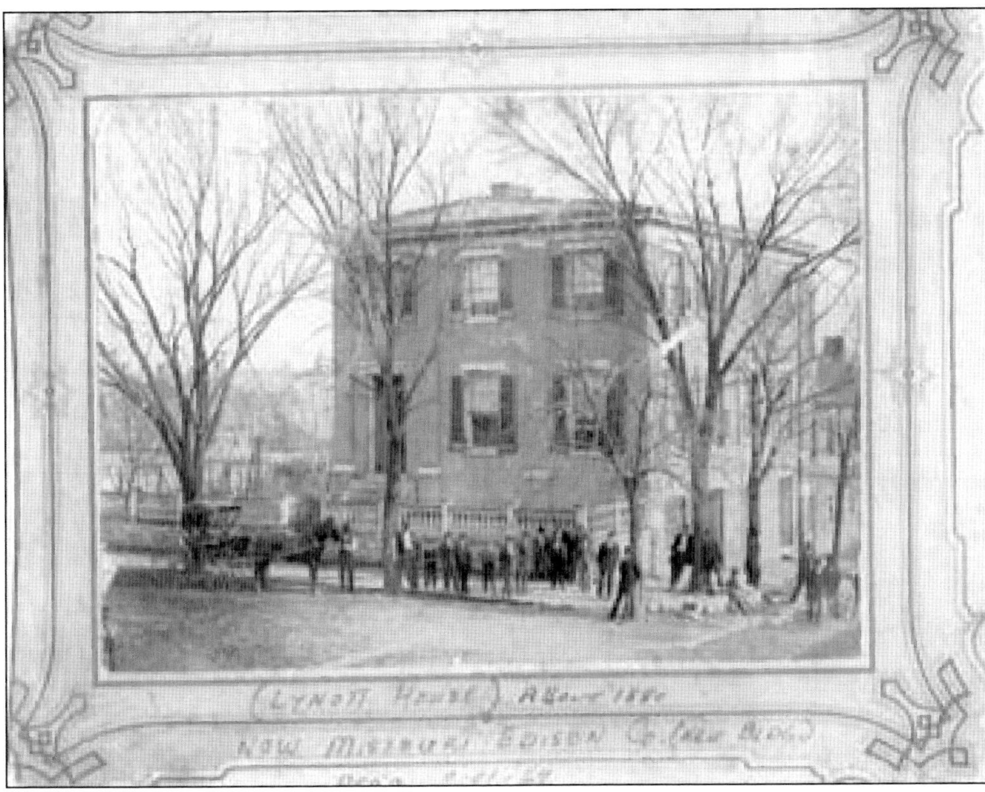

In 1862, this house was originally built in two sections at Third and South Carolina Streets by the Draper family. This stately showplace was owned by the Lynott family and became known as the Lynott House. Later, it housed apartments before eventually being demolished by the Missouri Edison Company in 1967 and rebuilt with bricks made in Virginia. It was purchased by the city and now houses city offices. The chamber of commerce conducts business here too. (Courtesy Betty Jane Allen.)

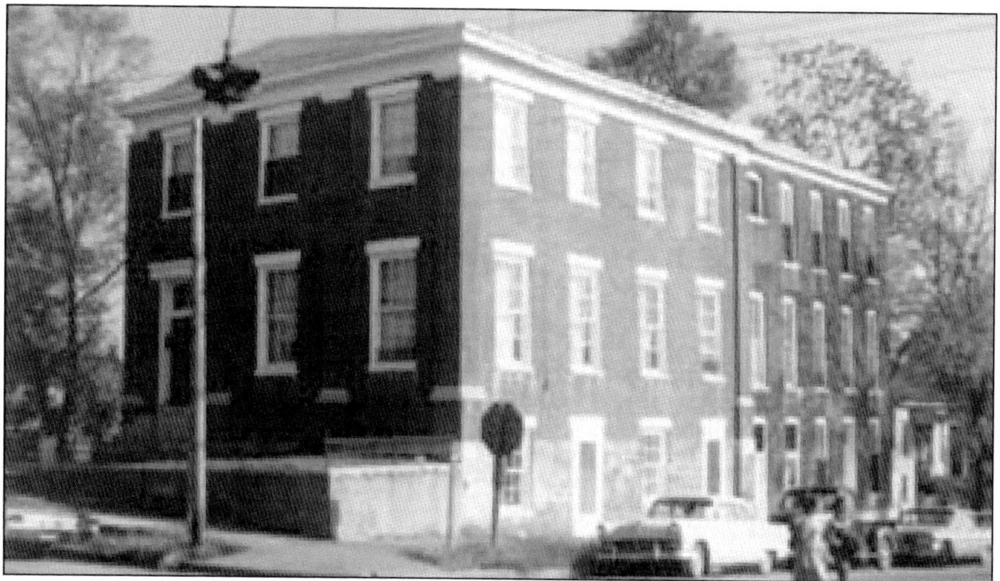

The old Lynott house is pictured as it appeared in the 1960s before razing. (Courtesy Louisiana Area Historical Museum.)

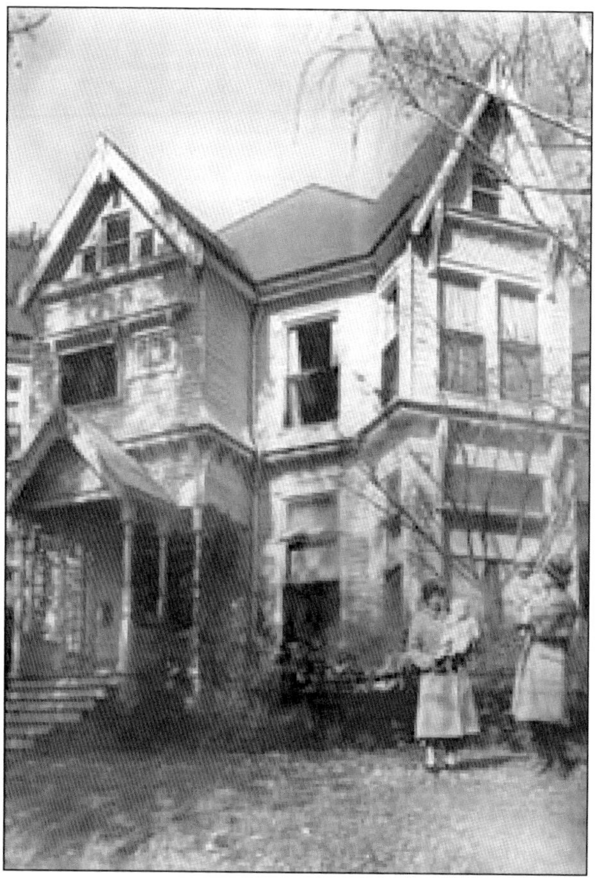

This house was built in 1891 by Albert Kuna Sr., a cabinet-maker who had emigrated from Bohemia in 1890. The house was for J.W. Crawford, the owner of one of Louisiana's early lumber companies. Designed as a showplace, it is a fine example of Eastern Victorian architecture. Three members of the Stark Bro's Nurseries & Orchards Co. have owned the house: William P. Stark, who sold it to his nephew, Lloyd Crow Stark, the 39th governor of Missouri (1937–1940), and his wife, Katherine; and Thomas W. Stark, a two-term mayor of Louisiana (1938–1942) and 20-year city councilman, and his wife, Alice. The house was listed in the Missouri Register of Historic Places on May 9, 1986, and in the National Register of Historic Places on December 21, 1987. Locally, it is referred to as the Stark House. Here, standing on the front lawn is Lloyd C. Stark and his wife, Katherine, holding their daughters Mary and Katherine. (Courtesy Anita Ludwig.)

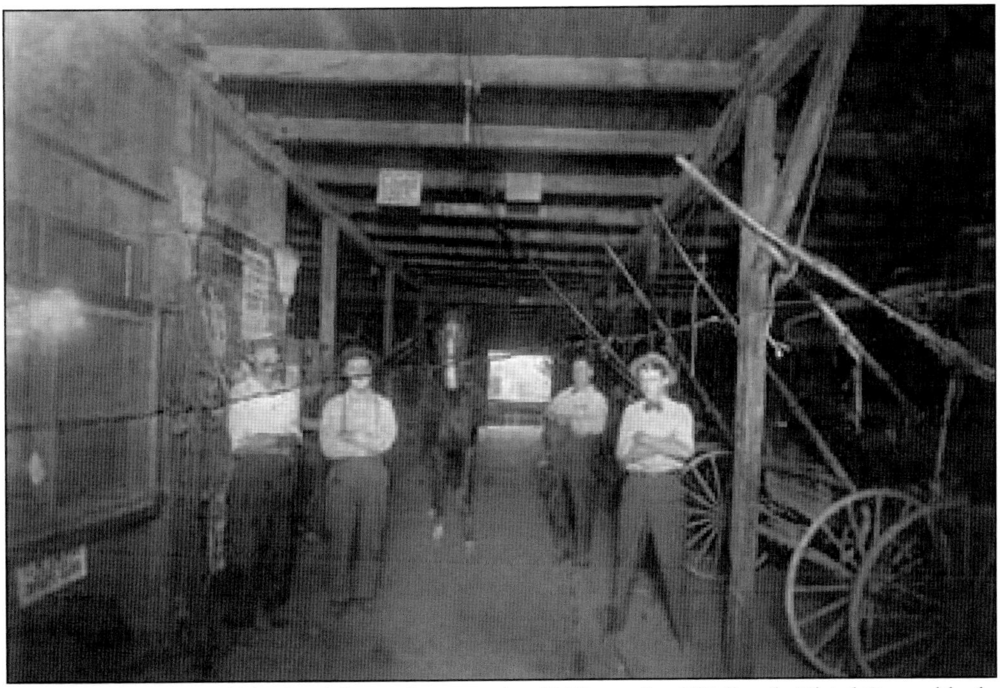

A. Hurley McDannold had a delivery barn in the 1900s in the 200 South Third Street block. He had horses, buggies, and hearses for hire. He also boarded horses and rigs and had a harness shop. John A. Lake, an undertaker, lived upstairs. The men in this photograph probably worked there, though their names are unknown. Livery stables were important; at one time, there were eight in town. (Courtesy Betty Jane Allen.)

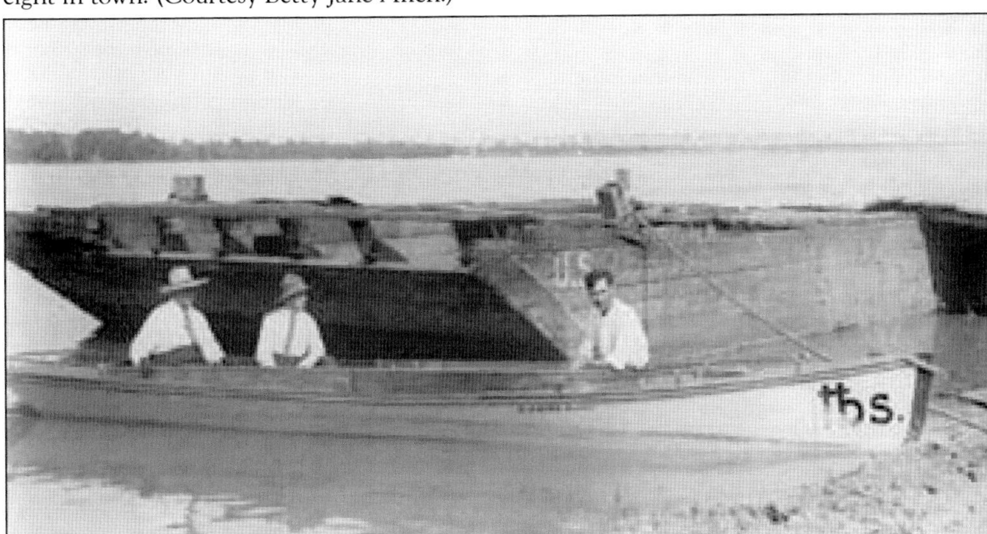

From left to right are William M. Pounds, his son Leonard Pounds, and Andy Wies. The elder Pounds hired Wies to build this boat for him. According to Leonard, his father signed his name "Lbs." The side of the boat reads "A.J. Wies, Builder." The photograph was taken at the riverbank near Louisiana and the railroad bridge is in the distance. Wies was the maternal grandfather of Francis L. "Pete" Johnson. (Courtesy Marilyn Johnson.)

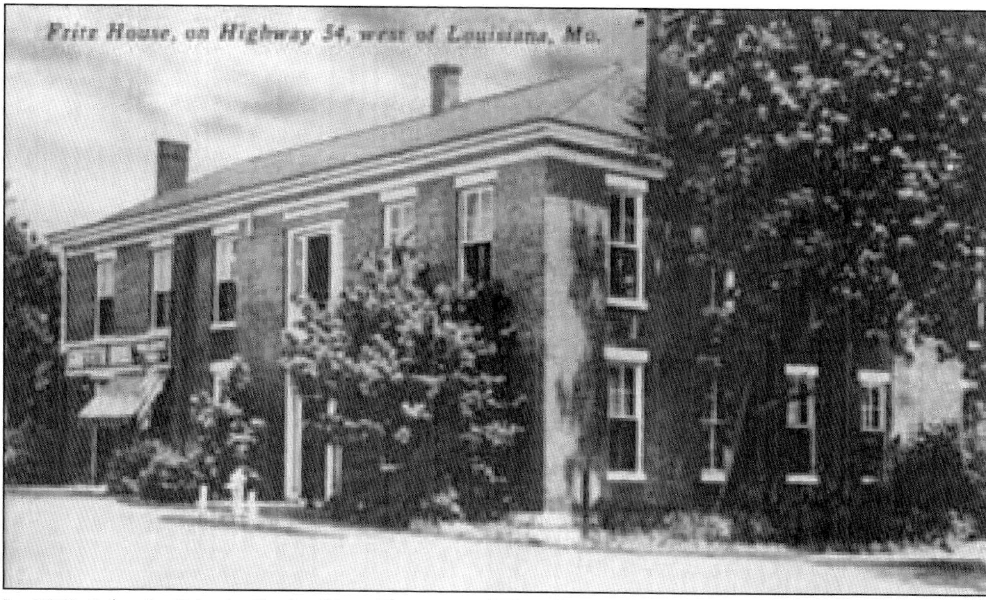

In 1859, John L. Fritz built the Fritz Tavern on West Georgia Street for travelers and stockmen. A racetrack—the first fairgrounds—was across the road. Union soldiers lived there during the Civil War. Much later, there was a grocery store downstairs and apartments above. Stark Bro's Nurseries & Orchards Co. eventually sold it to the Carpenters Union, and in April 1969, it was razed, and a new building is now located there. (Courtesy Betty Jane Allen.)

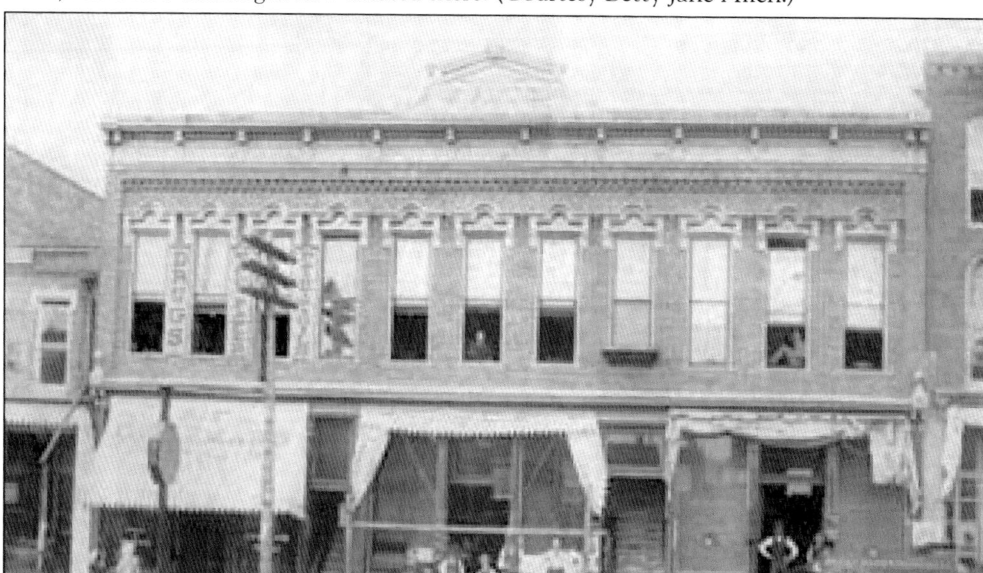

John L. Fritz was a prominent citizen who built three properties of importance: two taverns and one building downtown. This brick building was built in 1885 at 313 Georgia Street. It has been used by many stores and professions with upstairs apartments. Note the men in the upstairs windows. (Courtesy Betty Jane Allen.)

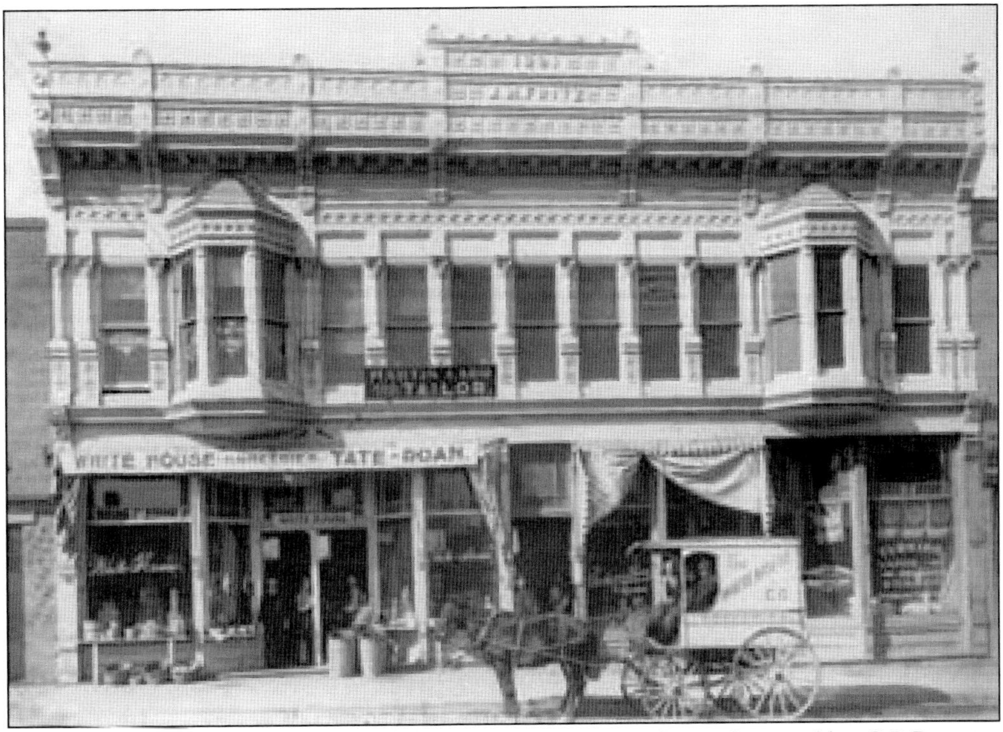

In 1891, John W. Fritz erected this brick building at 507 Georgia Street. It was sold to O.P. Benning and inherited by Benning's son Davis, who had a law office there for 15 years. In the late 1940s, Paul Burbridge bought it and ran a barbershop there for 20 years. It is currently owned by the Elks lodge. (Courtesy Louisiana Area Historical Museum.)

John L. Fritz operated this hotel on Water Street, known as the Fritz House. On November 16, 1867, the building burned down, but Fritz rebuilt and opened the new building on February 18, 1868. The family lived on one end and public accommodations were on the other. It was reported that escaping slaves were hidden in the cellar, fed, and sent northward at night. (Courtesy John Wood.)

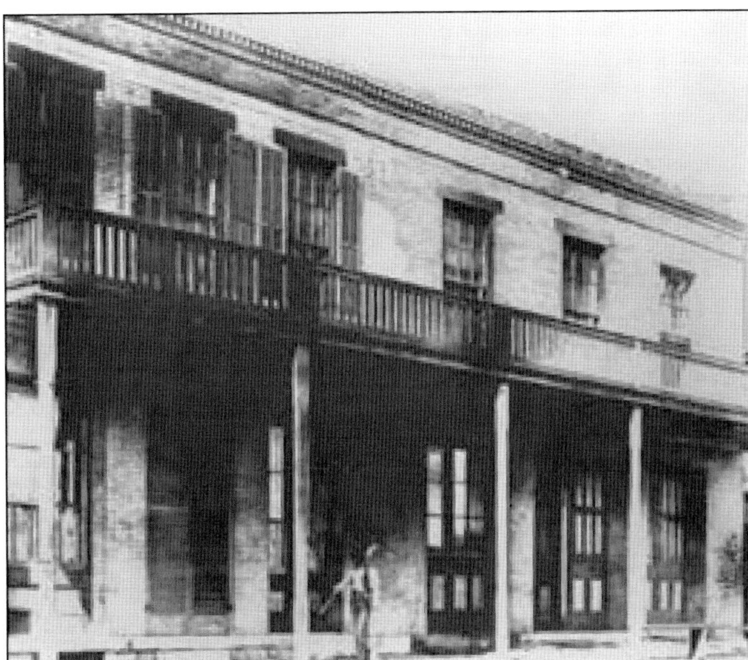

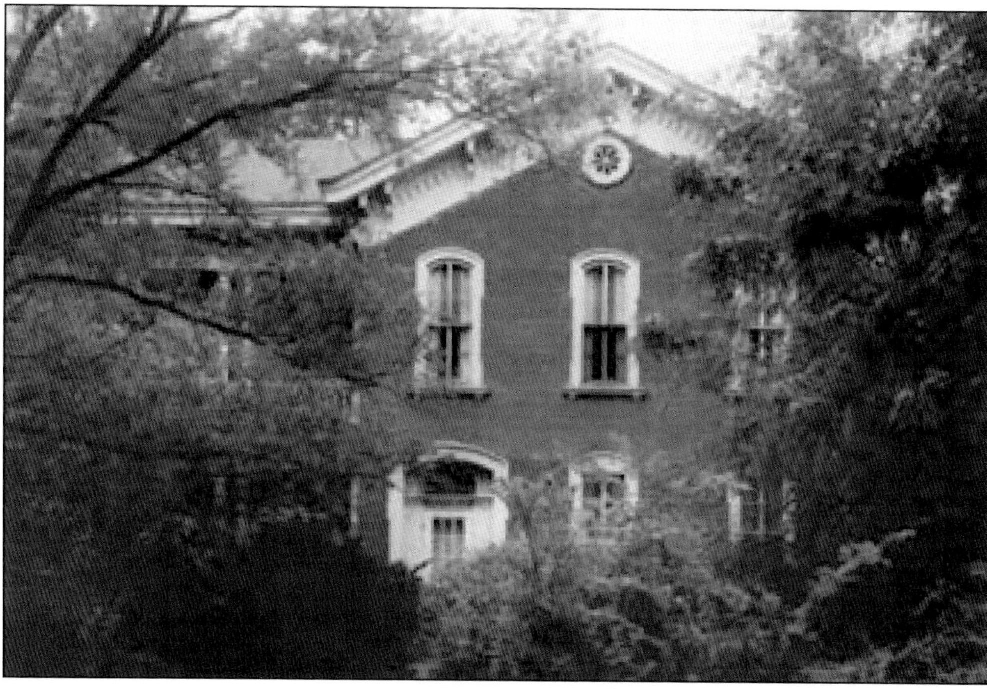

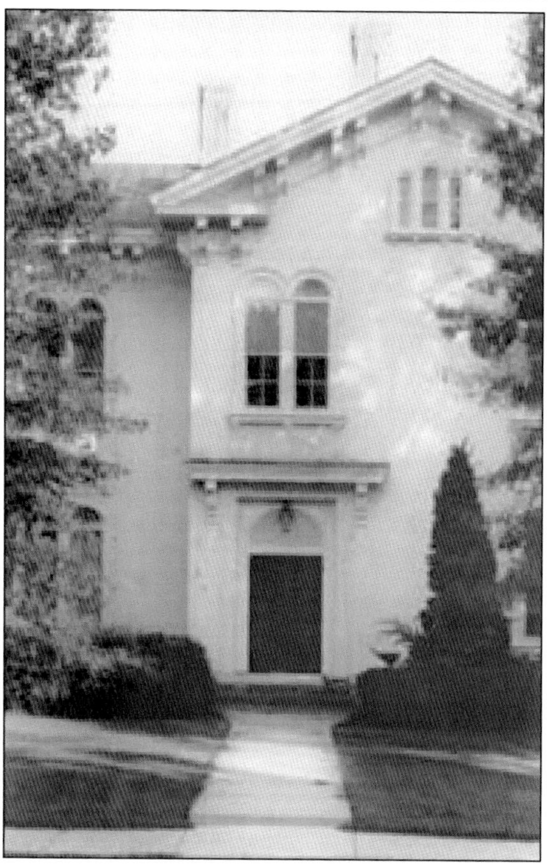

William C. Luce (1800–1884) came to Louisiana in 1840, bought the city mill, converted it into a flouring mill, and became a prosperous tobacco merchant. He built four houses for his family, known as the Luce Houses. The first house (above) was for his wife, Minerva, and their family. It was built by Powhatan Baird in 1857 at 1100 North Carolina Street. A cornfield surrounded it at that time. For many years, it was the home of Dr. Charles and Marie Meriwether and their son, Charles Jr. (Courtesy Betty Jane Allen.)

As the Luce family grew up and left the home place, William C. built homes for each of them. For his daughter Marian, who married Samuel Murray, he had Powhatan Baird build this house at 1210 Georgia Street. Later, Albert Pribe and his wife, Irma, enjoyed living here. It is now probably best known as the house with the Christmas ribbon, which is tastefully decorated every December by current owners Jim and Rose Osborn. (Courtesy Betty Jane Allen.)

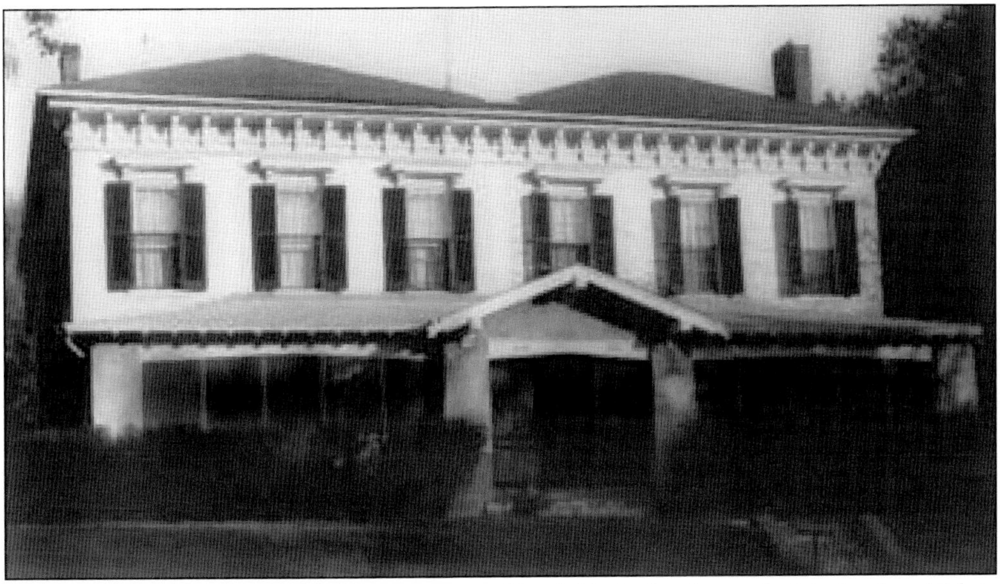

William C. Luce had acquired a large amount of land. He built a house for his daughter Helen, who married Archibald Van Horn, at 1016 South Carolina Street. The front porch was added in 1919. For many years, it was a duplex for R.R. Rule and E.A. Glenn and their descendants. (Courtesy Betty Jane Allen.)

William C. Luce was Homer's father. After Homer married, Levi Ruggles and his stepson, Powhatan Baird, built this house for him at 220 North Third Street. Homer's heirs sold it to David P. Dwyer, a Republican Missouri legislator. The third owner was John B. Henderson, a Republican senator. In 1933, after a Williamsburg trip, later owners Lawrence and Marie Stark made tasteful, major changes. In 1982, it was listed in the National Register of Historic Places. (Courtesy Betty Jane Allen.)

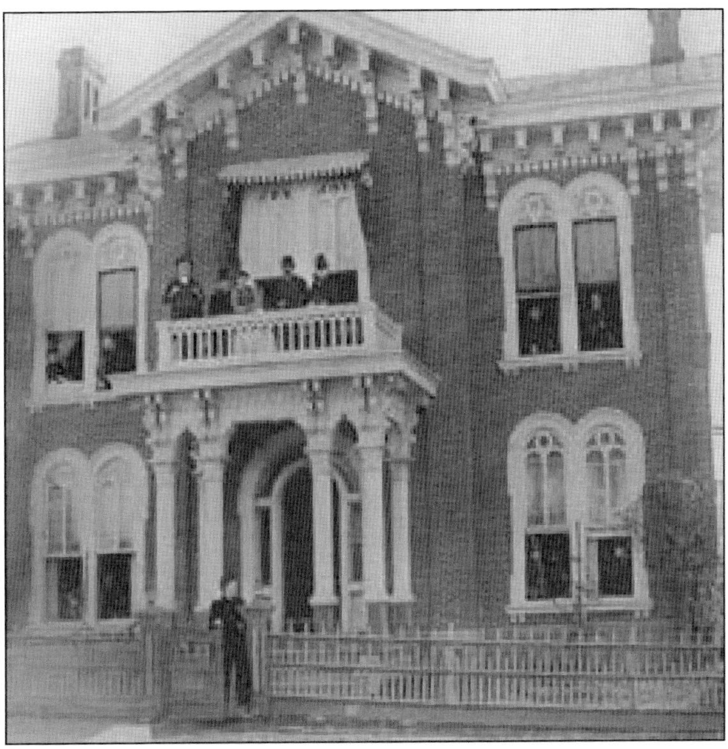

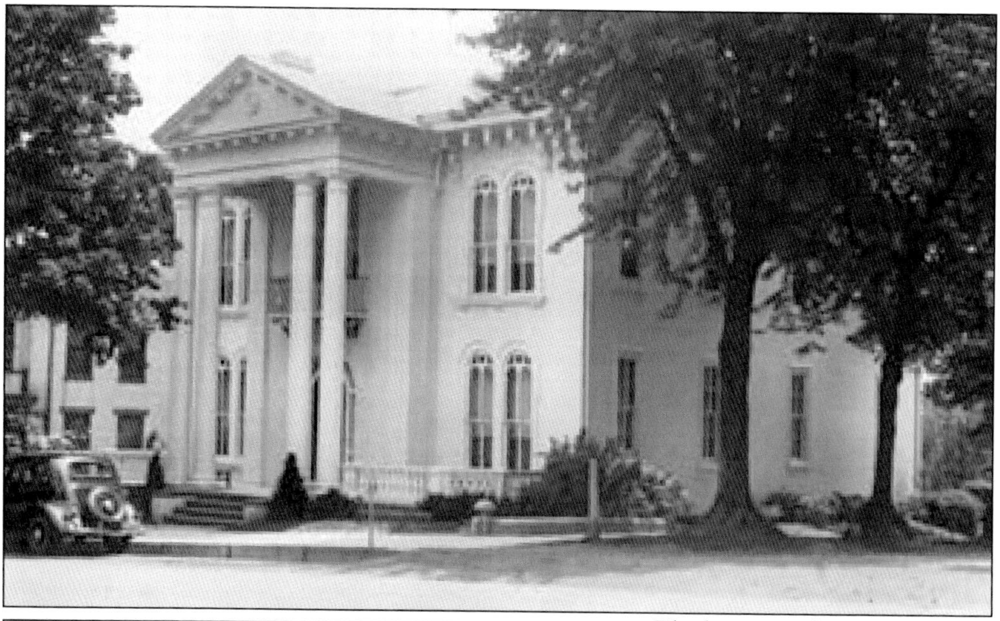

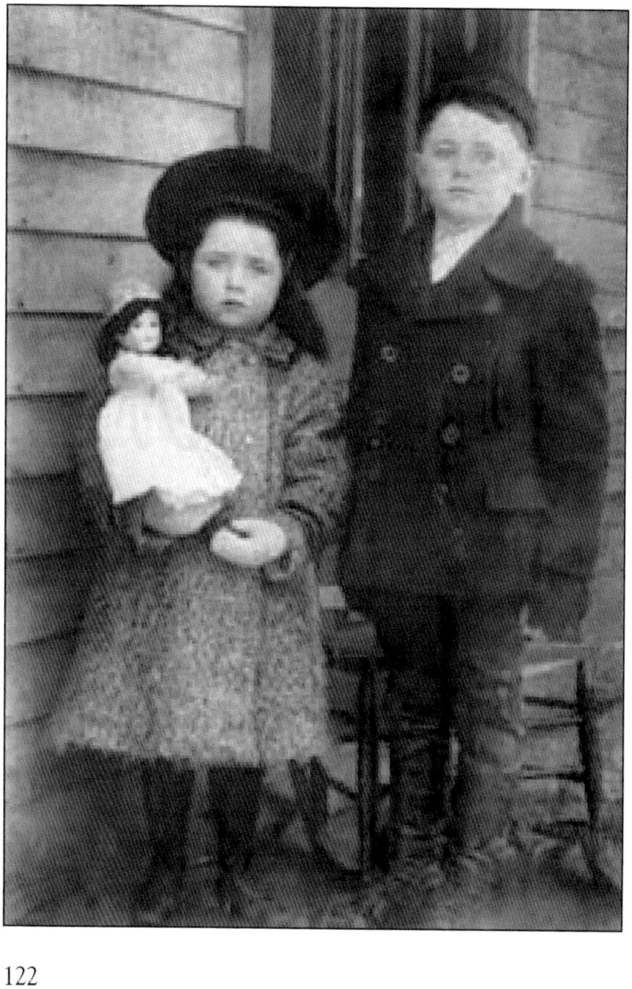

The house on the previous page, 220 North Third Street, is seen above after new owners Lawrence and Marie Stark returned from their trip to Williamsburg and renovated it extensively. (Courtesy Betty Jane Allen.)

Freda and Jim Roberts pose solemnly, perhaps on their way to Sunday school. They lived with their parents at 116 South Sixteenth Street. Freda married attorney Russell Benton in Kansas City where she taught grade school. Benton died very young. When Freda retired, she returned to Louisiana and lived in the Roberts' home place. She died in 2002 at almost 102 years old. Jim had a career in the Navy and relocated to California with his wife. They had no children. Their father, James, had worked at the Louisiana post office. The doll in this image is now owned by Trent Meyers. (Courtesy Trent Meyers.)

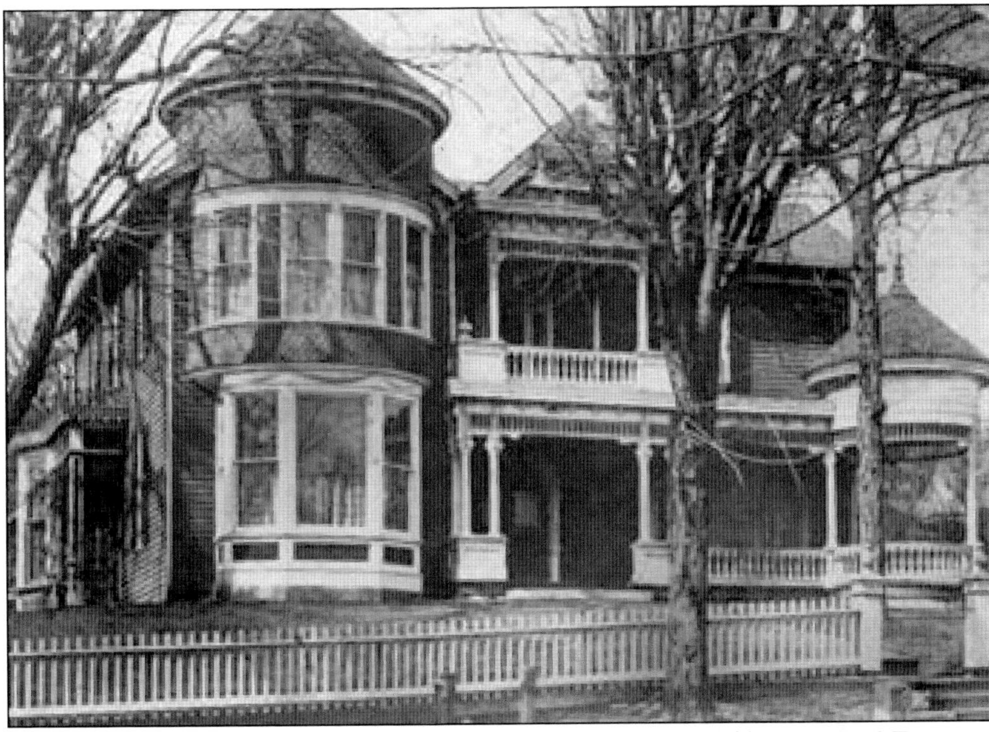

William N. Tinsley purchased four lots in 1875 and built this beautiful house at 1413 Tennessee Street. In 1895, he deeded the structure to his wife, Alice, "so that she may always have a home." He and A.J. McCune became associates of tobacco merchant Samuel Reid in 1882. Tinsley died in 1901, and Alice lived until 1939. Mark and Lydia Morris purchased the property in 1954 and lived there until 2010. (Courtesy Betty Jane Allen.)

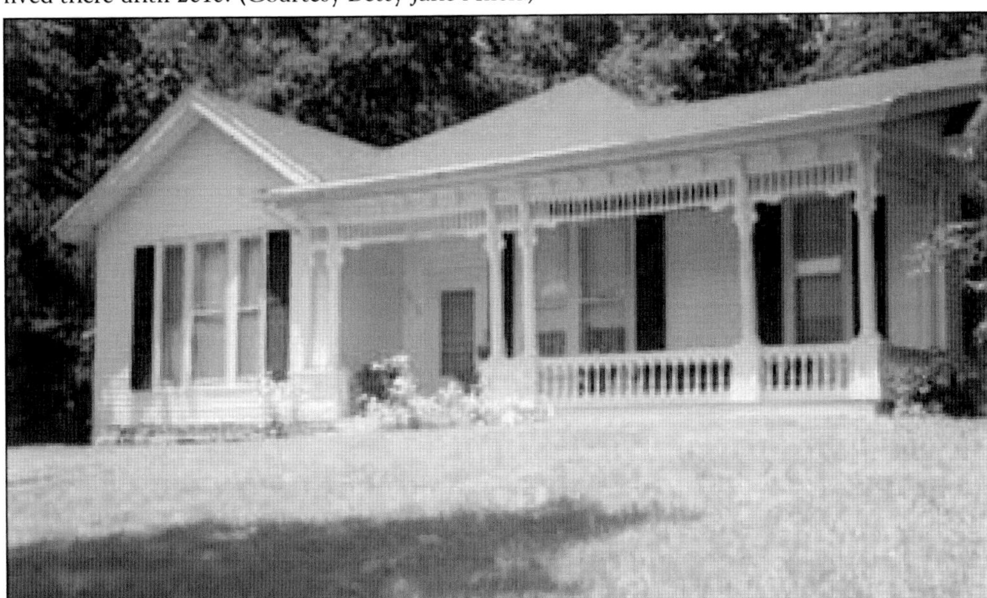

The house at 1413 Tennessee Street is seen here as it looked when the Morrises purchased it. (Courtesy Betty Jane Allen.)

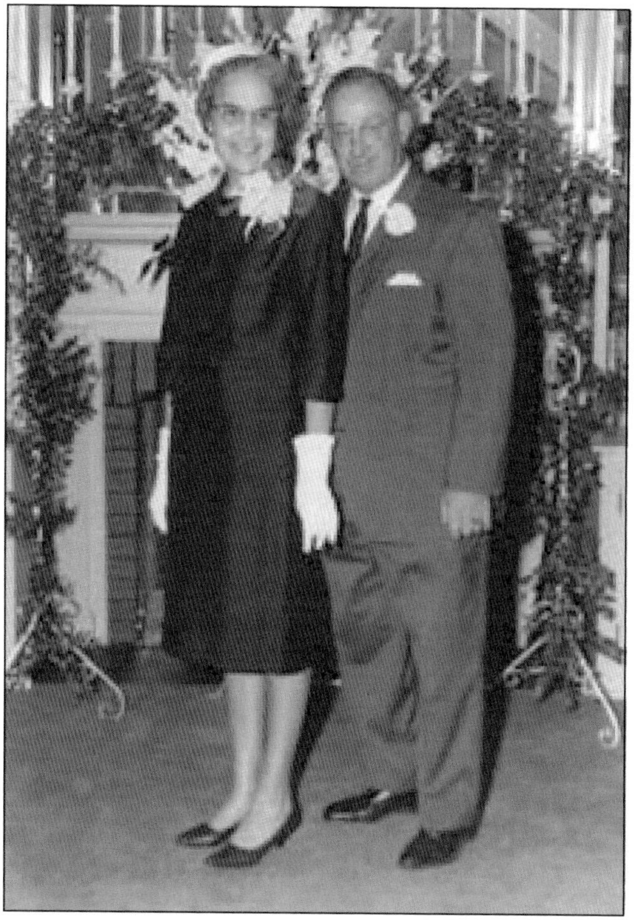

Charles L. Meriwether Jr. and Ione Pine were married on June 4, 1965. Meriwether drove a roving photographer around Louisiana for a week, providing him with the photographic material for a 1939 tape of the town for the local Rotary Club. In 1998, the club had the tape narrated and sold videos for a fundraiser, reordering three times to fill Christmas orders. Ione Meriwether worked for the telephone company for many years. (Courtesy Betty Jane Allen.)

The 50th wedding anniversary of William E. and Peggy Shannon Holliday was celebrated by their family, friends, and neighbors in 1937. W.E. "Ed" Holliday ran the ferryboat *Rover* with his brother and later by himself until 1929. The couple is seen in front of the house they built at 302 North Third Street. (Courtesy Eddie Holliday.)

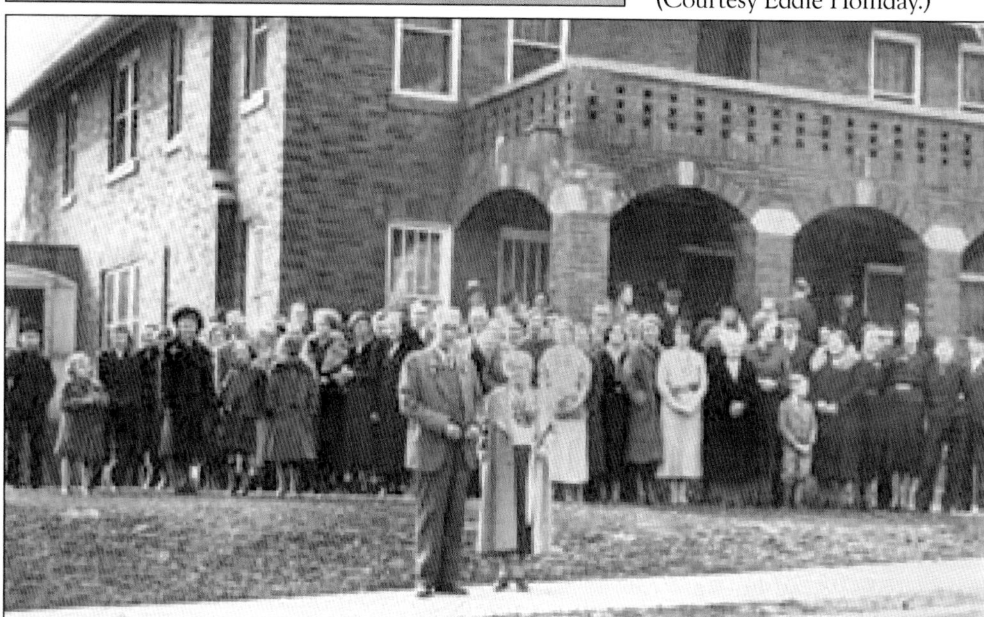

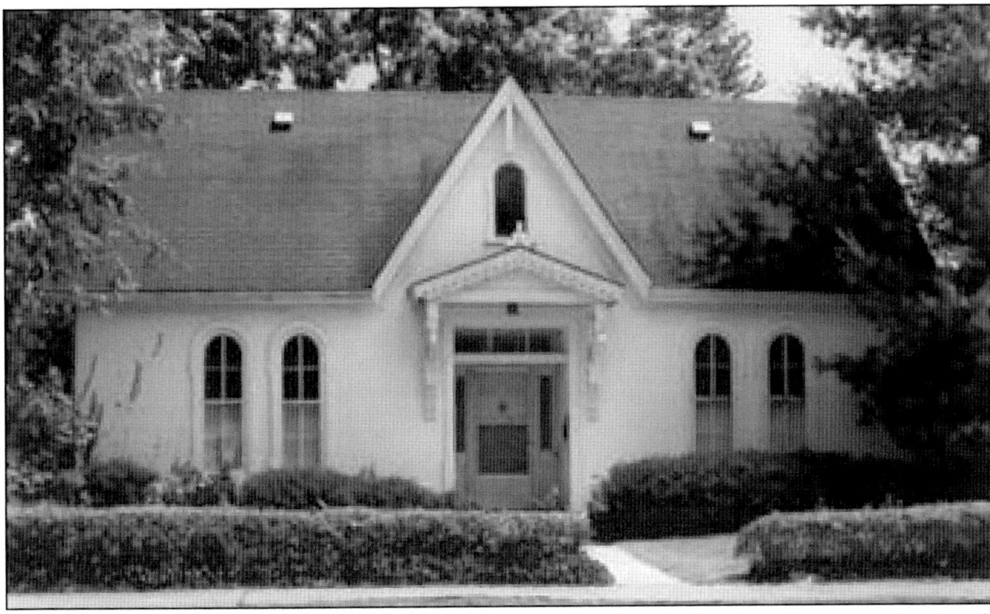

Conrad Smith (1821–1880) built this brick house at 720 South Carolina Street for his family in 1858. Today, it appears almost as it was then. Smith was appointed the superintendent of construction of the second Pike County courthouse by the county court in 1865, after the original courthouse burned. A descendant of his gave the county a copy of his courthouse plans. (Courtesy Betty Jane Allen.)

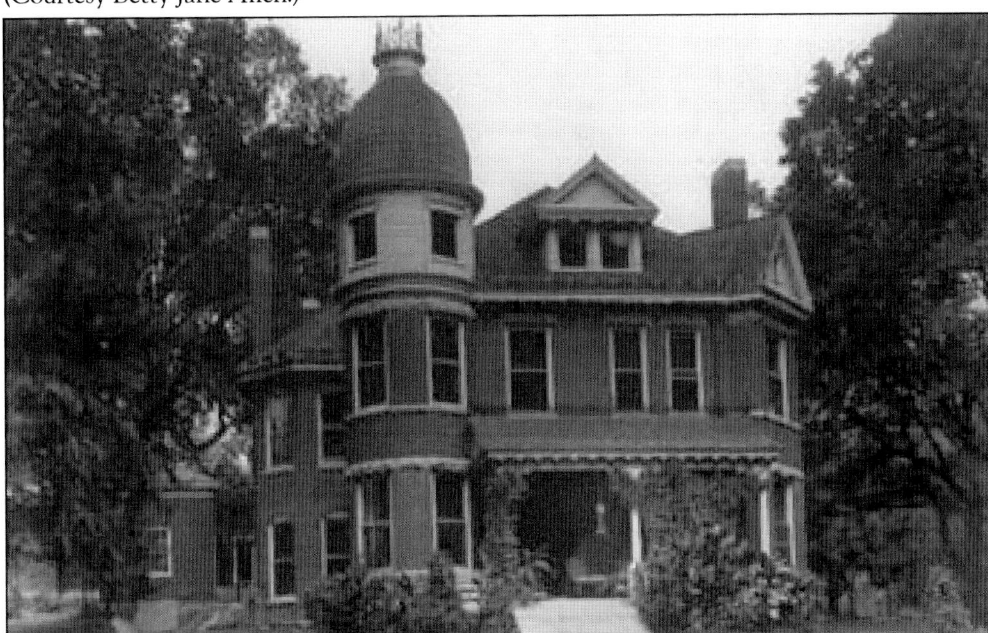

Belina Jackson and James H. Carstarphen were married at the home of Jackson's parents (on the following page), Julius and Hariett Jackson. They then built this beautiful brick house at 1805 Georgia Street in 1876, with lumber and millwork from her father's mill and bricks fired at the site. Belina and James Carstarphen raised three children here and are buried in the Jackson Cemetery. Dr. Joseph W. Martin and his wife, Janet, are the current owners. (Courtesy Betty Jane Allen.)

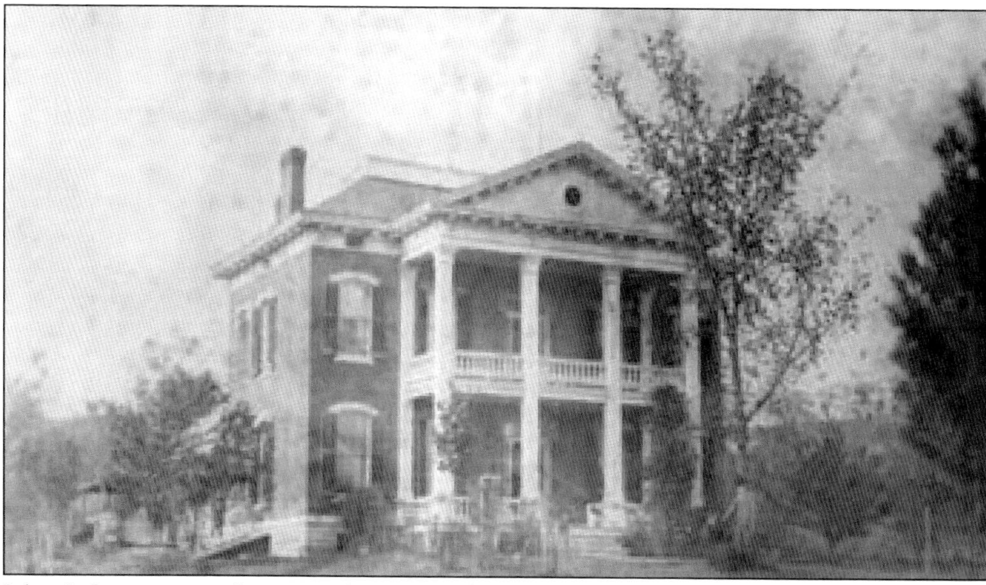

Julius Jackson came to Louisiana from Kentucky with his family in 1831 and built this house. His father, Christopher, was a first cousin of Pres. Andrew Jackson. Julius enlisted and served as a lieutenant under his cousin in the War of 1812. The house is a smaller replica of President Jackson's Hermitage. Julius and Harriett had eight children and their three daughters were married at the house. Many festive activities were enjoyed and many people of note were entertained; the Jacksons were an influential Missouri family. Christopher Jackson carefully selected and acquired more than 1,400 acres. The house is in the National Register of Historic Places. (Courtesy Dan DeCook.)

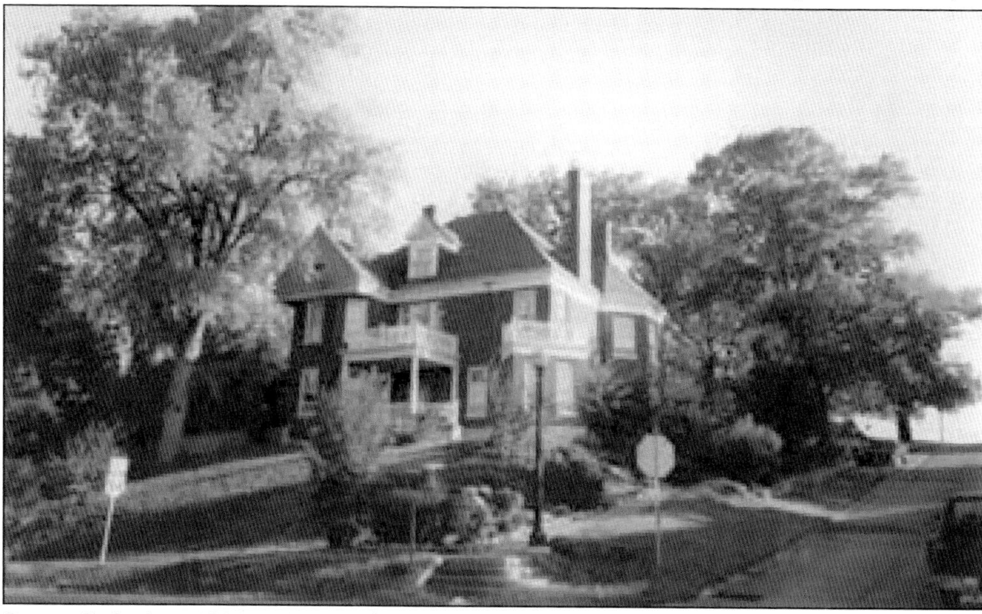

Originally built in 1894 at 601 North Third Street for Raymond H. Goodman, the chief cashier for the Bank of Louisiana, the Goodman-Stark house later became the home of Clarence M. Stark, the first president of Stark Bro's Nurseries & Orchards Co., which is credited with the discovery and promotion of the Red Delicious apple. The house is in the National Register of Historic Places. (Courtesy Betty Jane Allen.)

A Town of Beauty

The rolling hills along the Mississippi
Protect the lives of honorable souls.
Who through the centuries have dwelt
With promise in their hearts.

Louisiana was founded by proud people
Striving to create hopes for the future.
As the town grew with signs of greatness,
Stately homes were built and businesses flourished.

Families, faithful in their devotion
To chosen churches
Have shared a common need
For divine guidance.

Our town, how grand you stand,
Emblematic of all things dear.

—Grace Jane Catlett,
Louisiana High School class of 1942

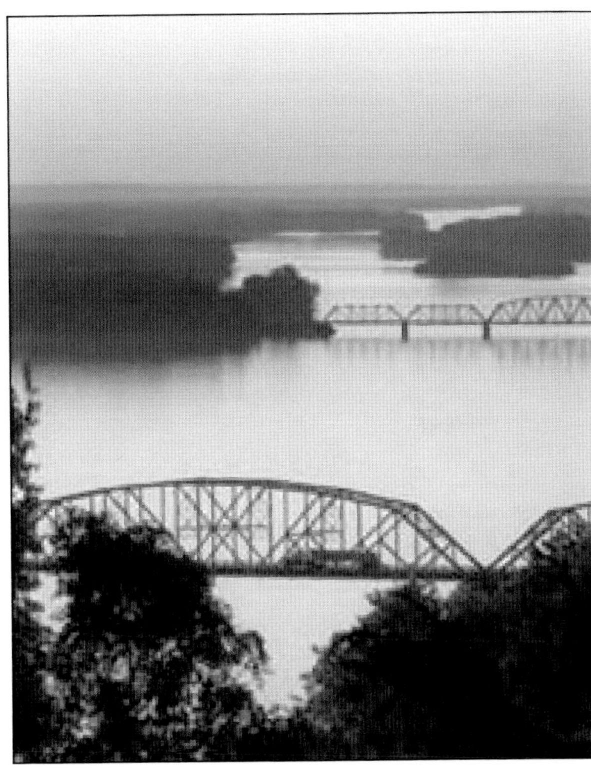

As this book comes to an end, "The City of Louisiana, Missouri, Missouri's Picturesque Rivertown"—the town motto—settles in quietly and peacefully. The railroad bridge in the background and the Champ Clark Bridge, can be seen crossing the mighty Mississippi River. (Courtesy Preserve Louisiana's Images.)